Praise For

Chinese through Scripture

Elegantly illustrated and highly accessible, this rich compendium includes luminous scripture verses, class devotionals, songs of praise, and a wide range of thoughtful discussion questions. Students will also enjoy the daily memory verses, prayer translations, and meditative writing exercises aimed at developing their vocabulary and overall Chinese language skills. *Chinese through Scripture*, a Christ-centered textbook with an accompanying workbook, is both edifying for the mind and nourishing for the soul.

—Karen An-hwei Lee, Provost of Wheaton College

***

Chinese through Scripture is the perfect book to allow intermediate-level students of Chinese to learn to express their Christian faith in the Chinese language, to prepare them for Christian ministry and outreach to Chinese speakers around the globe. Its rich content includes many Bible passages in Chinese with vocabulary notes, and the creative workbook helps the student master the material. Professor Wang's book fills a gap in the field of Chinese language instruction for Christian students of the language.

—Larry Herzberg, Professor Emeritus of Chinese, Calvin University; Author of *Basic Patterns of Chinese Grammar* (Stone Bridge Press) and *Writing Guide for Learners of Chinese* (Yale U. Press)

***

Professor Wang offers a timely contribution for Chinese language learners through her textbook, *Chinese through Scripture*. As an increasing number of individuals in the Chinese-speaking world proclaim the Christian faith, students of Chinese language and culture will need to understand the vocabulary and prose of the Bible. Professor Wang fills a critical gap in the literature by making such learning possible, memorable, and enjoyable. I cannot recommend this resource enough!

—Robert M. Lyons, Jr., Director of Academic Affairs, Georgetown University, SFS Asian Studies Program

***

Chinese through Scripture, which includes a textbook and workbook, is an innovative faith-informed curriculum that integrates content and language learning, Biblical wisdom, and Chinese language and culture. Professor Rose Wang engages learners and puts faith into action in her unique instructional design features throughout the units of study: *class devotionals; frequently quoted verses; covenantal promises; psalm readings; introductory readings; pre-reading questions reference verses for the text; themed text (character and pinyin versions); vocabulary; post-reading discussions; worship and praise; words and songs of praise; prayer passages*, and *exemplary prayers*. It is a well-scaffolded, pedagogically sound textbook for learning Chinese through Scripture; more and beyond, it is a celebration of spiritual formation in the author's guided design for learners.

—Jinhuei Enya Dai, Professor and Program Head of Chinese Studies Program, Middlebury Institute of International Studies at Monterey, CA; Author of *Life, Cognition and Teaching Chinese; Innovative Pedagogy and Ecological Perspectives; Interaction and Chinese Grammar Pedagogy I and II*

***

Chinese through Scripture is a breakthrough text which will inform and inspire Christian students of Chinese for decades to come. Born of extensive classroom experience, it methodically engages students with highly relevant content. While improving your Chinese level, it also prepares you to participate in a Chinese church community. I only wish it had been available back when I was a student!

—**Paul Condrell**, Former faculty colleague of Rose Wang; Marketing Director, Bibles, Tyndale House Publishers

***

It is a special thing to be taught by someone with both a deep passion and love for God and His Gospel, and an infectious joy in and love for the subject they teach. I have had the privilege of experiencing this under the instruction of Prof. Rose Wang, and now you will have that same opportunity. Her textbook and workbook, *Chinese through Scripture,* will stretch you to your limits as a language learner. It will not always be easy, but you will reach the end and find that your grasp of the Chinese language has improved dramatically. More than this, in studying this book, I believe you will see different facets of our Savior Jesus Christ, understanding and knowing Him in way you previously have not and, I hope, loving Him more than you did at the start. Within these pages, you will hear the voice of a professor who not only wants you to know and love her language, but who also wants you to know and love her God. I encourage you to make the most of this opportunity.

—**Brendan Keefer**, Computer Science Major, Wheaton College, 2022

Chinese
through
Scripture

TEXTBOOK
Simplified Characters

读圣经·学中文

Shuguang Wang

王曙光

Published by KHARIS PUBLISHING, an imprint of KHARIS MEDIA LLC.

Copyright © 2022 Shuguang Wang

ISBN-13: 978-1-63746-149-5

ISBN-10: 1-63746-149-6

Library of Congress Control Number: 2022949352

Interior design by Daini Eades (Liu)

Unless otherwise indicated all Scripture taken from the Holy Bible, New International Version for English and the Chinese Union Version with New Punctuation: CUNPSS-神，新标点和合本, 神版 for Chinese.

All KHARIS PUBLISHING products are available at special quantity discounts for bulk purchases for sales promotions, premiums, fund-raising, and educational needs. For details, contact:

Kharis Media LLC

Tel: 1-479-599-8657

support@kharispublishing.com

www.kharispublishing.com

This book is dedicated to

Dr. Philip C. Holtrop and Mrs. Marie Holtrop,
who were actively committed for some twenty-five years
to God's Kingdom work in China.

谨以此书献给
Philip C. Holtrop 博士和 Marie Holtrop 夫人，
感谢他们近二十五年来积极致力于神在中国的工作。

This book received
the Teaching Improvement and Innovation Grant (TIIG)
funded by Project Teacher Fund, and the support
of Academic & Institutional Technology (AIT)
from Wheaton College, Illinois.

With Deepest Appreciation

本书得到
伊利诺伊州惠顿大学教师计划工程项目
教学改进与创新基金的资助，
并获该校教育机构和学术教学技术部门的大力支持。

谨此谢忱！

Preface 前言

The task of writing this textbook has focused my mind on the experiences of a lifetime of language teaching and learning. It brings together my reflections as a teacher on the goals of language education and my ongoing discoveries as a learner of the relationship and connection between faith and knowledge.

I have been teaching Chinese since 2007 at Wheaton College, a Christian liberal arts college in Illinois, where the goals of language education are not only to develop students' linguistic and intercultural skills, but also to cultivate their understanding of God and Christian character formation through their study of a language.

Having been a teacher since the beginning of the Chinese program at Wheaton, I view my work as a mission to promote Christian liberal arts learning and my teaching as a God-given privilege that contributes to the realization of its intended educational goals. During this time, many students have expressed an interest in reading the Bible in Chinese, seeking to improve their Chinese language ability to communicate when sharing their Christian faith. The exploration of the resources available and my desire to craft an approach for the desired curriculum in my teaching context led to curriculum development and this textbook for a Wheaton course titled Chinese through Scripture.

The creation of this textbook brought forth new goals for me as a language teacher: to create thoughtful and meaningful material with the content and commitment of Christian faith, and to cultivate in students their aesthetic sensibility to see God's glory through language learning and to unleash students' artistic creativity to display God's truth and splendor in their works of language. To engage in this kind of teaching, I have sought to take into account the goal of human wholeness and the individual aspirations of my students. It was because of this new teaching perspective that I decided to write this textbook.

In addition, three timely inspirations also propelled me to write this textbook. The first came in 2007 with the call for the creation of a Chinese language program at Wheaton College as part of a future China Studies program. The next lay in increasing worldwide interest in learning Mandarin Chinese, my native language, which appeared to be growing in popularity with Christian learners, young and old, MKs and TCKs alike. A third reason grew from the realization that little was known among differences in the choices, experiences and difficulties that students encounter in learning CFL (Chinese as a Foreign Language) in Christian colleges and universities in countries where Chinese has been a recent addition to the curriculum. As a faculty member of a Christian college that emphasizes the integration of faith and learning and the development of a Christian worldview, I wanted to contribute to CFL teaching with this textbook by demonstrating what "Christian teaching" can look like at its best and by offering to CFL learners something directly applicable to their personal faith and to their ability to communicate in Chinese when sharing their faith.

This textbook and the approach to its creation is a study in faith-informed pedagogy, teaching in such a way that faith informs process, action, practice, and pedagogy. Though this kind of teaching is difficult because Christian practices make not only students but also teachers vulnerable to unpredictable encounters with God and others, it is rewarding for that very same reason. Having ventured down this pedagogical "road less traveled," the new pedagogical experiments I undertook led to the integration of faith and learning within the context of Chinese language learning. This integration is not the same as teaching Christian perspectives on the subject matter, it instead is a holistic approach that involves Christian faith in all aspects of the process.

Finally, because my career has been an unusually happy one, gratitude is also the leading sentiment evoking writing and making this textbook. I must also add that, as I have found after field-testing the textbook, there is still much room in it for further improvement. It is my hope and prayer that my role of a teacher will be that of a shepherd, inspiring my students to go in search of greener pastures, leading them in the right direction with deeper thinking, and always pointing them toward the Source of all Creation, in whom we live and move and have our being.

"你的言语一解开就发出亮光，使愚人通达。"
— 诗篇 119:130 (CUNPSS)

"The unfolding of your words gives light;
it gives understanding to the simple."
— Psalm 119:130 (NIV)

Acknowledgements 致谢

I could not have written this textbook without the support and participation of many people. First of all, I must thank all the students whom I have had the privilege of teaching at Wheaton College, especially those in my Chinese through Scripture class who responded to my idea of this textbook project and in turn persuaded me of its seriousness, shared their experiences and observations, and contributed to and tempered my enthusiasm. I am also deeply indebted to the academic scholars who have scaffolded my intellectual growth in the niche of foreign language education integrated with faith and learning in the past years, which eventually led to the writing of this book.

Special thanks are offered to Wheaton College's school administrators granting the Project Teacher Fund, The Teaching Improvement and Innovation Grant (TIIG), which enabled me to hire student workers to assemble and design course materials into a textbook. I would also like to thank Wheaton College's Academic & Institutional Technology (AIT) department for providing me with the access to Adobe InDesign software for this book project.

I received tremendous help from many Wheaton College students who made invaluable corrections and suggestions and assisted me with the designing work of this textbook. To name a few who were most instrumental in making this dream project a reality:

Renwei Chi (池仁威), a graduate student in Historical Theology (2021), who did the proofreading and critiquing on the lesson texts, for his meticulous proofreading of the final draft/manuscript, for his insights and expert knowledge of Christianity in China which have been incorporated into this work. He helped clarify many of my thoughts and gave the book a clearer framework. He did more than just editing the original manuscript—he became my teacher and editor as he put my thoughts into much better words.

Julia Damion (戴茱莉), a graduate student in TESOL (2019) and a student of Chinese through Scripture, who did some initial artwork for the book, for her loving support of the idea on the project.

Jillian Dowdy (邓佳靓), a Spanish and Chinese major (2019) and a student of Chinese through Scripture, who designed the initial layout of the book, for giving me the idea of turning my class presentation materials into a textbook, for her undying belief in this project.

Alice Jiang (蒋雅诗), a Philosophy major (2022), who did the foundational set of drawings and artwork for the book project, for her teaching assistant work on this project from the very beginning.

Brendan Keefer (柯宝恩), a Computer Science major (2022), who was involved in the final edits of the book. He added hyperlinks to the digital version of the book, formatted the supplemental materials, and helped proofread English sections.

Jack Meeker (杰克), a Bible and Theology major (2019), and a student of Chinese through Scripture, who organized the book pages, provided creative input, and imported and formatted lesson text, for his editorial input to an early draft and his many hours of rewriting and editing numerous drafts of the entire work, for his construction of the Appendix, for creating digital vocabulary and Bible reference resources and for his help with the supplemental materials. His insights were incorporated throughout this book.

Sophia Pelling (裴林慧), a Studio Art major (2024), who helped with the final edits of the book. She cleaned up final designs, helped with InDesign troubleshooting, proofread English sections, helped reformat the traditional character version of the book, and prepared the book for publishing.

Daini Liu (刘岱妮), a Biology and Studio Art major (2020), the main graphic designer for this book project, who selected the color palette and typography, redesigned the layout, and created illustrations and graphics for the book, for her creativity and artistic work. She incorporated the style of traditional Chinese art with modern Western designs, creating a visual voice to the reader with a sense of tranquility, harmony, refreshment, and trust. She also carefully considered page elements and composition to provide a natural flow and hierarchy of information so that students can navigate the textbook easily. Because of her labors, what you hold in your hands is much more than simply a book; it is also a work of art.

Lastly, a project of this character cannot be accomplished by one person alone. In the same way that many students at Wheaton College have shared every step with me during fieldwork and writing, my colleagues at Wheaton College have also offered me endorsement and enduring encouragement which gave me the faith to believe that this book could happen. I want to make mention of Dr. Christine Kepner, Associate Professor of Spanish at the department of Modern and Classical Languages, who with her special generosity, encouraged me in this path I had never before taken, read and edited my manuscript, and aided me with her thoughtful critique. I would also like to mention Dr. Emily McGowin, Assistant Professor of Theology at the department of Biblical and Theological Studies, who with her experience and expertise in religious studies and theology, proofread and edited the English translations of the Chinese texts.

But most of all, I am grateful to God, who is the reason for this book. I pray that more educators and learners will be able to benefit from using this textbook.

Shuguang (Rose) Wang 王曙光

Department of Modern and Classical Languages
Wheaton College, IL

v

Student Testimonials 学生嘉评

As a long-time student of Wang Laoshi, I was intrigued and enthusiastic when she proposed the idea of creating a textbook combining Biblical learning and Chinese language acquisition. Having taken her fantastic Chinese through Scripture class, I knew that the idea had a lot of potential and I encouraged her to make her idea a reality, offering my opinions on Chinese as a foreign language learner and assisting with the layout design. After months of planning, we drafted a prototype of what would become the textbook for Chinese through Scripture. I am proud to know that Wang Laoshi's passions for both Biblical and language education will be available to educators and learners alike via this unique textbook.

– Jillian Dowdy (邓佳靓)
Spanish & Chinese Major,
Wheaton College, 2019

My role in this project involved organizing, designing, and editing lesson content. By far, my favorite part of this experience has been the amazing relationships that have flourished under the wise and passionate leadership of Professor Wang, whose devotion to both Christ and Chinese language education is a daily encouragement. This project is significant because it fills a gaping void in Chinese language education: Chinese language materials about Christianity. This book merges Biblical truth with devotional encouragement, enabling language learners to understand Christianity and articulate it in Chinese. Between the Scriptural content and educational exercises, this book forges in the language learner a passion for both the Chinese language and the Living God.

– Jack Meeker (杰克)
Bible & Theology Major,
Wheaton College, 2019

As the main graphic designer for this book project, my role included developing the overall style, designing the content layout and covers, and creating illustrations and graphics. This textbook project has been an excellent opportunity for me to practice what I learned about art and design, to use my bilingual skills, and to integrate faith and learning. For example, when creating the unit cover illustrations, I incorporated traditional Chinese elements with modern Western designs and Biblical symbolism. By providing these thoughtful content format and visual designs, I aimed to make the textbook content more appealing and engaging for the students rather than distracting. I enjoyed creating aesthetic and functional designs that enhance language learners' experiences with this book.

– Daini Liu (刘岱妮)
Studio Art and Biology Major,
Wheaton College, 2020

Special Thanks 特别感谢

Special recognition goes to the following student readers of the Chinese through Scripture class at Wheaton College (IL), who reviewed the manuscript, suggested improvements, and offered comments in their participation of the field testing of this book project:

Mae Z. Brown 潘照苏

Katrina Chan 陈婉薇

Eliana Chow 周恩霖

John Chu 朱明恩

William DiGena 狄伟仁

Eric Fan 范佳欣

Rebecca Hofer 何蓓嘉

Matthew Hudson 何拓胜

Noelle Jepsen 叶璞真

Catherine Kok 郭秦怡

Joshua Lee 李大君

Jack Meeker 杰克

Philip Merrifield 梅林

Genesis Morris 乔娜思

Kezia Nathaniel 可嘉

Darrin Pollino 彭德君

Joshua Treadway 崔嘉许

Peter Soung 宋培德

Eui Rin Um 严义邻

Cassia Waligora 王珍珠

Luke Witzig 卫泽辉

Cody Wollin 温正雄

Introduction 简介

Unlike any other Chinese language textbook, Chinese through Scripture integrates the Bible into the teaching and learning of Chinese. It is aimed at intermediate level high school or college students or independent learners who have acquired about 500 Chinese characters in reading and is designed for those who wish to expand their understanding and gain new insights into the reception and translation of the Bible by reading it in another language, and for those who desire to learn and use Chinese for ministry and Christian outreach.

This textbook not only teaches the basics of the language, but also introduces basic Christian terms and statements about God, Jesus, worship, and prayer, as well as major Christian themes in Chinese. It teaches vocabulary on biblical topics, enabling learners to become conversant in sharing the Gospel and talking about Christianity in Chinese. It provides pinyin or phonetic pronunciation support of unfamiliar words for self-study. English translation of the themed texts is also included in the appendix to aid language comprehension.

The great variety of genres in the Bible, such as poetry, biographies, prose, stories, and more offer a rich repository of such content. Scripture is the essence of the craft of this textbook. More than 600 scriptures alone are included and referenced. Texts, including Bible verses, prayers and stories chosen for the lessons, are familiar to learners with basic background knowledge of the Bible.

This textbook contains a total of six units on the topics of God's Word (the Bible), the Triune God, Scripture Alone, God's Saving Grace, Justification by Faith, and Glory (Be to God). These six units can be used or studied consecutively, in any order, or independently. The units can be used for individual learning or in a class. Each unit has three lessons followed by a wrap-up as a summary of the unit. The preparatory unit can serve as foundational content for the subsequent content, including classification of the books of the Old and New Testaments, core vocabulary for Bible study, a guide to Chinese Bible translations, and an overview of the Bible. Each unit includes related verses themed around the texts of the lessons for reference, questions and conversation starters for sharing the Bible and Christian faith.

Examples of conversion prayers, explanations of the meaning of the Gospel, supplementary reading of the gospel stories, lists of Biblical study terms, and special notes explaining the development of dozens of selected Chinese characters such as "God", "Sin", "Sacrifice", "Covenant", "Lamb" and "Righteousness" are available as free download supplemental materials and extended learning resources for the study.

This textbook also comes with a workbook that correlates with the lessons and provides learners with language practice in reading and writing. Discussion of traditional Chinese thoughts and Chinese folk religion in the workbook invites learners to make connections between Chinese language and culture and their own linguistic and religious heritage. With cultural topics discussed from a Christian perspective, the learning materials in the workbook equip learners with practical tools for cultural insights and Christian discourse in preparation for cross-cultural mission trips or ministry work.

The explicit pedagogical orientation in both the textbook and the workbook facilitates the teaching, learning and assessment of the language. Almost all sections in the textbook and the workbook are labeled with headings such as "Name the Book of the Bible," "Write the Verse of the Unit," "Put the Verses in Order," "Recite the Key Verse," and "Write down in Chinese What You Want to Pray to God" to make it easy for learners to understand the structure of the information. A daily class devotional is programmed into the course material to maximize student participation.

For assessment, this textbook classifies questions into five categories as warm-up, pre-reading, and post-reading activities followed by unit and reflective discussions. Daily Bible verse memory and copy work, Bible vocabulary acquisition, words and songs of praise, keyword search, psalm reading, prayer items, Bible storytelling and other kinds of alternative assessment tasks are also included in the textbook and the workbook.

By using the widely known Chinese Union Version translation of the Bible, learners have easy access to numerous online audio productions of the Chinese Bible for listening practice. Online Quizlet flashcards correspond to the vocabulary words of each lesson for language practice.

The design of physical features including clear layout and illustrations, use of colors, diagrams, pictures, and other visual representations was carefully considered to make the textbook and workbook visually appealing and engaging, with attention to the typeface and font size that allows for minimal eyestrain and an effortless Chinese reading experience. Illustration of the unit cover pages alludes to its biblical theme and features common Chinese natural elements. Traditional Chinese art combined with modern western designs, biblical symbolism, and rice paper textures on the page background create an organic look and a visual signal to the reader of a sense of tranquility, harmony, refreshment, and trust. The design of this book is diversified in terms of content selection and pedagogical method; its appearance and layout are innovative, aesthetic, and attractive, so that students will not only be interested in reading but also will have a sense of visual delight when doing so.

Chinese through Scripture is written from the perspective of a language teacher. Such a perspective, though limited, is a privileged one. It is my hope that this textbook will turn conversational Chinese into transformational Chinese as it teaches learners how to communicate the love of Christ through a rich variety of Scripture passages, challenging educational exercises, and basic information about Christianity.

Unit Cover Illustration
单元封面设计

The introductory page for each unit features a piece of traditional Chinese artwork that alludes to the unit theme to enhance the instructional design.

Learning Objectives
学习目的

The list of skills covered in the unit that clarifies the learning objectives and helps students focus their study and take responsibility for their own learning.

Unit Title
单元标题

Unit titles are presented in Chinese characters arranged vertically.

Seal Stamp
封面印章

Traditional characters in the seal stamp are used to create decorative calligraphy that corelates with the unit title in traditional typography.

Unit Verse
单元经文

Each unit begins with a Bible verse that reflects the unit's theme and introduces students to the unit's content and main message.

独一真神
Unit 1
第一单元

Learning Objectives
学习目的

In this unit, you will learn to...
- Understand basic Christian terminology
- Use basic terms for God and Jesus
- Make basic statements about God and Jesus
- Talk about reverence and thankfulness to God
- Discuss your personal understanding of who God is

rèn shi nǐ dú yí de zhēn shén bìng qiě rèn shi nǐ suǒ chāi lái de yē sū jī dū zhè jiù shì yǒng shēng
认识你独一的真神，并且认识你所差来的耶稣基督，这就是永生。
—约翰福音17:3

Key terms
关键词汇

A short list of keywords that highlights the theme of the unit.

Warm-up Questions
热身问题

A preparatory activity to engage and aid students to interact in the study of the unit topic.

Key Verse Reading
经文细读

Each unit begins with a selected Bible passage that introduces a question related to a key biblical concept or a key term of the unit for discussion and to aid understanding.

Unit Preview
预备学习

Unit preview provides a manageable amount of information that connects to the unit as a jump-off point and an important preview tool.

Unit 1：预备学习
第 一 单 元

guān jiàn cí huì
关键词汇 Key Terms

shìjiè	shén	cúnzài	jī dū tú	xìn
世界	神	存在	基督徒	信
(world	God	existence	Christian	believe)

rè shēn wèn tí
热身问题 Warm-up Questions

1. 世界上真的有神吗？
2. 我们人如何能知道神的存在？
3. 如果有人问你基督徒信什么，你怎么回答？

jīng wén xì dú
经文细读 Key Verse Reading

shén duì mó xī shuō wǒ shì zì yǒu yǒng yǒu de yòu shuō nǐ yào duì yǐ sè liè rén zhè yàng shuō
神对摩西说："我是自有永有的"；又说："你要对以色列人这样说：
nà zì yǒu de dǎ fā wǒ dào nǐ men zhè lǐ lái
'那自有的打发我到你们这里来。'"
—出埃及记 3:14

God said to Moses, "I AM WHO I AM. This is what you are to say to the Israelites: I Am has sent me to you.
— Exodus 3:14

12

Lesson Title
课文标题
Lesson titles are presented in Chinese characters arranged horizontally.

Class Devotional
课堂灵修
A featured Bible passage related to the topic of each lesson provides additional reading practice and creates a devotional routine in the classroom.

Daily Memory Verse
每日经文背诵
A topic-related Bible verse to be memorized for the purpose of building biblical literacy.

Frequently Quoted Verse
圣经金句
Each lesson selects a frequently-quoted Bible verse to practice Chinese character recognition and acquisition, and to read for enjoyment and encouragement.

Sample page (page 13):

Lesson 1 第一课: 自有永有

课堂灵修 Class Devotional

我是阿拉法，我是俄梅戛；我是首先的，我是末后的；我是初，我是终。

—启示录 22:13

Daily Memory Verse

主神说："我是阿拉法，我是俄梅戛，是昔在、今在、以后永在的全能者。"

—启示录 1:8

圣经金句 Frequently Quoted Verse

你，惟独你是耶和华！你造了天和天上的天，并天上的万象，地和地上的万物，海和海中所有的；这一切都是你所保存的。

—尼希米记 9:6

You alone are the Lord. You made the heavens, even the highest heavens, and all their starry host, the earth and all that is on it, the seas and all that is in them. You give life to everything.

—Nehemiah 9:6

13

Covenantal Promise
盟约应许
Each lesson includes one of God's covenant promises to humankind, a very important theme in the Bible, for reading comprehension and practice.

Psalm Reading
诗篇集锦
Each lesson incudes a portion of a selected psalm with word assonance, alliteration, use of repetition or the piling up of synonyms and complements to be read aloud for language practice and enjoyment.

Sample page (page 14):

盟约应许 Covenantal Promise

神人之约

神说："我们要照着我们的形象、按着我们的样式造人，使他们管理海里的鱼、空中的鸟、地上的牲畜，和全地，并地上所爬的一切昆虫。"神就照着自己的形象造人，乃是照着他的形象造男造女。神就赐福给他们，又对他们说："要生养众多，遍满地面，治理这地，也要管理海里的鱼、空中的鸟，和地上各样行动的活物。"

—创世记 1:26-28

God's Covenant with Mankind

Then God said, "Let us make mankind in our image, in our likeness, so that they may rule over the fish in the sea and the birds in the sky, over the livestock and all the wild animals, and over all the creatures that move along the ground." So God created mankind in his own image, in the image of God he created them; male and female he created them. God blessed them and said to them, "Be fruitful and increase in number; fill the earth and subdue it. Rule over the fish in the sea and the birds in the sky and over every living creature that moves on the ground."

—Genesis 1:26-28

诗篇集锦 Psalm Reading

May his name endure forever;
may it continue as long as the sun.
Then all nations will be blessed through him,
and they will call him blessed.
Praise be to the Lord God,
the God of Israel,
who alone does marvelous deeds.

—Psalm 72:17-18—

他的名要存到永远，
要留传如日之久。
人要因他蒙福；
万国要称他有福。
独行奇事的耶和华
以色列的神是应当称颂的！

—诗篇 72:17-18—

14

Introductory Reading
课文预读

An introduction to the text of each lesson by pre-teaching of potentially difficult concepts and vocabulary, identifying key words, activating prior knowledge, and providing background support to stimulate interest.

Pre-reading Questions
预读问题

A preparatory activity to engage students and help them interact with the subsequent learning of the text.

Reference Verses for the Text
参考经文

Scripture passages referenced in the text are cited with the abbreviated names, chapter numbers, and the verse numbers of the books in the Bible. Chapters and verses are separated by colons.

课文预读 Introductory Reading

上帝是神，
是真神，
是万军的神。
耶和华是祂的名号，
是神永久的名字，
也是神永远被记念的名。
世世代代的人都要这样称呼祂。
耶和华是首先的，是末后的；
祂是以色列的王，
是以色列的救赎主。
祂是亚伯拉罕的神，
是以撒的神，是雅各的神。
除祂以外，再没有真神。
谁能像耶和华？
一切荣耀都归给祂的名！

神的名

shàngdì shì shén,
shì zhēnshén,
shì wàn jūn de shén.
yēhéhuá shì tā de míng hào,
shì shén yǒngjiǔ de míngzi,
yě shì shén yǒngyuǎn bèi jì niàn de míng.
shìshì dàidài de rén dōu yào zhèyàng chēnghu tā.
yēhéhuá shì shǒuxiān de, shì mòhòu de;
tā shì yǐsèliè de wáng,
shì yǐsèliè de jiùshú zhǔ
tā shì yàbólāhǎn de shén,
shì yǐsā de shén, shì yǎgè de shén.
chú tā yǐwài, zài méiyǒu zhēnshén.
shéi néng xiàng yēhéhuá?
yíqiè róngyào dōu guī gěi tā de míng!

预读问题 Pre-reading Questions

1. 上帝是谁?
2. "耶和华"是谁的名字?
3. 上帝是怎样的神?

参考经文 Reference Verses for the Text

出3:14-15；赛42:8, 44:6；何12:5

15

Themed Text
主题课文

In the formatted text of each lesson, names of places and people are underlined, new vocabulary bolded, and special notes highlighted in red and marked with asterisks. Each text written in Chinese characters has its corresponding pinyin text and English translation to provide phonetic guidance and to help with reading comprehension.

Special Notes on the Text
课文特注

Key vocabulary words and phrases requiring explanation are marked with pinyin and noted.

主题课文 Themed Text

圣经告诉我们只有一位真神。神说："我是**首先**的，我是**末后**的，除我以外再没有真神。"

圣经还向我们**启示**了这位神的名字，叫做"**耶和华***"。这个名字在圣经里出现了上千次，是"**自有永有***"的意思，也就是说，神是自存者，是存在的**独一源头***。所以，神在圣经中启示祂*自己为自有永有的独一真神。

神在圣经中还有许多别的**称谓**，例如上帝、主、**全能者**、**创造主**和**牧者**。但圣经中人**称呼**神最多的还是"神（上帝）"或"耶和华"。

课文特注

* "**耶和华**" yēhéhuá: 有些基督教书籍上也使用"雅威"(yǎwēi)，是 YHWH 的音译，是"上"(zhù)的意思。

* "**自有永有**"zì yǒu yǒng yǒu: "I AM WHO I AM"

* "祂" tā 为神或主耶稣的"他"代名词。本书引用的经文中依和合本照旧用"他"。

16

课文词汇 Vocabulary
kè wén cí huì

1.	首先	shǒu xiān	(Adj) first of all
2.	末后	mò hòu	(Adj) last of all
3.	启示	qǐ shì	(V) to reveal
4.	耶和华	yē hé huá	(N) Yahweh
5.	永	yǒng	(Adj) forever, permanent
6.	独一	dú yī	(Adj) only, sole
7.	源头	yuán tóu	(N) source, beginning
8.	称谓	chēng wèi	(N) title, salutation

Vocabulary
课文词汇
The vocabulary introduced in the textbook is selected based on its unit themes and lesson topics. The vocabulary list includes Chinese characters, pinyin, part of speech, and English definition. A Chinese-English and English-Chinese glossary arranged in pinyin and English alphabetical order respectively is included at the end of the book.

读后讨论 Post-reading Discussion
dú hòu tǎo lùn

1. 我们如何称呼神的名?
2. 神给自己的名字是什么意思?
3. 新旧约中人对神有哪些称谓? 称呼最多的是什么?

Post-reading Discussion
读后讨论
Discussions concerning the subject or theme of the lesson appear after the lesson text for speaking practice. These topic-related questions help derive the intended meaning and increase student engagement and participation.

敬拜赞美 Worship and Praise
jìng bài zàn měi

Goodness of the Lord

Let the name of the Lord be praised,
both now and forevermore.
From the rising of the sun to the place where it sets,
the name of the Lord is to be praised.
The Lord is exalted over all the nations,
his glory above the heavens.

— Psalm 113: 2-4 —

耶和华的良善
yē hé huá de liáng shàn

耶和华的名是应当称颂的,
yēhéhuá de míng shì yīngdāng chēngsòng de
从今时直到永远
cóng jīn shí zhídào yǒngyuǎn
从日出之地到日落之处,
cóng rìchū zhī dì dào rìluò zhī chù
耶和华的名是应当赞美的!
yēhéhuá de míng shì yīngdāng zànměi de
耶和华超乎万民之上;
yēhéhuá chāohū wànmín zhī shàng
他的荣耀高过诸天。
tā de róngyào gāo guò zhū tiān

— 诗篇 113:2-4 —

Worship and Praise
敬拜赞美
Verses of praise are embedded in each lesson as part of worship and a joyful recounting of God's goodness to enrich the lesson, personalize the learning experience and bring honor to God.

诗章颂词 Words and Songs of Praise
shī zhāng sòng cí

三一颂

赞美真神万福之源,
世上万民都当颂扬,
天使天军赞美主名,
赞美圣父圣子圣灵。
阿们。

— Doxology
(浸信会版本)

Words and Songs of Praise
诗章颂词
Incremental readings of psalms, hymns, and songs with pinyin and English translation are organized and broken down into digestible subsegments that help retain knowledge for better language practice.

Sample page (top)

shī wén dǎo gào
诗文祷告 Prayer Passage

                                yán shí   shān zhài   qiú   yuán gù
因为你是我的岩石，我的山寨；所以，求你为你名的缘故
yǐn dǎo   zhǐ diǎn
引导我，指点我。   —诗篇 31:3

Since you are my rock and my fortress, for the sake of your name lead and
guide me.
                                                — Psalms 31:3

qí dǎo fàn wén
祈祷范文 Exemplary Prayer

赛 45:5；撒下 7:22；太 6:9

zhǔ   nǐ dú   shén yē hé huá   quán dì
主啊，祢是独一的真神，耶和华祢的名在全地多么的美，没有可比
                                                    běn
祢的。祢在时间空间以上、以先、以外，祢本为大。求祢帮助我们更多
地认识祢，看见祢的大能，只认祢为独一真神，让祢来作我们的主人。
fèng yē sū jī dū   dǎo gào á
奉主耶稣基督的名祷告，阿们。

21

Prayer Passage
诗文祷告
Short prayer text passages for
additional reading practice and
articulate expression.

Exemplary Prayer
祈祷范文
Prayer texts written as examples
to reinforce learned concepts and
vocabulary.

Sample page (bottom)

Unit 1: 综合提要
zōng hé tí yào
Wrap-up

dān yuán jiǎn yào
单元简要 Unit Summary

神是存在的，   shén shì cúnzài de,
他不是宇宙的一部分，   三   tā búshì yǔzhòu de yí bùfèn,
他是宇宙的创造者。   sān   tā shì yǔzhòu de chuàngzàozhě.
我们要敬拜神，   位   wǒmen yào jìngbài shén,
因为他是真神，是爱的神， wèi yīnwèi tā shì zhēnshén, shì ài de shén,
是创造万物的神，是可靠的神。yī shì chuàngzào wànwù de shén, shì kěkào de shén,
我们要感谢神，   tǐ   wǒmen yào gǎnxiè shén,
因为他赐给我们生命和慈爱， 体   yīnwèi tā cì gěi wǒmen shēngmìng hé cí'ài,
赐给我们圣经，赐给我们圣灵，   cì gěi wǒmen shèngjīng, cì gěi wǒmen shèngling,
赐给我们救主耶稣，   cì gěi wǒmen jiùzhǔ yēsū,
赦免我们的罪，   shèmiǎn wǒmen de zuì,
让我们有智慧、有力量，   ràng wǒmen yǒu zhìhuì, yǒu lìliàng,
让我们知道我们是神的儿女。   ràng wǒmen zhīdào wǒmen shì shén de érnǚ.

zì cí jí jiě
字词集解 Word Explanation

sān wèi yī tǐ
三位一体 (Trinity)
jìngbài yì   yī
我们敬拜一体三位，三位一体的神。父是神，子是神，圣灵也是
            yī   yí xìng   yì róngyào   yì
神。不是三神，而是一神。父、子、圣灵同一神性，同一荣耀，也同一
héng zhī zūnyán
永恒之尊严。
                                            yà   xiū
                            —《亚他那修信经》(Athanasian Creed)

40

Wrap-up
综合提要
Each unit concludes with a
wrap-up which summarizes
the unit for review and further
clarification.

Word Explanation
字词集解
A deeper explanation of a
key word or phrase from
the unit.

Follow-up Questions
问题跟踪

More challenging questions for discussion on the content of the learned unit that can be tailored for multi-level learners.

Scripture Response Reading
经文回应

A selected key verse that sums up the themes of the unit and serves as a transition to the next unit.

Bible Story Reading
故事阅读

A Bible story for reading practice, vocabulary acquisition, and exposure to global features of the language including sentence structure, narrative, sequencing events, and much more.

---

wèn tí gēn zōng
问题跟踪 Follow-up Questions

1. 基督徒信的神是一位怎样的神?

2. "道成肉身"是什么意思?

3. 圣灵充满的表现是怎样的?

4. 为什么说信徒的身子是"圣灵的殿"? (林前6:19)

5. 基督教的"三位一体"是什么意思?

jīng wén huí yìng
经文回应 Scripture Response Reading

cóng gǔ yǐ lái， rén wèi céng tīng jiàn、 wèi céng ěr wén、 wèi céng yǎn jiàn
从 古 以 来， 人 未 曾 听 见、 未 曾 耳 闻、 未 曾 眼 见

zài nǐ yǐ wài yǒu shéme shén wèi děnghòu tā de rén xíngshì
在 你 以 外 有 什 么 神 为 等 候 他 的 人 行 事。

—— 以赛亚书 64:4 ——

Since ancient times no one has heard, no ear has perceived, no eye has seen any God besides you, who acts on behalf of those who wait for him.
—— Isaiah 64:4 ——

---

gù shì yuè dú
故事阅读 Bible Story Reading

shén chuàng zào tiān dì
神创造天地
(创1:1-2:4)

起初神创造天地，把天空下面的水聚在一处，成为海洋，使陆地出现。然后神说："地上要生出青草、蔬菜和树木。"于是，事就这样 成了。

神又造了两个大光体，大的管理白天，是太阳；小的管理黑夜，是月亮。又造了星星，把它们安放在天空。

神又说："水里、空中和地

Qǐchū shén chuàngzào tiāndì, bǎ tiānkōng xiàmiàn de shuǐ jù zài yí chù, chéngwéi hǎiyáng, shǐ lùdì chūxiàn. Ránhòu shén shuō: "Dìshàng yào shēng chū qīngcǎo, shūcài hé shùmù "

Yúshì, shì jiù zhèyàng chéng le.

Shén yòu zào le liǎng gè dà guāngtǐ, dà de guǎnlǐ báitiān, shì tàiyáng; xiǎode guǎnlǐ hēiyè, shì yuèliàng. Yòu zào le xīngxing, bǎ tāmen ānfàng zài tiānkōng.

上，要有多种能活动的生物。"于是，事情又照神所说的成就了。

最后，神照着自己的形象创造了人，有男，有女。祂看着祂所造的一切都很好。

这样，六天之中天地万物都造齐了。第七天，神完成了祂所作的工，休息了。

Shén yòu shuō: "shuǐ lǐ, kōngzhōng hé dìshàng, yào yǒu duōzhǒng néng huó dòng de shēngwù." Yúshì, shì qíng yòu zhào shén suǒ shuō de chéngjiù le.

Zuìhòu, shénzhàozhe zìjǐ de xíng xiàng chuàngzàole rén, yǒu nán, yǒu nǚ. Tā kàn zhe tā suǒ zào de yíqiè dōu hěn hǎo.

Zhèyàng, liù tiān zhī zhōng tiándì wànwù dōu zào qí le. Dì qī tiān, shén wánchéng le tā suǒzuò de gōng, xiūxi le.

Table of Contents 目录

神 的 话 语

shén de huà yǔ
神 的 话 语
Pre-Unit
yù bèi dān yuán
预 备 单 元

Learning Objectives
xué xí mù dì
学 习 目 的

In this unit, you will learn to...

* Identify various translations of the Chinese Bible
* Navigate the Chinese Bible
* Understand basic Christian terminology in Chinese
* Name the books of the Bible in Chinese
* Locate any book or verse in the Chinese Bible

rènshi yēhéhuá róngyào de zhīshi yào chōngmǎn biàndì hǎoxiàng shuǐ chōngmǎn yánghǎi yìbān
认识耶和华荣耀的知识要充满遍地，好像水充满洋海一般。

—哈巴谷书 2:14

shèng jīng dān cí

圣经单词 Key Terms for Bible Reading

圣经	shèng jīng	(N)	Bible/Holy Scripture	福音	fúyīn	(N)	Gospel
译本	yì běn	(N)	translation	保罗书信	bǎo luó shū xìn	(N)	Pauline Epistles
旧约	jiù yuē	(N)	Old Testament	普通书信	pǔ tōng shū xìn	(N)	General Epistles
新约	xīn yuē	(N)	New Testament	启示	qǐshì	(N)	revelation
书卷	shū juàn	(N)	book	圣经故事	shèng jīng gù shi	(N)	Bible story
经文	jīng wén	(N)	scripture verse	叙述	xùshù	(N/V)	narrative; to narrate
章	zhāng	(N)	chapter	讲道	jiǎng dào	(N/V)	sermon; to preach
节	jié	(N)	verse	基督教	jī dū jiào	(N)	Christianity
预言	yù yán	(N/V)	prophecy; to predict	教义	jiào yì	(N)	doctrine
诗篇	shī piān	(N)	psalm	教会	jiào huì	(N)	church
箴言	zhēn yán	(N)	proverb	信条	xìn tiáo	(N)	creed
比喻	bǐyù	(N/V)	parable; to compare...to...	纲要	gāng yào	(N)	outline
律法	lù fǎ	(N)	law	盟约	méng yuē	(N)	covenant
摩西五经	mó xī wǔ jīng	(N)	Pentateuch	十诫	shí jiè	(N)	Ten Commandments
历史	lì shǐ	(N)	history	神迹	shén jì	(N)	miraculous sign
诗歌	shī gē	(N)	poetry	使徒	shǐtú	(N)	apostle
智慧文学	zhì huì wén xué	(N)	wisdom literature	先知	xiān zhī	(N)	prophet

cí xìng

词性 Parts of Speech

(N)	Noun	名词		(Adv)	Adverb	副词
(Pr)	Pronoun	代词		(M)	Measure word	量词
(Pn)	Proper Noun	专有名词		(Conj)	Conjunction	连词
(V)	Verb	动词		(Prep)	Preposition	介词
(Adj)	Adjective	形容词		(Part)	Particle	助词

课堂用语 Class Expressions

我们来讨论一下单元热身问题。 — Let's discuss our unit warm-up questions.

我们来看一下单元关键词汇。 — Let's take a look at the key terms for our unit.

我们来做课堂灵修。 — Let's do our class devotional.

我们来背诵一下我们的每日经文。 — Let's recite our daily memory verse.

请把圣经拿出来，我们来读经。 — Please take out your Bible. Let's read.

请打开圣经，翻到创世记一章一节。 — Please open your Bible to Genesis 1:1.

我们来查一查相关经文。 — Let's look up the related verses in the Bible.

请念一下这节/段经文。 — Please read this verse/paragraph.

请读第一节至第五节。 — Please read verses 1 to 5.

我们来读一个圣经故事。 — Let's read a Bible story.

我们来听一首诗歌。 — Let's listen to a hymn.

我们来唱诗敬拜。 — Let us sing and worship.

请大家来分享一下。 — Let's share with each other.

我们来一起祷告。 — Let's pray together.

请为……代祷。 — Please pray for…

专用标志 Special Markings

本书中符号《》代表书名。名称下加横线，代表专有人名或地名。课文中以红色突出显示的词或短语是特别注明的词语，粗体是出现在生词表中的字词。

In this book, the 《》 symbol represents the title of a book. Words underlined indicate proper names for a specific person or place. The words or phrases highlighted in red correspond with a special note, and the words in bold appear in the vocabulary list.

圣经目录—旧约 Old Testament Books

1	创世记	chuàng shì jì	（创）	Genesis
2	出埃及记	chū āi jí jì	（出）	Exodus
3	利未记	lì wèi jì	（利）	Leviticus
4	民数记	mín shù jì	（民）	Numbers
5	申命记	shēn mìng jì	（申）	Deuteronomy
6	约书亚记	yuē shū yà jì	（书）	Joshua
7	士师记	shì shī jì	（士）	Judges
8	路得记	lù dé jì	（得）	Ruth
9	撒母耳记上	sā mǔ'ěr jì shàng	（撒上）	1 Samuel
10	撒母耳记下	sā mǔ'ěr jì xià	（撒下）	2 Samuel
11	列王纪上	liè wáng jì shàng	（王上）	1 Kings
12	列王纪下	liè wáng jì xià	（王下）	2 Kings
13	历代志上	lì dài zhì shàng	（代上）	1 Chronicles
14	历代志下	lì dài zhì xià	（代下）	2 Chronicles
15	以斯拉记	yǐ sī lā jì	（拉）	Ezra
16	尼希米记	ní xī mǐ jì	（尼）	Nehemiah
17	以斯帖记	yǐ sī tiē jì	（斯）	Esther
18	约伯记	yuē bó jì	（伯）	Job
19	诗篇	shī piān	（诗）	Psalms
20	箴言	zhēn yán	（箴）	Proverbs
21	传道书	chuán dào shū	（传）	Ecclesiastes
22	雅歌	yǎ gē	（歌）	Song of Songs
23	以赛亚书	yǐ sài yà shū	（赛）	Isaiah
24	耶利米书	yē lì mǐ shū	（耶）	Jeremiah
25	耶利米哀歌	yē lì mǐ āi gē	（哀）	Lamentations
26	以西结书	yǐ xī jié shū	（结）	Ezekiel
27	但以理书	dàn yǐ lǐ shū	（但）	Daniel
28	何西阿书	hé xī'ā shū	（何）	Hosea
29	约珥书	yuē ěr shū	（珥）	Joel
30	阿摩司书	ā mó sī shū	（摩）	Amos
31	俄巴底亚书	é bā dǐ yà shū	（俄）	Obadiah
32	约拿书	yuē ná shū	（拿）	Jonah
33	弥迦书	mí jiā shū	（弥）	Micah
34	那鸿书	nà hóng shū	（鸿）	Nahum
35	哈巴谷书	hǎ bā gǔ shū	（哈）	Habakkuk
36	西番雅书	xī fān yǎ shū	（番）	Zephaniah
37	哈该书	hā gāi shū	（该）	Haggai
38	撒迦利亚书	sā jiā lì yǎ shū	（亚）	Zechariah
39	玛拉基书	mǎ lā jī shū	（玛）	Malachi

圣经目录—新约 New Testament Books

1	马太福音	mǎ tài fú yīn	（太）	Matthew
2	马可福音	mǎ kě fú yīn	（可）	Mark
3	路加福音	lù jiā fú yīn	（路）	Luke
4	约翰福音	yuē hàn fú yīn	（约）	John
5	使徒行传	shǐ tú xíng zhuàn	（徒）	Acts
6	罗马书	luó mǎ shū	（罗）	Romans
7	哥林多前书	gē lín duō qián shū	（林前）	1 Corinthians
8	哥林多后书	gē lín duō hòu shū	（林后）	2 Corinthians
9	加拉太书	jiā lā tài shū	（加）	Galatians
10	以弗所书	yǐ fú suǒ shū	（弗）	Ephesians
11	腓立比书	féi lì bǐ shū	（腓）	Philippians
12	歌罗西书	gē luō xī shū	（西）	Colossians
13	帖撒罗尼迦前书	tiē sā luō ní jiā qián shū	（帖前）	1 Thessalonians
14	帖撒罗尼迦后书	tiē sā luō ní jiā hòu shū	（帖后）	2 Thessalonians
15	提摩太前书	tí mó tài qián shū	（提前）	1 Timothy
16	提摩太后书	tí mó tài hòu shū	（提后）	2 Timothy
17	提多书	tí duō shū	（多）	Titus
18	腓利门书	féi lì mén shū	（门）	Philemon
19	希伯来书	xī bó lái shū	（来）	Hebrews
20	雅各书	yǎ gè shū	（雅）	James
21	彼得前书	bǐ dé qián shū	（彼前）	1 Peter
22	彼得后书	bǐ dé hòu shū	（彼后）	2 Peter
23	约翰一书	yuē hàn yī shū	（约一）	1 John
24	约翰二书	yuē hàn èr shū	（约二）	2 John
25	约翰三书	yuē hàn sān shū	（约三）	3 John
26	犹大书	yóu dà shū	（犹）	Jude
27	启示录	qǐ shì lù	（启）	Revelation

徒4:12；罗10:17；提后3:16-17；彼后1:20-21

圣经的六十六卷书是由四十位左右不同的作者用希伯来语、亚拉姆语和希腊语在大约一千四百多年的时间里写成的。圣经是神所启示的话，用来教导门徒，培养和预备信徒。圣经并不是仅仅由人类智慧所建立，而是由神启示的，并将永远持续下去。

The 66 books of the Bible were written over approximately 1,400 years by 40 different authors or so in Hebrew, Aramaic, and Greek. The 66 books of the Bible are the inspired words of God that are used to make disciples, and to develop and train believers. The Bible was not created by mere human wisdom but was inspired by God and will last forever.

虽然圣经谈到很多话题，但其中心思想是耶稣基督(犹太人的弥赛亚)来到世上，赐给我们永生的救恩。只有通过耶稣基督，我们才能得救。"可见信道是从听道来的，听道是从基督的话来的。"

While the Bible addresses many topics, its central message is that Jesus Christ (the Jewish Messiah) came into the world to provide the way of salvation for us. It is only through Jesus Christ that we can be saved. "Faith comes from hearing the message, and the message is heard through the word about Christ."

shèng jīng dà gāng
圣经大纲 Bible Outline

1. 摩西五经   1. 福音书
2. 历史书   2. 使徒行传
3. 诗歌与智慧书   3. 保罗书信
4. 先知书   4. 普通书信
                      5. 启示录

yì běn zhǐ dǎo
译本指导 A Chinese Bible Translation Guide

Commonly Used Abbreviations for Chinese Bible Translations:

hé hé běn
和合本 Chinese Union Version: CUV (CUVS, CUVT, CUVMPS, CUVMPT)

hé hé běn xiū dìng bǎn
和合本修订版 Revised Chinese Union Version: RCUV (RCUVS, RCUVT)

xīn biāo diǎn hé hé běn
*****新标点和合本** Chinese Union Version with New Punctuation: CUNPSS - 神/上帝

xīn yì běn
新译本 Chinese New Version: NCV (NCVS, NCVT) or CNV (CNVS, CNVT)

dāngdài shèngjīng
当代圣经 Chinese Contemporary Bible: CCB

zhōngwén biāozhǔn yìběn
中文标准译本 Chinese Standard Bible: CSB (CSBS, CSBT)

*除非另有说明，本书所有经文均取自英文新国际版圣经和中文新标点和合本--神版圣经。

*Unless otherwise indicated, all Scripture verses in this book are taken from the New International Version (NIV) of the Bible in English and the Chinese Union Version with New Punctuation (CUNPSS) of the Bible in Chinese.

Note on "Shén" and "Shàngdì" Editions of the Bible:

"Shangdi" is an ancient name for God that originated in the Chinese language and culture. "Shen" is a generic term for God. The "Shen" edition is more commonly used but neither of the translations should cause any interpretation issues unless the reader is from a background that has certain connotations regarding the generic term for God.

本书中凡是称呼"神"的地方，也可以称"上帝"。

Where "神 shén" is used in this book, "上帝 shàngdì" can also be used.

书卷类别 Books of the Bible

圣经六十六卷书含旧约和新约两部分。旧约有三十九卷书，新约有二十

七卷书。旧约和新约书卷各有四个主要的分类：

The Bible includes 66 books and consists of two parts, the Old Testament and New Testament. The Old Testament includes 39 books, and the New Testament includes 27 books. The Old and New Testaments each include four major divisions of books.

类别	旧约	类别	新约
摩西五经	The Pentateuch 创世记、出埃及记、利未记、民数记和申命记	福音书	The Gospels 马太福音、马可福音、路加福音、约翰福音
历史书	The Historical Books 约书亚记、士师记、路得记、撒母耳记上下、列王纪上下、历代志上下、以斯拉记，尼希米记和以斯帖记	历史书	The Historical Book 使徒行传
诗歌与智慧书	Poetry and Wisdom Books 约伯记、诗篇、箴言、传道书、雅歌（或所罗门之歌）	书信	The Epistles 十三封保罗书信（罗马书、哥林多前后书、加拉太书、以弗所书、腓立比书、歌罗西书、帖撒罗尼迦前后书、提摩太前后书、提多书和腓利门书）和八封一般书信（希伯来书、雅各书、彼得前后书、约翰一二三书和犹大书）
先知书	The Prophets 五卷大先知书（以赛亚、耶利米、耶利米哀歌、以西结和但以理）和十二卷小先知书（何西阿，约珥，阿摩司，俄巴底亚、约拿、弥迦、那鸿、哈巴谷、西番雅、哈该、撒迦利亚和玛拉基）	先知书	The Prophetic Book 启示录

单元简要 Unit Summary

神的话记在一本书里头，

这本书就是圣经。

圣经告诉我们：

神造天地和万物。

圣经告诉我们：

神的救恩和祂的爱。

圣经是一本关于生命意义的书，

是充满智慧的书。

shén
神

de
的

huà
话

shén de huà jì zài yìběn shū lǐ tou,

zhè běn shū jiù shì shèngjīng.

shèngjīng gàosu wǒmen:

shén zào tiāndì hé wànwù.

shèngjīng gàosu wǒmen:

shén de jiù ēn hé tā de ài.

shèngjīng shì yìběn guānyú shēngmìng yìyì de shū,

shì chōngmǎn zhìhuì de shū.

wèn tí gēn zōng
问题跟踪 Follow-up Questions

1. 圣经是一本什么样的书？

2. 圣经告诉我们什么？

3. 圣经的旧约和新约书卷各有几个主要分类？

4. 圣经的旧约和新约书卷是怎么分类的？

经文游踪 Cite the Verse

tài chū yǒu dào　dào yǔ shén tóng zài　dào jiù shì shén

"太初有道，道与神同在，道就是神。"

xiāng guān jīng wén
相关经文 Related Verses

诗119:105；箴30:5；

赛40:8；约8:47；林前2:4-5；来11:3

xuān dú mò xiǎng
宣读默想 Read and Meditate

dāng yòng gè yàng de zhì huì　bǎ jī dū de dào lǐ fēng fēng fù fù de cún zài xīn

"当用各样的智慧，把基督的道理丰丰富富地存在心

lǐ　yòng shī zhāng　sòng cí　líng gē　bǐ cǐ jiào dǎo　hù xiāng quàn jiè

里。用诗章、颂词、灵歌，彼此教导，互相劝戒，

xīn bèi ēn gǎn　gē sòng shén

心被恩感，歌颂神。"

— 歌罗西书 3:16

Let the message of Christ dwell among you richly as you teach and admonish one another with all wisdom through psalms, hymns, and songs from the Spirit, singing to God with gratitude in your hearts.

— Colossians 3:16

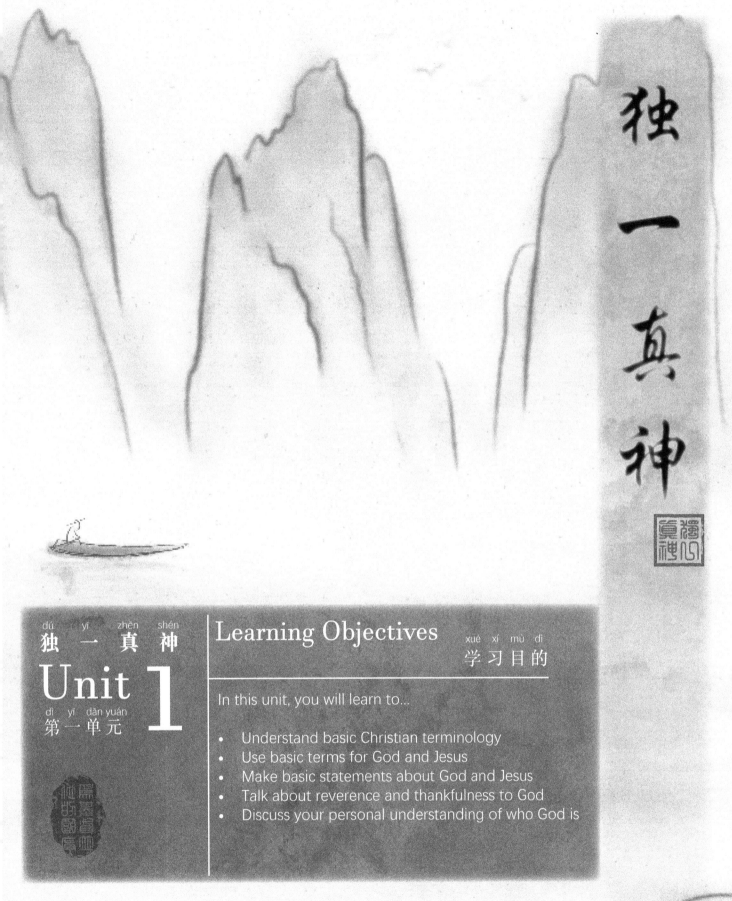

独 一 真 神

dú yī zhēn shén
独 一 真 神
Unit 1
dì yī dān yuán
第 一 单 元

Learning Objectives
xué xí mù dì
学 习 目 的

In this unit, you will learn to...

- Understand basic Christian terminology
- Use basic terms for God and Jesus
- Make basic statements about God and Jesus
- Talk about reverence and thankfulness to God
- Discuss your personal understanding of who God is

rènshi nǐ dúyī de zhēn shén bìng qiě rèn shi nǐ suǒ chāi lái de yē sū jī dū   zhè jiù shì yǒngshēng
认识你独一的真神，并且认识你所差来的耶稣基督，这就是永生。

—约翰福音17:3

Unit 1：预备学习
第一单元

guān jiàn cí huì
关键词汇 Key Terms

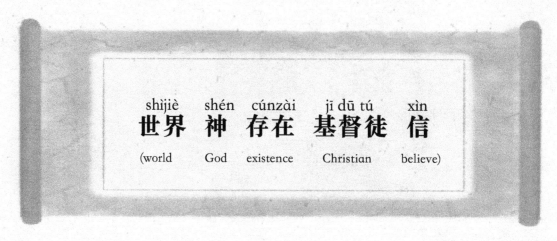

shìjiè	shén	cúnzài	jī dū tú	xìn
世界	神	存在	基督徒	信
(world	God	existence	Christian	believe)

rè shēn wèn tí
热身问题 Warm-up Questions

1. 世界上真的有神吗？

2. 我们人如何能知道神的存在？

3. 如果有人问你基督徒信什么，你怎么回答？

jīng wén xì dú
经文细读 Key Verse Reading

shén duì mó xī shuō   wǒ shì zì yǒu yǒng yǒu de   yòu shuō   nǐ yào duì yǐ sè liè rén zhè yàng shuō
神对摩西说："我是自有永有的"；又说："你要对以色列人这样说：

nà zì yǒu de dǎ fā wǒ dào nǐ men zhè lǐ lái
'那自有的打发我到你们这里来。'"   — 出埃及记 3:14

God said to Moses, "I AM WHO I AM. This is what you are to say to the Israelites: 'I Am has sent me to you.'"

— Exodus 3:14

12

Lesson 1
第一课

自有永有
zì yǒu yǒng yǒu

课堂灵修 Class Devotional

wǒ shì ā lā fǎ　wǒ shì é méi jiá　wǒ shì shǒu xiān de　wǒ shì mò hòu de　wǒ shì chū
我是阿拉法，我是俄梅戛；我是首先的，我是末后的；我是初，

wǒ shì zhōng
我是终。

— 启示录 22:13

Daily Memory Verse

每日经文背诵
měi rì jīng wén bèi sòng

zhǔ shén shuō　　wǒ shì ā lā fǎ　　wǒ shì é méi jiá
主神说："我是阿拉法，我是俄梅戛，

shì xī zài　　jīn zài　　yǐ hòu yǒng zài de quán néng zhě
是昔在、今在、以后永在的全能者。

— 启示录 1:8

shèng jīng jīn jù
圣经金句 Frequently Quoted Verse

nǐ　wéi dú nǐ shì yē hé huá　nǐ zào le tiān hé tiānshàng de tiān　bìng tiānshàng de wànxiàng
你，惟独你是耶和华！你造了天和天上的天，并天上的万象，

dì hé dì shàng de wànwù　hǎi hé hǎizhōng suǒyǒu de　zhè yí qiè dōu shì nǐ suǒ bǎocún de
地和地上的万物，海和海中所有的；这一切都是你所保存的。

— 尼希米记 9:6

You alone are the Lord. You made the heavens, even the highest heavens, and all their starry host, the earth and all that is on it, the seas and all that is in them. You give life to everything.

— Nehemiah 9:6

shén rén zhī yuē
神人之约

神说："我们要照着我们的形象、按着我们的样式造人，使他们管理海里的鱼、空中的鸟、地上的牲畜，和全地，并地上所爬的一切昆虫。"

神就照着自己的形象造人，乃是照着他的形象造男造女。神就赐福给他们，又对他们说："要生养众多，遍满地面，治理这地，也要管理海里的鱼、空中的鸟，和地上各样行动的活物。"

— 创世记 1:26-28

God's Covenant with Mankind

Then God said, "Let us make mankind in our image, in our likeness, so that they may rule over the fish in the sea and the birds in the sky, over the livestock and all the wild animals, and over all the creatures that move along the ground." So God created mankind in his own image, in the image of God he created them; male and female he created them. God blessed them and said to them, "Be fruitful and increase in number; fill the earth and subdue it. Rule over the fish in the sea and the birds in the sky and over every living creature that moves on the ground."

— Genesis 1:26-28

shī piān jí jǐn
诗篇集锦 Psalm Reading

他的名要存到永远，
要留传如日之久。
人要因他蒙福；
万国要称他有福。
独行奇事的耶和华—
以色列的神是应当称颂的！

May his name endure forever;
may it continue as long as the sun.
Then all nations will be blessed through him,
and they will call him blessed.
Praise be to the Lord God,
the God of Israel,
who alone does marvelous deeds.

— Psalm 72:17-18 —

— 诗篇 72:17-18 —

课文预读 Introductory Reading

上帝是神，

是真神，

是万军的神。

耶和华是祂的名号，

是神永久的名字，

也是神永远被记念的名，

世世代代的人都要这样称呼祂。

耶和华是首先的，是末后的；

祂是以色列的王，

是以色列的救赎主。

祂是亚伯拉罕的神，

是以撒的神，是雅各的神。

除祂以外，再没有真神。

谁能像耶和华？

一切荣耀都归给祂的名！

shén
de
míng

神
的
名

shàngdì shì shén,

shì zhēn shén,

shì wàn jūn de shén.

yēhéhuá shì tā de míng hào,

shì shén yǒngjiǔ de míngzi,

yě shì shén yǒngyuǎn bèi jì niàn de míng,

shìshì dàidài de rén dōu yào zhèyàng chēnghu tā.

yēhéhuá shì shǒuxiān de, shì mòhòu de;

tā shì yǐsèliè de wáng,

shì yǐsèliè de jiù shú zhǔ.

tā shì yàbólāhàn de shén,

shì yǐsā de shén, shì yǎgè de shén.

chú tā yǐ wài, zài méi yǒu zhēn shén.

shéi néng xiàng yēhéhuá?

yí qiè róngyào dōu guī gěi tā de míng!

预读问题 Pre-reading Questions

1. 上帝是谁？

2. "耶和华"是谁的名字？

3. 上帝是怎样的神？

参考经文 Reference Verses for the Text

出3:14-15；赛42:8, 44:6；何12:5

圣经告诉我们只有一位真神。神说："我是**首先**的，我是**末后**的，除我以外再没有真神。"

圣经还向我们**启示**了这位神的名字，祂的名字叫"**耶和华**[*]"。这个名字在圣经里出现了上千次，是"**自有永有**[*]"的意思，也就是说，神是自存者，是存在的**独一源头**。所以，神在圣经中启示祂[*]自己为自有永有的独一真神。

神在圣经中还有许多别的**称谓**，例如**上帝、主、全能者、创造主**和**牧者**。但圣经中人**称呼**神最多的还是"神（上帝）"或"耶和华"。

课文特注

* "耶和华"yēhéhuá：有些基督教书籍上也使用"雅威"yǎwēi，是YHWH的音译，是"主"（zhǔ）的意思。

* "自有永有"zì yǒu yǒng yǒu："I AM WHO I AM"

* "祂"tā 为神或主耶稣的"他"代名词。本书引用的经文中依和合本照旧用"他"。

shèngjīng gàosu wǒmen zhǐyǒu yí wèi zhēnshén. shén shuō: "wǒ shì **shǒuxiān** de, wǒ shì **mòhòu** de, chú wǒ yǐwài zài méiyǒu zhēnshén."

shèngjīng hái xiàng wǒmen **qǐshì** le zhè wèi shén de míngzi, jiàozuò "**yēhéhuá***". zhège míngzi zài shèngjīng lǐ chūxiàn le shàng qiān cì, shì "zìyǒu**yǒng**yǒu*" de yìsi, yě jiùshì shuō, shén shì zì cún zhě, shì cúnzài de **dúyī yuántóu**. suǒyǐ, shén zài shèngjīng zhōng qǐshì tā* zìjǐ wéi zìyǒuyǒngyǒu de dúyī zhēn shén.

shén zài shèngjīng zhōng hái yǒu xǔduō bié de **chēngwèi**, lìrú **shàngdì, zhǔ, quánnéngzhě, chuàngzàozhǔ** hé **mùzhě**. dàn shèngjīng zhōng rén **chēnghu** shén zuìduō de háishì "shén (shàngdì)" huò "yēhéhuá".

Special Notes on Text

* Jehovah/Yahweh: Some Christian books also use "yǎwēi," which is a transliteration of YHWH and means "Lord."

* zìyǒuyǒngyǒu: "I AM WHO I AM"

* tā 祂 (He) is synonymous with "tā 他" for God or Jesus Christ. For the scriptures quoted in this book, "他" is still used according to the Chinese Union Version translation of the Bible.

1.	首先	shǒu xiān	(Adj)	first of all
2.	末后	mò hòu	(Adj)	last of all
3.	启示	qǐ shì	(V)	to reveal
4.	耶和华	yē hé huá	(N)	Yahweh
5.	永	yǒng	(Adj)	forever, permanent
6.	独一	dú yī	(Adj)	only, sole
7.	源头	yuán tóu	(N)	source, beginning
8.	称谓	chēng wèi	(N)	title, salutation
9.	上帝	shàng dì	(N)	God (also 神)
10.	主	zhǔ	(N)	the Lord
11.	创造主	chuàngzàozhǔ	(N)	Creator
12.	全能者	quánnéngzhě	(N)	Almighty
13.	牧者	mù zhě	(N)	shepherd
14.	称呼	chēng hu	(V)	to call, to address

读后讨论 Post-reading Discussion

1. 我们如何称呼神的名?

2. 神给自己的名字是什么意思?

3. 新旧约中人对神有哪些称谓?人称呼神最多的是什么?

jìng bài zàn měi
敬拜赞美 Worship and Praise

Goodness of the Lord

Let the name of the Lord be praised,
both now and forevermore.
From the rising of the sun to the place where it sets,
the name of the Lord is to be praised.
The Lord is exalted over all the nations,
his glory above the heavens.

— Psalm 113: 2-4 —

yē hé huá de liáng shàn
耶和华的良善

yēhéhuá de míng shì yīngdāng chēngsòng de
耶和华的名是应当称颂的,

cóng jīn shí zhídào yǒngyuǎn
从今时直到永远!

cóng rìchū zhī dì dào rìluò zhī chù
从日出之地到日落之处,

yēhéhuá de míng shì yīngdāng zànměi de
耶和华的名是应当赞美的!

yēhéhuá chāohū wànmín zhī shàng
耶和华超乎万民之上;

tā de róngyào gāo guò zhū tiān
他的荣耀高过诸天。

— 诗篇 113:2-4 —

三一颂

赞美真神万福之源，

世上万民都当颂扬，

天使天军赞美主名，

赞美圣父圣子圣灵。

阿们。

—浸信会版本

Sān Yī Sòng

zànměi zhēnshén wànfú zhī yuán,

shìshàng wànmín dōu dāng sòngyáng,

tiānshǐ tiānjūn zànměi zhǔ míng,

zànměi shèngfù shèngzǐ shènglíng.

āmen.

Doxology

Praise God, from whom all blessings flow;

Praise Him, all creatures here below;

Praise Him above, ye heavenly host;

Praise Father, Son, and Holy Ghost.

Amen.

　　因为你是我的岩石，我的山寨；所以，求你为你名的缘故

引导我，指点我。

—诗篇 31:3

Since you are my rock and my fortress, for the sake of your name lead and

guide me.

— Psalm 31:3

qí dǎo fàn wén
祈祷范文 Exemplary Prayer

赛45:5；撒下7:22；太6:9

　　主啊，祢是独一的真神，耶和华祢的名在全地多么的美，没有可比

祢的。祢在时间空间以上、以先、以外，祢本为大。求祢帮助我们更多

地认识祢，看见祢的大能，只认祢为独一真神，让祢来作我们的主人。

奉主耶稣基督的名祷告，阿们。

Lesson 2: 道成肉身
第二课
dào chéng ròu shén

课堂灵修 Class Devotional
kè táng líng xiū

chú le wǒ yǐ wài   zài méi yǒu shén   wǒ shì gōng yì de shén   yòu shì jiù zhǔ   chú le wǒ yǐ wài
除了我以外，再没有神；我是公义的神，又是救主；除了我以外，

zài méi yǒu bié shén
再没有别神。

— 以赛亚书 45:21

Daily Memory Verse

每日经文背诵
měi rì jīng wén bèi sòng

yīn wèi zhǐ yǒu yí wèi shén   zài shén hé rén zhōng jiān   zhǐ yǒu
因为只有一位神，在神和人中间，只有

yí wèi zhōngbǎo   nǎi shì jiàng shì wéi rén de jī dū yē sū
一位中保，乃是降世为人的基督耶稣。

— 提摩太前书 2:5

圣经金句 Frequently Quoted Verse
shèng jīng jīn jù

fán rèn yē sū wéi shén ér zi de   shén jiù zhù zài tā lǐ miàn   tā yě zhù zài shén lǐ miàn
凡认耶稣为神儿子的，神就住在他里面，他也住在神里面。

— 约翰一书 4:15

If anyone acknowledges that Jesus is the Son of God, God lives in them and they in God.

— 1 John 4:15

22

盟约应许 Covenantal Promise

méng yuē yīng xǔ

伊甸之约
yī diàn zhī yuē

耶和华神用地上的尘土造人，将生气吹在他鼻孔里，他就成了有灵
yē hé huá shén yòng chén tǔ zào jiāng chuī bí kǒng chéng líng

的活人，名叫亚当。耶和华神将那人安置在伊甸园，使他修理，看守。
huó yà dāng ān zhì yī diàn yuán shǐ xiū lǐ kān shǒu

耶和华神吩咐他说："园中各样树上的果子，你可以随意吃，只是分别善
fēn fù gè shù guǒ suí yì fēn bié shàn

恶树上的果子，你不可吃，因为你吃的日子必定死！"
è bì dìng sǐ

— 创世记 2:7，15-17

The Edenic Covenant

Then the Lord God formed a man from the dust of the ground and breathed into his nostrils the breath of life, and the man became a living being. The Lord God took the man and put him in the Garden of Eden to work it and take care of it. And the Lord God commanded the man, "You are free to eat from any tree in the garden; but you must not eat from the tree of the knowledge of good and evil, for when you eat from it you will certainly die."

— Genesis 2:7, 15-17

诗篇集锦 Psalm Reading

shī piān jí jǐn

Give praise to the Lord,

proclaim his name;

make known among the nations what he has done.

Sing to him, sing praise to him;

tell of all his wonderful acts.

Glory in his holy name

— Psalm 105:1-3 —

你们要称谢耶和华，
nǐmen yào chēngxiè yēhéhuá

求告他的名，
qiúgào tā de míng

在万民中传扬他的作为！
zài wànmín zhōng chuányáng tā de zuòwéi

要向他唱诗歌颂，
yào xiàng tā chàngshī gēsòng

谈论他一切奇妙的作为！
tánlùn tā yíqiè qímiào de zuòwéi

要以他的圣名夸耀！
yào yǐ tā de shèngmíng kuāyào

— 诗篇 105:1-3 —

课文预读 Introductory Reading

神爱世上的人，

将祂的独生爱子耶稣赐给我们。

神的儿子为了爱我们，

离开天堂来到世界上，

神成为人，道成了肉身。

耶稣为了爱我们，

为我们舍命，死在十字架上，

做我们的救主，

赐给我们新生命。

世上的国成了主所立的基督的国，

耶稣基督是我们永永远远的王。

我们信靠耶稣，

心里就有耶稣的生命，

也有耶稣的真理，

更有最美的福音盼望。

神 的 儿 子
shén de ér zi

shén ài shìshàng de rén,

jiāng tā de dú shēng ài zǐ yēsū cìgěi wǒmen.

shén de érzi wèile ài wǒmen,

líkāi tiāntáng lái dào shìjiè shàng,

shén chéngwéi rén, dào chéngle ròushēn.

yēsū wèile ài wǒmen,

wèi wǒmen shěmìng, sǐ zài shízìjià shàng,

zuò wǒmen de jiùzhǔ,

cì gěi wǒmen xīn shēngmìng.

shìshàng de guó chéngle zhǔ suǒ lì de jīdū de guó,

yēsū jīdū shì wǒmen yǒngyǒng yuǎnyuǎn de wáng.

wǒmen xìn kào yēsū,

xīnlǐ jiù yǒu yēsū de shēngmìng,

yěyǒu yēsū de zhēnlǐ,

gèng yǒu zuìměi de fúyīn pànwàng.

预读问题 Pre-reading Questions

1. 我们怎么知道神爱世人？

2. 神的儿子为什么要死在十字架上？

3. 我们人为什么要信靠耶稣？

参考经文 Reference Verses for the Text

约1:1-5，14，14:6；路2:11；可1:1；启11:15，17:14

太初，道已经存在，道与神同在，道就是神，万物是藉着祂造的。在祂里面有**生命**，这生命是**人类**的**光**。世界是藉着祂造的，世界却不认识祂。

这道就是**耶稣基督**[*]，是神的独生爱子。神为了爱我们，将祂的**独生子**耶稣基督赐给我们，道成肉身，成为人的样式，住在我们中间。耶稣**降生**时**天使宣告**："今天在大卫的城里，为你们生了**救主**[*]，就是主基督"。神的儿子[*]耶稣这名告诉我们祂是来作我们的救主，是要叫我们得着生命。

耶稣说："我就是**道路**、**真理**、生命；若不藉着我，没有人能到父那里去。"我们如**信靠**耶稣，在我们里面就有耶稣的生命和真理，更有最美的**盼望**。末日，藉着耶稣我们就可以到天父那里去。

所以，耶稣基督是真神，是"万王之王，万主之主"。主耶稣再来时，世上的国就要成为神的国，祂要作王，直到永永远远。

课文特注

* 新约中人对耶稣的称谓，最多的是"基督"（jīdū）和"主"（zhǔ），其他还有"救主"（jiùzhǔ）和"圣子"（shèngzǐ）等。

* "耶稣"yēsū：意思是"救主"（jiùzhǔ）（太1:21）

* "基督"jīdū：是由希腊文"Christos"音译而来，是希伯来文"弥赛亚"（mísàiyà）的希腊文翻译。中文圣经里译为"受膏者"（shòugāozhě）。

* "神的儿子"shén de érzi：旧约中神称自己的选民以色列人为神的儿子，指这百姓是为神所治理的。新约中耶稣被称为神的儿子，是指父神的独生子，具有百分之百的神性。

tàichū, dào yǐjīng cúnzài, dào yǔ shén tóng zài, dào jiùshì shén, wànwù shì jièzhe tā zào de. zài tā lǐmiàn yǒu **shēngmìng**, zhè shēngmìng shì **rénlèi** de **guāng**. shìjiè shì jièzhe tā zào de, shìjiè què bú rènshi tā.

zhè dào jiùshì **yēsū jīdū***, shì shén de dú shēng ài zǐ. shén wèi le ài wǒmen, jiāng tā de **dúshēngzǐ** yēsū jīdū cìgěi wǒmen, dào chéng ròushēn, chéngwéi rén de yàngshì, zhù zài wǒmen zhōngjiān. yēsū **jiàngshēng** shí **tiānshǐ xuāngào**: "jīntiān zài dàwèi de chéng lǐ, wèi nǐmen shēng le **jiùzhǔ***, jiùshì zhǔ jīdū". shén de érzi* zhè míng gàosu wǒmen tā shì lái zuò wǒmen de jiùzhǔ, shì yào jiào wǒmen dézháo shēngmìng.

yēsū shuō: "wǒ jiùshì **dàolù**, **zhēnlǐ**, shēngmìng; ruò bú jièzhe wǒ, méiyǒu rén néng dào fù nàlǐ qù". wǒmen rúguǒ **xìnkào** yēsū, zài wǒmen lǐmiàn jiù yǒu yēsū de shēngmìng hé zhēnlǐ, gèng yǒu zuìměi de **pànwàng**. mòrì, jièzhe yēsū wǒmen jiù kěyǐ dào tiānfù nàlǐ qù.

suǒyǐ, yēsū jīdū shì zhēnshén, shì "wàn wáng zhī wáng, wàn zhǔ zhī zhǔ". zhǔ yēsū zài lái shí, shìshàng de guó jiù yào chéngwéi shén de guó, tā yào zuò wáng, zhídào yǒng yǒng yuǎn yuǎn.

Special Notes on Text

* The most common names for Jesus in the New Testament are "Christ"(jīdū) and "Lord"(zhǔ). Other names include "Savior"(jiùzhǔ) and "Son of God"(shèngzǐ).

* yēsū (Jesus) means "Savior"(jiùzhǔ) (Mt 1:21)

* jīdū (Christ) is transliterated from the Greek word "Christos," which is the Greek translation of the Hebrew word "Messiah"(mísàiyà), which is in turn translated as "Anointed One"(shòugāozhě) in the Chinese Bible.

* shén de érzi (Son of God): In the Old Testament, God called His chosen people, Israel, the sons of God, referring to this people as governed by God. In the New Testament, Jesus is called the Son of God, referring to the only begotten Son of God the Father, who is wholly (lit. "one hundred percent") divine.

1.	生命	shēng mìng	(N)	life
2.	人类	rén lèi	(N)	humanity
3.	光	guāng	(N)	light
4.	独生子	dú shēng zǐ	(N)	only begotten son
5.	耶稣	yē sū	(N)	Jesus
6.	基督	jī dū	(N)	Christ
7.	降生	jiàng shēng	(V)	to be born
8.	天使	tiān shǐ	(N)	angel
9.	宣告	xuān gào	(V)	to announce
10.	救主	jiù zhǔ	(N)	Savior
11.	道路	dào lù	(N)	way
12.	真理	zhēn lǐ	(N)	truth
13.	信靠	xìn kào	(V)	to rely on
14.	盼望	pàn wàng	(N)	hope

读后讨论 Post-reading Discussion

dú hòu tǎo lùn

1. 耶稣基督是谁？

2. 除了"主"、"救主"以外，圣经里对耶稣基督还有什么称呼？

3. 耶稣基督为什么"降世为人"？

敬拜赞美 Worship and Praise

jìng bài zàn měi

A Psalm of Thanksgiving

Shout for joy to the Lord, all the earth.

Worship the Lord with gladness;

come before him with joyful songs.

Know that the Lord is God.

It is he who made us, and we are his;

we are his people, the sheep of his pasture.

Enter his gates with thanksgiving

and his courts with praise;

give thanks to him and praise his name

— Psalm 100:1-4 —

赞美之诗

zàn měi zhī shī

pǔ tiānxià dāng xiàng yēhéhuá huānhū
普天下当向耶和华欢呼！

nǐmen dāng lèyì shì fèng yēhéhuá
你们当乐意事奉耶和华，

dāng lái xiàng tā gē chàng
当来向他歌唱！

nǐmen dāng xiǎode yēhéhuá shì shén
你们当晓得耶和华是神！

wǒmen shì tā zào de yěshì shǔ tā de
我们是他造的，也是属他的；

wǒmen shì tā de mín yěshì tā cǎochǎng de yáng
我们是他的民，也是他草场的羊。

dāng chēngxiè jìnrù tā de mén
当称谢进入他的门；

dāng zànměi jìnrù tā de yuàn
当赞美进入他的院。

dāng gǎnxiè tā, chēngsòng tā de míng
当感谢他，称颂他的名！

—诗篇 100:1-4 —

三一颂

赞美真神万福之根，

地上生灵当赞主恩，

天上万军颂赞主名，

赞美圣父圣子圣灵。

阿们。

—宣道出版社《生命圣诗》版本

Sān Yī Sòng

zànměi zhēnshén wànfú zhī gēn,

dìshàng shēnglíng dāng zàn zhǔ ēn,

tiānshàng wànjūn sòngzàn zhǔ míng,

zànměi shèngfù shèngzǐ shènglíng.

āmen.

Doxology

Praise God, from whom all blessings flow;

Praise Him, all creatures here below;

Praise Him above, ye heavenly host;

Praise Father, Son, and Holy Ghost.

Amen.

_{yē hé huá}　_{qiú jiāng}　_{dào zhǐ jiào}　　_{zhào}　_{zhēn lǐ}
耶和华啊，求你将你的道指教我；我要照你的真理行；求

_{shǐ}　_{zhuān jìng wèi}
你使我专心敬畏你的名！
　　　　　　　　　　　　　　　　　　　　　　　　—诗篇 86:11

Teach me your way, Lord, that I may rely on your faithfulness; give me an un-
divided heart, that I may fear your name.
　　　　　　　　　　　　　　　　　　　　　　　　— Psalm 86:11

_{qí dǎo fàn wén}
祈祷范文 Exemplary Prayer

罗11:36；林前8:6；来1:3

_{yē sū}　_{wàn zhī}　　　_{héděng bǎoguì}　　　　_{běn}　_{nǐ}　　　_{jiè}
耶稣，万名之上的名，何等宝贵的名，万有都本于祢，万物都是藉着

_{shén tǐ xiàng}　　_{dú}　　_{jiàngbēi chéngwéi}　　　_{dāng}
祢来的。神本体的真像，神的独生子，祢降卑成为人子，来到我们当中，

_{dài zì yóu}　_{ān níng.}　　　　_{bié wú cì}　_{zhěngjiù}　_{yuàn róngyào guī}　_{shèng}　_{zhǔ}
带来自由和安宁。天下人间，别无赐下拯救，愿荣耀都归祢的圣名。主耶

_{shèngjīng hé}　　　　　　　　　　　　　　　　_{mìng}
稣，祢是圣经的核心，愿祢在今天和以后的每一天也成为我们生命的中

_{fèng}　_{dǎogào}　_ā
心。奉祢的名祷告，阿们。

Lesson 3: 圣灵运行
第三课
shèng líng yùn xíng

课堂灵修 Class Devotional

dàn wǒ yào cóng fù nà lǐ chāi bǎo huì shī lái　　jiù shì cóng fù chū lái zhēnlǐ de shènglíng　tā　lái le
但我要从父那里差保惠师来，就是从父出来真理的圣灵；他来了，

jiù yào wèi wǒ zuò jiànzhèng
就要为我做见证。

—— 约翰福音 15:26

---— Daily Memory Verse —---

每
日　mēi rì jīng wén bèi sòng
经
文
背
诵

shén shì gè líng　　suǒ yǐ bài tā　de bì　xū yòng xīn líng
神是个灵，所以拜他的必须用心灵
hé chéngshí bài　tā
和诚实拜他。

—— 约翰福音 4:24

圣经金句 Frequently Quoted Verse

jiù rú shēn zi shì yí gè　　què yǒu xǔ duō zhī tǐ　　ér qiě zhī tǐ suī duō　　réng shì yí gè
就如身子是一个，却有许多肢体；而且肢体虽多，仍是一个

shēn zi　　jī dū yě shì zhè yàng
身子；基督也是这样。

—— 哥林多前书 12:12

Just as a body, though one, has many parts, but all its many parts form one body, so it is with Christ.

—— 1 Corinthians 12:12

盟约应许 Covenantal Promise

yà dāng zhī yuē
亚当之约

神对女人说：我必多多加增你怀胎的苦楚；你生产儿女必多受苦楚。你必恋慕你丈夫；你丈夫必管辖你。又对亚当说：你既听从妻子的话，吃了我所吩咐你不可吃的那树上的果子，地必为你的缘故受咒诅；你必终身劳苦才能从地里得吃的。地必给你长出荆棘和蒺藜来；你也要吃田间的菜蔬。你必汗流满面才得糊口，直到你归了土，因为你是从土而出的。你本是尘土，仍要归于尘土。

— 创世记 3:16-19

The Adamic Covenant

To the woman he said, "I will make your pains in childbearing very severe; with painful labor you will give birth to children. Your desire will be for your husband, and he will rule over you." To Adam he said, "Because you listened to your wife and ate fruit from the tree about which I commanded you, 'You must not eat from it,' "Cursed is the ground because of you; through painful toil you will eat food from it all the days of your life. It will produce thorns and thistles for you, and you will eat the plants of the field. By the sweat of your brow you will eat your food until you return to the ground, since from it you were taken; for dust you are and to dust you will return.

— Genesis 3:16-19

诗篇集锦 Psalm Reading

You have searched me, Lord, and you know me.
 You know when I sit and when I rise;
 you perceive my thoughts from afar.
You discern my going out and my lying down;
 you are familiar with all my ways.

— Psalm 139:1-3 —

耶和华啊，你已经鉴察我，认识我。
我坐下，我起来，你都晓得；
你从远处知道我的意念。
我行路，我躺卧，你都细察；
你也深知我一切所行的。

— 诗篇 139:1-3 —

课文预读 Introductory Reading

神就是爱，

住在爱里面的，就住在神里面。

耶稣将自己的生命给我们，

也将祂的平安和喜乐赐给我们。

只要我们信靠祂，

就能得到新的生命，平安和喜乐。

我们所以知道神住在我们里面，

是因为神所赐的圣灵。

这圣灵是神的灵，

它能感动人的心，

启示人的心，

和安慰人的心，

住在每一个信耶稣的人的心中。

圣灵让人也知道、也信，

有真正的平安喜乐和盼望。

shén
神
de
的
líng
灵

shén jiù shì ài,

zhù zài ài lǐmiàn de, jiù zhù zài shén lǐmiàn.

yēsū jiāng zìjǐ de shēngmìng gěi wǒmen,

yě jiāng tā de píng'ān hé xǐlè cìgěi wǒmen.

zhǐyào wǒmen xìn kào tā,

jiù néng dédào xīn de shēngmìng, píng'ān hé xǐlè.

wǒmen suǒyǐ zhīdao shén zhù zài wǒmen lǐmiàn,

shì yīnwèi shén suǒ cì de shènglíng.

zhè shènglíng shì shén de líng,

tā néng gǎndòng rén de xīn,

qǐshì rén de xīn,

hé ānwèi rén de xīn,

zhù zài měi yí gè xìn yēsū de rén de xīnzhōng.

shènglíng ràng rén yě zhīdao, yě xìn,

yǒu zhēnzhèng de píng'ān xǐlè hé pànwàng.

预读问题 Pre-reading Questions

1. 耶稣赐给我们什么？

2. 圣灵的工作是什么？

3. 我们怎么才可以得到真正的平安喜乐？

参考经文 Reference Verses for the Text

弥5:2；太28:19；约4:24；10:30；15:26；罗8:9；

西1:15；约一4:15

圣经告诉我们神是从**亘古**到永远都存在的神，是**无所不能、无所不知、无所不在**的神。神只有一位，有三个**位格**：圣父、圣子和圣灵*。圣子由圣父所生，圣灵由圣父而出。我们从圣经中还知道神是灵，是**无限的**，**永恒的**，是不**改变**的。

基督是神，祂的**根源**从太初就有。所以保罗说，"爱子是那不能看见之神的像，是首生的，在一切被造的以先。"耶稣也说："我与父原为一。"所以，"凡认耶稣为神儿子的，神就住在他里面，他也住在神里面"。

耶稣**应许**赐给我们的"保惠师*"是从父出来真理的圣灵，也是基督的灵。圣灵住在信靠耶稣的人心中，**感动**、启示、和**安慰**人的心，赐平安和喜乐，智慧和盼望。"如果神的灵住在我们心里，我们就不属肉体，乃属圣灵了。"

所以，圣父是神，圣子是神，圣灵也是神，是"**三位一体***"同受**敬拜**，同享**尊荣**，同有**权柄**的神。

课文特注

* "灵"líng：这个字的希伯来文是"ruach"，希腊文是"pneuma"。在这两种文字中都是"风"（fēng）的意思。

* "保惠师"bǎohuìshī：英文是"安慰者"（ānwèizhě），中文可翻译为"帮助者"（bāngzhùzhě），希腊语是"parakeletos"，即"请来站在旁边的一位"的意思。

* "三位一体"sān wèi yì tǐ：一位神，三个位格，即圣父、圣子和圣灵，中文简称"三一"。

主题课文 Themed Text

shèngjīng gàosu wǒmen shén shì cóng **gèngǔ** dào yǒngyuǎn dōu cúnzài de shén, shì **wúsuǒbùnéng, wúsuǒbùzhī, wúsuǒbúzài** de shén. shén zhǐyǒu yí wèi, yǒu sān gè **wèigé**: shèngfù, shèngzǐ hé shènglíng*. shèngzǐ yóu shèngfù suǒ shēng, shènglíng yóu shèngfù ér chū. wǒmen cóng shèngjīng zhōng hái zhīdào shén shì líng, shì **wúxiàn de, yǒnghéng de**, shì bù **gǎibiàn** de.

jīdū shì shén, tā de **gēnyuán** cóng tàichū jiù yǒu. suǒyǐ <u>bǎoluó</u> shuō, "àizǐ shì nà bùnéng kànjiàn zhī shén de xiàng, shì shǒushēng de, zài yíqiè bèi zào de yǐxiān." yēsū yě shuō: "wǒ yǔ fù yuán wéi yī." suǒyǐ "fán rèn yēsū wéi shén érzi de, shén jiù zhù zài tā lǐmiàn, tā yě zhù zài shén lǐmiàn".

yēsū **yīngxǔ** cì gěi wǒmen de "bǎohuìshī*" shì cóng fù chūlái zhēnlǐ de shènglíng, yěshì jīdū de líng. shènglíng zhù zài xìnkào yēsū de rén xīnzhōng, **gǎndòng**, qǐshì, hé **ānwèi** rén de xīn, cì píng'ān hé xǐlè, zhìhuì hé pànwàng. "rúguǒ shén de líng zhù zài wǒmen xīnlǐ, wǒmen jiù bù shǔ ròutǐ, nǎi shǔ shènglíng le."

suǒyǐ, shèngfù shì shén, shèngzǐ shì shén, shènglíng yěshì shén, shì "**sānwèiyìtǐ***" tóng shòu **jìngbài**, tóng xiǎng **zūnróng**, tóng yǒu **quánbǐng** de shén.

Special Notes on Text

* líng (Spirit) is "ruach" in Hebrew and "pneuma" in Greek. It means "breath," "wind," or some invisible moving force (fēng) in both languages.

* bǎo huìshī (advocate): The English word for bǎohuìshī is "comforter" (ānwèizhě), which can be translated as "helper" (bāngzhùzhě) in Chinese. Its Greek word is "parakeletos," which means "one who is summoned or called to one's side" (qǐnglái zhànzài pángbiān de yíwèi), especially called to one's aid.

* sānwèiyìtǐ (Trinity) means one God, three persons, namely the Father, the Son, and the Holy Spirit. It is abbreviated as "sānyī" in Chinese.

1.	亘古	gèn gǔ	(N)	throughout time
2.	无所不能	wú suǒ bù néng	(Adj)	omnipotent
3.	无所不知	wú suǒ bù zhī	(Adj)	omniscient
4.	无所不在	wú suǒ bù zài	(Adj)	omnipresent
5.	位格	wèi gé	(N)	person
6.	无限的	wúxiàn de	(Adj	infinite
7.	永恒的	yǒnghéng de	(Adj)	everlasting
8.	改变	gǎi biàn	(V)	to change
9.	根源	gēn yuán	(N)	source, origin
10.	应许	yīng xǔ	(V)	to promise
11.	感动	gǎn dòng	(V)	to touch, to affect
12.	安慰	ān wèi	(V)	to comfort
13.	敬拜	jìng bài	(V)	to worship
14.	尊荣	zūn róng	(N)	rank and honor
15.	权柄	quán bǐng	(N)	authority, power

读后讨论 Post-reading Discussion

1. 圣灵是谁？

2. 圣灵怎样在人心里工作？

3. 耶稣说"我与父原为一"，这话是什么意思？ （约10:30）

jìng bài zàn měi

敬拜赞美 Worship and Praise

shén de měi shàn
神的美善

wǒ yào shíshí chēngsòng yēhéhuá
我要时时称颂耶和华；

zànměi tā de huà bì cháng zài wǒ kǒuzhōng
赞美他的话必常在我口中。

The LORD is Good

wǒ de xīn bì yīn yēhéhuá kuāyào
我的心必因耶和华夸耀；

I will extol the Lord at all times;

qiānbēi rén tīngjiàn jiù yào xǐlè
谦卑人听见就要喜乐。

his praise will always be on my lips.

I will glory in the Lord;

nǐmen hé wǒ dāng chēng yēhéhuá wéi dà
你们和我当称耶和华为大，

let the afflicted hear and rejoice.

Glorify the Lord with me;

yìtóng gāojǔ tā de míng.
一同高举他的名。

let us exalt his name together.

— Psalm 34:1-3 —

— 诗篇 34:1-3 —

三一颂

普天之下万国万民，

齐声赞美父、子、圣灵，

三位一体同荣同尊，

万有之源，万福之本。

阿们。

—中国基督教协会版本

Sān Yī Sòng

pǔ tiān zhī xià wànguó wànmín,

qíshēng zànměi fù、 zǐ、 shènglíng,

sānwèiyìtǐ tóng róng tóng zūn,

wànyǒu zhī yuán, wànfú zhī běn.

āmen.

Doxology

All creatures here below,

Praise Father, Son, and the Holy Ghost,

Three in One in the same glory and same honor,

the source of everything, the source of all blessings.

Amen.

但你—耶和华（yē hé huá）是我四围的盾牌（dùn pái），是我的荣耀（róng yào），又是叫我抬（tái）起头来的。我用我的声音（shēng）求（qiú）告耶和华，他就从他的圣山上应允（yìng yǔn）我。

—诗篇 3:3-4

But you, Lord, are a shield around me, my glory, the One who lifts my head high. I call out to the Lord, and he answers me from his holy mountain.

— Psalm 3:3-4

腓4:13；弗2:19-20；诗62:6

神（shén）啊，求祢（qiú nǐ）藉着（jí zhe）居住（jū zhù）和运行（yùn xíng）在我们里面（lǐ miàn）那基督（jī dū）的灵（líng）使（shǐ）我们里面刚（gāng）强（qiáng）。靠（kào）着祢加（jiā）给我们力量（lì liàng），我们凡（fán）事都能作。祢在基督里建造（jiàn zào）我们，我们有基督耶稣（yē sū）祂自己（tā zì jǐ）为房角石（fáng jiǎo shí）。祂是我们盼望得到（pànwàng dé dào）的最可靠、最真实（zuì shí）、和最稳固（wěn gù）的根基（gēn jī）。祂是我们的磐石（pán shí），我们的拯救（zhěngjiù），是我们的高台（gāo tái），是我们患（huàn）难（nàn）中随（suí）时的帮助（bāng zhù）。我们感谢（gǎn xiè）祢，愿（yuàn）我们凡事都荣耀（róngyào）祢！奉（fèng）耶稣基督的名祈（qí）求，阿（ā）们。

单元简要 Unit Summary
dān yuán jiǎn yào

神是存在的，

祂不是宇宙的一部分，

祂是宇宙的创造者。

我们要敬拜神，

因为祂是真神，是爱的神，

是创造万物的神，是可靠的神。

我们要感谢神，

因为祂赐给我们生命和慈爱，

赐给我们圣经，赐给我们圣灵，

赐给我们救主耶稣，

赦免我们的罪，

让我们有智慧、有力量，

让我们知道我们是神的儿女。

三位一体
sān wèi yì tǐ

shén shì cúnzài de,

tā búshì yǔzhòu de yí bùfèn,

tā shì yǔzhòu de chuàngzàozhě.

wǒmen yào jìngbài shén,

yīnwèi tā shì zhēnshén, shì ài de shén,

shì chuàngzào wànwù de shén, shì kěkào de shén.

wǒmen yào gǎnxiè shén,

yīnwèi tā cìgěi wǒmen shēngmìng hé cí'ài,

cìgěi wǒmen shèngjīng, cìgěi wǒmen shènglíng,

cìgěi wǒmen jiùzhǔ yēsū,

shèmiǎn wǒmen de zuì,

ràng wǒmen yǒu zhìhuì, yǒu lìliàng,

ràng wǒmen zhīdao wǒmen shì shén de érnǚ.

字词集解 Word Explanation
zì cí jí jiě

三位一体 (Trinity)
sān wèi yì tǐ

我们敬拜一体三位，三位一体的神。父是神，子是神，圣灵也是神。不是三神，而是一神。父、子、圣灵同一神性，同一荣耀，也同一永恒之尊严。

— 《亚他那修信经》 (Athanasian Creed)

问题跟踪 Follow-up Questions

1. 基督徒信的神是一位怎样的神?

2. "道成肉身"是什么意思?

3. 圣灵充满的表现是怎样的?

4. 为什么说信徒的身子是"圣灵的殿"? （林前6:19）

5. 基督教的"三位一体"是什么意思?

jīng wén huí yìng
经文回应 Scripture Response Reading

cóng gǔ yǐ lái　　rén wèi céng tīng jiàn　wèi céng ěr wén　　wèi céng yǎn jiàn
从 古 以 来 ，人 未 曾 听 见、 未 曾 耳 闻、 未 曾 眼 见

zài nǐ　yǐ wài yǒu shéme shén wèi děnghòu tā de rén xíngshì
在 你 以 外 有 什 么 神 为 等 候 他 的 人 行 事。

— 以赛亚书 64:4 —

Since ancient times no one has heard, no ear has perceived,
no eye has seen any God besides you, who acts on behalf of
those who wait for him.

— Isaiah 64:4 —

shén chàng zào tiān dì
神创造天地
（创1:1-2:4）

起初神创造天地，把天空下面的水聚在一处，成为海洋，使陆地出现。然后神说："地上要生出青草、蔬菜和树木。"于是，事就这样成了。

神又造了两个大光体，大的管理白天，是太阳；小的管理黑夜，是月亮。又造了星星，把它们安放在天空。

神又说："水里、空中和地上，要有多种能活动的生物。"于是，事情又照神所说的成就了。

最后，神照着自己的形象创造了人，有男，有女。祂看着祂所造的一切都很好。

这样，六天之中天地万物都造齐了。第七天，神完成了祂所作的工，休息了。

Qǐchū shén chuàngzào tiāndì, bǎ tiān kōng xiàmiàn de shuǐ jù zài yí chù, chéngwéi hǎi yáng, shǐ lùdì chūxiàn. Ránhòu shén shuō: "Dìshàng yào shēngchū qīngcǎo, shūcài hé shù mù." Yúshì, shì jiù zhèyàng chéng le.

Shén yòu zào le liǎng gè dà guāngtǐ, dà de guǎnlǐ báitiān, shì tàiyáng; xiǎode guǎnlǐ hēiyè, shì yuèliàng. Yòu zào le xīng xīng, bǎ tāmen ānfàng zài tiānkōng.

Shén yòu shuō:"shuǐ lǐ, kōngzhōng hé dì shàng, yàoyǒu duōzhǒng néng huódòng de shēngwù." Yúshì, shì qíng yòu zhào shén suǒ shuō de chéngjiù le.

Zuìhòu, shénzhàozhe zìjǐ de xíng xiàng chuàngzàole rén, yǒu nán, yǒu nǚ. Tā kàn zhe tā suǒ zào de yíqiè dōu hěn hǎo.

Zhèyàng, liù tiān zhī zhōng tiāndì wànwù dōu zào qí le. Dì qī tiān, shén wánchéng le tā suǒzuò de gōng, xiūxi le.

唯独圣经

wéi dú shèng jīng
唯 独 圣 经
Unit 2
dì èr dàn yuán
第二单元

Learning Objectives
xué xi mù dì
学习目的

In this unit, you will learn to...

* Describe what the Bible is and its importance
* Name all the books of the Bible
* Understand the arrangement of the Bible
* Use basic Christian terminology about the Bible
* Discuss the purpose of the Bible

shèngjīng dōu shì shén suǒ mòshì de yú jiàoxùn   dū zé   shǐ rén guī zhèng jiàodǎo rén xué yì dōu shì yǒuyì de
圣经都是神所默示的，于教训、督责、使人归正、教导人学义都是有益的。

一提摩太后书 3:16

Unit 2: 预备学习
第二单元
yù bèi xué xí

关键词汇 Key Terms
guān jiàn cí huì

zuòzhě	rénwù	nèiróng	juéduì	quánwēi
作者	人物	内容	绝对	权威
(author	character	content	absolute	authority)

热身问题 Warm-up Questions
rè shēn wèn tí

1. 圣经的作者是谁？（圣经是谁写的？）

2. 圣经的中心人物是谁？

3. 圣经的内容真的可靠吗？圣经有绝对的权威吗？

经文细读 Key Verse Reading
jīng wén xì dú

shèngjīng dōu shì shén suǒ mòshì de yú jiào xùn   dū zé   shǐ rén guī zhèng jiàodǎo rén xué yì dōu
圣经都是神所默示的，于教训、督责、使人归正、教导人学义都
shì yǒu yì de
是有益的。

— 提摩太后书 3:16

All Scripture is God-breathed and is useful for teaching, rebuking, correcting and training in righteousness.

— 2 Timothy 3:16

Lesson 1: 神的默示
第一课
shén de mò shì

课堂灵修 Class Devotional

wǒ shí zài gàosu nǐ men jiù shì dào tiāndì dōu fèi qù le lù fǎ de yì diǎn yí huà yě bù néng fèi
我实在告诉你们，就是到天地都废去了，律法的一点一画也不能废

qù dōu yào chéng quán
去，都要成全。

— 马太福音 5:18

Daily Memory Verse

每日经文背诵
měi rì jīng wén bèi sòng

cǎo bì kū gān huā bì diāo cán wéiyǒu wǒmen shén de huà
草必枯干，花必凋残，惟有我们神的话
bì yǒngyuǎn lì dìng
必永远立定。

— 以赛亚书 40:8

shèng jīng jīn jù

圣经金句 Frequently Quoted Verse

yīn wèi chū yú shén de huà méi yǒu yí jù bú dài néng lì de
因为，出于神的话，没有一句不带能力的。

— 路加福音 1:37

For no word from God will ever fail.

— Luke 1:37

盟约应许 Covenantal Promise

神与挪亚立约

看哪，我要使洪水泛滥在地上，毁灭天下；凡地上有血肉、有气息的活物，无一不死。我却要与你立约；你同你的妻，与儿子儿妇，都要进入方舟。

— 创世记 6:17-18

God's Covenant with Noah

I am going to bring floodwaters on the earth to destroy all life under the heavens, every creature that has the breath of life in it. Everything on earth will perish. But I will establish my covenant with you, and you will enter the ark—you and your sons and your wife and your sons' wives with you.

— Genesis 6:17-18

诗篇集锦 Psalm Reading

Teach me, Lord,

the way of your decrees,

that I may follow it to the end.

Give me understanding,

so that I may keep your law and obey it

with all my heart.

Direct me in the path of your commands,

for there I find delight.

— Psalm 119:33-35 —

耶和华啊，

求你将你的律例指教我，

我必遵守到底！

求你赐我悟性，

我便遵守你的律法，

且要一心遵守。

求你叫我遵行你的命令，

因为这是我所喜乐的。

— 诗篇 119:33-35 —

课文预读 Introductory Reading

圣经是神的话，

神的话不是神话，

因为它是从神而来的。

神用祂的话造天、造地和万物，

祂的话一出，事情就成了。

圣经说的，就是神所说的，

它是"活神的活道"，

是作者们被圣灵感动默示，

写下成文的神的话。

它是神赐给人类的启示，

记载人类的起源，

人生的意义和人生的结局。

它也是神对祂自己的启示，

让我们明白祂为人预备的救恩，

所以圣经还是一本"救恩之书"。

神 shén
的 de
启 qǐ
示 shì

shèngjīng shì shén de huà,

shén de huà búshì shénhuà,

yīnwèi tā shì cóng shén ér lái de.

shén yòng tā de huà zào tiān, zào dì hé wànwù,

tā de huà yì chū, shìqíng jiù chéng le.

shèngjīng shuō de, jiù shì shén suǒ shuō de,

tā shì "huó shén de huó dào",

shì zuòzhěmen bèi shènglíng gǎndòng mò shì,

xiě xià chéng wén de shén de huà.

tā shì shén cìgěi rénlèi de qǐshì,

jìzǎi rénlèi de qǐyuán,

rénshēng de yìyì hé rénshēng de jiéjú.

tā yěshì shén duì tā zìjǐ de qǐshì,

ràng wǒmen míngbái tā wéi rén yùbèi de jiù ēn,

suǒyǐ shèngjīng hái shì yì běn "jiù ēn zhī shū".

预读问题 Pre-reading Questions

1. 神在圣经里向我们启示什么？

2. 圣经是一本什么样的书？

3. 圣经想要让人明白什么？

参考经文 Reference Verses for the Text

创2:7；出32:16；约20:22；提后3:16

圣经*是一本非常独特的书，全书是由数十位作者写成。这些作者的**身份**和**年龄**各不相同，有的是**祭司**、**君王**、先知，有的是牧人、**渔夫**、**农夫**。他们所处的**时代背景**和写作地点也不相同。有的写在西奈*的**旷野**，有的写在耶路撒冷***圣殿**，有的写在巴比伦*的河边，还有的写在罗马*的**监狱**里。从写第一卷创世记到最后一卷启示录，中间经过了一千多年，但是全部圣经的内容却前后**连贯**，成为一本完整的书。

正因为这样，我们说圣经都是神所**默示***的，是圣灵藉着人手所写的。默示的意思是被吹入，神把祂的话语吹入到人里面，即圣灵默示人所要说出和写下的。这就**意味**着圣经出自神，是神的话，是祂赐给人类的启示，是不改变的。

所以，圣经是一部神的书，是神启示的真理，但也是一部人的书，是人记录的事实。圣经因此是神奇妙的道写成文字的特别启示，既是神的书，也是人的书。虽然圣经是用人的语言叙述的，但它却具有属神的**权威**。

课文特注

* "圣经"shèngjīng：来自希腊文 Biblos，是"书"的意思。

* 西奈 xī nài：Sinai

* 耶路撒冷 yēlùsālěng：Jerusalem

* 巴比伦 bābǐlún：Babylon

* 罗马 luómǎ：Rome

* "默示"mòshì：多数英文版本把它翻译成"God-breathed"，即神直接呼出祂的话语。但也有人认为是"吹入"的意思，认为是神把祂的话语吹入到人里面。

shèngjīng* shì yì běn fēicháng dútè de shū, quánshū shì yóu shù shí wèi zuòzhě xiěchéng de. zhèxiē zuòzhě de **shēnfèn** hé **niánlíng** gè bù xiāngtóng, yǒude shì **jìsī**, **jūnwáng**, xiānzhī, yǒude shì mùrén, **yúfū**, **nóngfū**. tāmen suǒ chǔ de **shídài bèijǐng** hé xiězuò dìdiǎn yě bù xiāngtóng. yǒude xiě zài <u>xī nài</u>* de **kuàngyě**, yǒude xiě zài <u>yēlùsālěng</u>* **shèngdiàn**, yǒude xiě zài <u>bābǐlún</u>* de hé biān, hái yǒude xiě zài <u>luómǎ</u>* de **jiānyù** lǐ. cóng xiě dì yī juàn chuàngshìjì dào zuìhòu yí juàn qǐshìlù, zhōngjiān jīngguò le yì qiān duō nián, dànshì quánbù shèngjīng de nèiróng què qiánhòu **liánguàn**, chéngwéi yì běn wánzhěng de shū.

zhèng yīnwèi zhèyàng, wǒmen shuō shèngjīng dōu shì shén suǒ **mòshì*** de, shì shènglíng jièzhe rén shǒu suǒ xiě de. mòshì de yìsi shì bèi chuīrù, shén bǎ tā de huàyǔ chuīrù dào rén lǐmiàn, jí shènglíng mòshì rén suǒyào shuō chū hé xiě xià de nèiróng. zhè jiù **yìwèi** zhe shèngjīng chūzì shén, shì shén de huà, shì tā cì gěi rén lèi de qǐshì, shì bù gǎibiàn de.

suǒyǐ, shèngjīng shì yí bù shén de shū, shì shén qǐshì de zhēnlǐ, dàn yěshì yí bù rén de shū, shì rén jìlù de shìshí. shèngjīng yīncǐ shì shén qímiào de dào xiěchéng wénzì de tèbié qǐshì, jìshì shén de shū, yěshì rén de shū. suīrán shèngjīng shì yòng rén de yǔyán xùshù de, dàn tā què jùyǒu shǔ shén de **quánwēi**.

Special Notes on Text

* shèngjīng (Bible): from the Greek word "Biblos," meaning "book."

* xīnài: Sinai

* yēlùsālěng: Jerusalem

* bābǐlún: Babylon

* luómǎ: Rome

* mòshì (God-breathed): Most English versions translate this as "God-breathed," that is, God breathed out His Word directly. Another translation is "breathed into": that God breathes His Word into people.

1.	身份	shēn fèn	(N)	identity
2.	年龄	nián líng	(N)	age
3.	祭司	jì sī	(N)	priest
4.	君王	jūn wáng	(N)	king, lord
5.	渔夫	yú fū	(N)	fisherman
6.	农夫	nóng fū	(N)	farmer
7.	时代	shí dài	(N)	era
8.	背景	bèi jǐng	(N)	background
9.	旷野	kuàng yě	(N)	wilderness
10.	圣殿	shèng diàn	(N)	temple
11.	监狱	jiān yù	(N)	prison
12.	连贯	lián guàn	(Adj)	coherent
13.	默示	mò shì	(V)	to imply, to reveal
14.	意味	yì wèi	(V)	to mean
15.	权威	quán wēi	(N)	authority

读后讨论 Post-reading Discussion

1. "圣经是神所默示的"是什么意思？

2. 圣经是在什么背景下写的？

3. 圣经先后写作的年代有多久？

jìng bài zàn měi
敬拜赞美 Worship and Praise

God's Glory in Creation

The heavens declare the glory of God;

the skies proclaim the work of his hands.

Day after day they pour forth speech;

night after night they reveal knowledge.

They have no speech,

they use no words;

no sound is heard from them.

Yet their voice goes out into all the earth,

their words to the ends of the world.

— Psalm 19: 1-4 —

shén de chuàng zào
神的创造

zhū tiān shùshuō shén de róngyào
诸天述说神的荣耀；

qióngcāng chuányáng tā de shǒuduàn
穹苍传扬他的手段。

zhè rì dào nà rì fā chū yányǔ
这日到那日发出言语；

zhè yè dào nà yè chuán chū zhīshì
这夜到那夜传出知识。

wú yán wú yǔ
无言无语，

yě wú shēngyīn kě tīng
也无声音可听。

tā de liàng dài tōng biàn tiānxià
它的量带通遍天下，

tā de yányǔ chuán dào dì jí
它的言语传到地极。

— 诗篇 19:1-4 —

主祷文

所以，你们祷告要这样说：

我们在天上的父：

愿人都尊你的名为圣。

愿你的国降临；

愿你的旨意行在地上，如同行在天上。

我们日用的饮食，今日赐给我们。

免我们的债，如同我们免了人的债。

不叫我们遇见试探，救我们脱离凶恶。

因为国度、权柄、荣耀，全是你的，直到永远。

阿们！

— 马太福音 6:9-13

Zhǔ Dǎo Wén

suǒyǐ, nǐmen dǎogào yào zhèyàng shuō:

wǒmen zài tiānshàng de fù:

yuàn rén dōu zūn nǐ de míng wèi shèng.

yuàn nǐ de guó jiànglín;

yuàn nǐ de zhǐyì xíng zài dìshàng, rú tóng xíng zài tiānshàng.

The Lord's Prayer

This, then, is how you should pray:

Our Father in heaven,

hallowed be your name,

your kingdom come,

your will be done, on earth as it is in heaven.

诗文祷告 Prayer Passage

耶和华啊，求你将你的道指示我，将你的路教训我！求你
以你的真理引导我，教训我，因为你是救我的神。我终日等候
你。

— 诗篇 25:4-5

Show me your ways, Lord, teach me your paths. Guide me in your truth and
teach me, for you are God my Savior, and my hope is in you all day long.

— Psalm 25:4-5

qí dǎo fàn wén

祈祷范文 Exemplary Prayer

太5:43；路10:27；提后3:16

主啊，我们为着祢默示的话语感谢祢。愿祢所呼出的话语成为我们
每日生活的基石，滋养、挑战，并带领我们爱神和爱祢的邻舍。当我们
每天读祢的话语时，求祢引导我们进入祢的真理，按着我们的需要装备
我们，好使我们忠心为祢而活。奉耶稣的名求，阿们。

Lesson 2: 神的应许
第二课

课堂灵修 Class Devotional
kè táng líng xiū

wǒmen jiǎng de nǎi shì cóngqián suǒ yǐncáng shén àomì de zhìhuì jiù shì shén zài wànshì yǐqián yù

我们讲的，乃是从前所隐藏、神奥秘的智慧，就是神在万世以前预

dìng shǐ wǒmen dé róngyào de

定使我们得荣耀的。

— 歌林多前书 2:7

Daily Memory Verse

每日经文背诵
měi rì jīng wén bèi sòng

tiān dì yào fèi qù wǒ de huà què bù néng fèi qù

天地要废去，我的话却不能废去。

— 马太福音 24:35

圣经金句 Frequently Quoted Verse
shèng jīng jīn jù

rén huó zhe bú shì dān kào shíwù nǎi shì kào shén kǒulǐ suǒ chū de yíqiè huà

人活着，不是单靠食物，乃是靠神口里所出的一切话。

— 马太福音 4:4

Man shall not live on bread alone, but on every word that comes from the mouth of God.

— Matthew 4:4

nuó yà zhī yuē
挪亚之约

xiǎo yù nuó yà   yǔ   yì lì yuē bìng

神晓谕挪亚和他的儿子说："我与你们和你们的后裔立约，并与你们

yí qiè huó wù   fēi niǎo shēng chù   shòu   fán fāng zhōu

这里的一切活物—就是飞鸟、牲畜、走兽，凡从方舟里出来的活物—立

                  xiě ròu   bèi hóng miè jué   huǐ huài

约。我与你们立约，凡有血肉的，不再被洪水灭绝，也不再有洪水毁坏

dì

地了。"

— 创世记 9:8-11

The Noahic Covenant

Then God said to Noah and to his sons with him: "I now establish my covenant with you and with your descendants after you and with every living creature that was with you—the birds, the livestock and all the wild animals, all those that came out of the ark with you—every living creature on earth. I establish my covenant with you: Never again will all life be destroyed by the waters of a flood; never again will there be a flood to destroy the earth."

— Genesis 9:8-11

shī piān jí jǐn
诗篇集锦 Psalm Reading

He provided redemption for his people;

he ordained his covenant forever—

holy and awesome is his name.

The fear of the Lord is the beginning of wisdom;

all who follow his precepts have good understanding.

To him belongs eternal praise.

— Psalm 111:9-10 —

tā xiàng bǎixìng shīxíng jiùshú
他向百姓施行救赎，

mìngdìng tā de yuē
命定他的约，

zhídào yǒngyuǎn
直到永远；

tā de míng shèng ér kě wèi
他的名圣而可畏。

jìngwèi yēhéhuá shì zhìhuì de kāiduān
敬畏耶和华是智慧的开端；

fán zūnxíng tā mìnglìng de shì cōngmíng rén
凡遵行他命令的是聪明人。

yēhéhuá shì yǒngyuǎn dāng zànměi de
耶和华是永远当赞美的！

— 诗篇 111:9-10 —

课文预读 Introductory Reading

神的话道成文字，

写成圣经，

是完美的真理。

神的儿子基督耶稣，

道成肉身，成为人子，

是完美的救主。

圣经的中心内容，

就是向人类启示这位救主。

圣经的中心人物，

就是成为肉身的"道"基督。

圣经的主题，

就是基督耶稣的救恩。

成文的道，完美的救恩启示，

是神的道，

永永远远地记在圣经里。

_{shén}
神
_{de}
的
_{jiù}
救
_{ēn}
恩

shén de huà dào chéng wénzì,

xiě chéng shèngjīng,

shì wánměi de zhēnlǐ.

shén de érzi jīdū yēsū,

dàochéng ròushēn chéng wéi rénzǐ,

shì wánměi de jiùzhǔ.

shèngjīng de zhōngxīn nèiróng,

jiù shì xiàng rénlèi qǐshì zhè wèi jiùzhǔ.

shèngjīng de zhōngxīn rénwù,

jiù shì chéng wéi ròushēn de "dào" jīdū.

shèngjīng de zhǔtí,

jiù shì jīdū yēsū de jiù ēn.

chéng wén de dào wánměi de jiù ēn qǐshì,

shì shén de dào,

yǒngyǒng yuǎnyuǎn de jì zài shèngjīng lǐ.

_{yù dú wèn tí}
预读问题 Pre-reading Questions

1. 圣经的中心内容是什么？

2. 道成肉身的"道"是什么意思？

3. 圣经的主题是什么？

_{cān kǎo jīng wén}
参考经文 Reference Verses for the Text

赛42:8-9；彼后1:20-21；林后1:20；可10:45；
约10:9，14:6；路19:10

"圣经上所有的预言没有可随私意解说的；因为预言从来没有出于人意的，乃是人被圣灵感动，说出神的话来。"神还是与人立约的神，祂不但把自己的话默示给圣经作者，而且与祂的**子民立约**。所以，约是神启示自己的方式之一。

圣经的旧约*记录有关主耶稣**降临**前的故事，是关于一位弥赛亚*来救赎<u>以色列</u>，成为人类未来的希望和救赎的预言。新约*则是记录有关主耶稣降临之后的故事，包括了耶稣降生后的有关**记载**及使徒的书信等，告诉我们耶稣就是旧约启示的弥赛亚。也就是说，耶稣基督*是全部圣经的中心，因为祂不但**成全**了旧约圣经中神与祂的子民的约定，而且祂自己也与人立新的约。"神的应许不论有多少，在基督都是是的。"

耶稣基督说了没有人敢说的话："我就是道路，真理，生命；若不藉着我，没有人能到父那里去。""我就是门；凡从我进来的，必然得救。"祂还说："人看见了我，就是看见了父。""人子来，为要**寻找拯救失丧**的人，并且**舍命**作多人的**赎价**。"祂的一切话语都向我们**显明**，祂就是我们的救主，能把我们从**罪恶**与**灭亡**中拯救出来。所以，耶稣基督是神给我们最大的应许，也是最大的**奇迹**。

课文特注

* "旧约"jiùyuē：在耶稣降生前，先知们把神的信息带给人们。这些先知用希伯来文写下旧约全书。

* "弥赛亚"mísàiyà 是希伯来文"mishiah"的音译。在旧约中"弥赛亚"的意思是"受膏者"（shòugāozhě），是指在以色列人中受膏作君王或祭司的。

* "新约"xīnyuē：耶稣的门徒用希腊文写下新约全书。

* 耶稣基督的生年为公历元年。"公元"写作 A.D.，也就是拉丁文的 Anno Domini，意思为"主的生年"。

57

shèngjīng shàng suǒyǒu de yùyán méiyǒu kě suí sīyì jiěshuō de; yīnwèi yùyán cónglái méiyǒu chūyú rényì de, nǎi shì rén bèi shènglíng gǎndòng, shuōchū shén de huà lái." shén háishì yǔ rén lìyuē de shén, tā búdàn bǎ zìjǐ de huà mò shì gěi shèngjīng zuòzhě, érqiě yǔ tā de **zǐmín lìyuē**. suǒyǐ, yuē shì shén qǐshì zìjǐ de fāngshì zhī yī.

shèngjīng de jiùyuē* jìlù yǒuguān zhǔ yēsū **jiànglín** qián de gùshì, shì guānyú yí wèi mísàiyà* lái jiùshú yǐsèliè, chéngwéi rénlèi wèilái de xīwàng hé jiùshú de yùyán. xīnyuē* zé shì jìlù yǒuguān zhǔ yēsū jiànglín zhīhòu de gùshì, bāokuò le yēsū jiàngshēng hòu de yǒuguān **jìzǎi** jí shǐtú de shūxìn děng, gàosu wǒmen yēsū jiùshì jiùyuē qǐshì de mísàiyà. yě jiùshì shuō, yēsū jīdū shì quánbù shèngjīng de zhōngxīn, yīnwèi tā búdàn **chéngquán** le jiùyuē shèngjīng zhōng shén yǔ tā de zimín de yuēdìng, érqiě tā zìjǐ yě yǔ rén lì xīn de yuē. shén de yīngxǔ, búlùn yǒu duōshǎo, zài jīdū dōu shì shì de.

yēsū jīdū shuō le méiyǒu rén gǎn shuō de huà: "wǒ jiùshì dàolù, zhēnlǐ, shēngmìng; ruò bú jièzhe wǒ, méiyǒu rén néng dào fù nàlǐ qù." "wǒ jiùshì mén; fán cóng wǒ jìnlái de, bìrán déjiù." tā hái shuō: "rén kànjiàn le wǒ, jiùshì kànjiàn le fù." "rénzǐ lái, wèi yào **xúnzhǎo zhěngjiù shīsàng** de rén, bìngqiě **shěmìng** zuò duō rén de **shújià**." tā de yíqiè huàyǔ dōu xiàng wǒmen **xiǎnmíng**, tā jiùshì wǒmen de jiùzhǔ, néng bǎ wǒmen cóng **zuì'è** yǔ **mièwáng** zhōng zhěngjiù chūlái. suǒyǐ, yēsū jīdū shì shén gěi wǒmen zuì dà de yīngxǔ, yěshì zuìdà de **qíjì**.

Special Notes on Text

* jiùyuē (Old Testament): Before the birth of Jesus, the prophets brought God's message to people. These prophets wrote the entire Old Testament in Hebrew (xībóláiwén).

* xīnyuē (New Testament): The disciples of Jesus wrote the entire New Testament in Greek (xīlàwén).

* mísàiyà (Messiah) is the transliteration of the Hebrew word "mishiah." In the Old Testament, the word "messiah" means "the anointed" (shòugāozhě), meaning one who is anointed as a king or priest among the Israelites.

* The birth year of Jesus Christ is the first year of the Gregorian calendar (gōnglìyuánnián), "A.D." (gōngyuán), which is also known as Anno Domini, meaning "the year of the Lord's birth" (zhǔ de shēng nián) in Latin.

1. 子民　zǐ mín　(N)　the people

2. 立约　lì yuē　(V)　to make a covenant

3. 降临　jiàng lín　(V)　to come down

4. 记载　jì zǎi　(N)　record

5. 成全　chéng quán　(V)　to help complete

6. 寻找　xún zhǎo　(V)　to search

7. 拯救　zhěng jiù　(V)　to save

8. 失丧　shī sàng　(Adj)　lost

9. 舍命　shě mìng　(V)　to sacrifice oneself

10. 赎价　shú jià　(N)　ransom price

11. 显明　xiǎn míng　(V)　to show, to demonstrate

12. 罪恶　zuì'è　(N)　sin

13. 灭亡　miè wáng　(V)　to perish

14. 奇迹　qí jì　(N)　miracle

读后讨论 Post-reading Discussion

dú hòu tǎo lùn

1. 我们怎样知道圣经是神的话？

2. 圣经中旧约和新约都记录了什么故事？

3. 圣经中神给了我们什么最大的应许？为什么？

敬拜赞美 Worship and Praise

jìng bài zàn měi

Praise to God for His Deliverance

As for God, his way is perfect:
The Lord's word is flawless;
he shields all who take refuge in him.
For who is God besides the Lord?
And who is the Rock except our God?

— Psalm 18:30-31 —

称颂神的拯救
chēngsòng shén de zhěngjiù

zhì yú shén   tā de dào shì wánquán de
至于神，他的道是完全的；

yēhéhuá de huà shì liàn jìng de
耶和华的话是炼净的。

fán tóukào tā de
凡投靠他的，

tā biàn zuò tāmen de dùnpái
他便作他们的盾牌。

chú le yēhéhuá   shéi shì shén ne
除了耶和华，谁是神呢？

chú le wǒmen de shén   shéi shì pánshí ne
除了我们的神，谁是磐石呢？

— 诗篇 18:30-31 —

60

主祷文

所以、你们祷告要这样说：

我们在天上的父：

愿人都尊你的名为圣。

愿你的国降临；

愿你的旨意行在地上、如同行在天上。

我们日用的饮食，今日赐给我们。

免我们的债，如同我们免了人的债。

不叫我们遇见试探，救我们脱离凶恶。

因为国度、权柄、荣耀，全是你的、直到永远。

阿们！

— 马太福音 6:9-13

Zhǔ Dǎo Wén

wǒmen rì yòng de yǐnshí, jīnrì cìgěi wǒmen.
miǎn wǒmen de zhài, rútóng wǒmen miǎn le rén de zhài.

The Lord's Prayer

Give us today our daily bread.
And forgive us our debts, as we also have forgiven our debtors.

我一心寻求了你；求你不要叫我偏离你的命令。我将你的

话藏在心里，免得我得罪你。耶和华啊，你是应当称颂的！求

你将你的律例教训我！

— 诗篇 119:10-12

I seek you with all my heart; do not let me stray from your commands. I have hidden your word in my heart that I might not sin against you. Praise be to you, Lord; teach me your decrees.

— Psalm 119:10-12

qí dǎo fàn wén
祈祷范文 Exemplary Prayer

创15:5，17:5，28:14；罗4:13；启5:9-13

天上的神啊，诸天诉说祢的荣耀，众星都是祢的杰作！请帮助我们

向世界彰显祢的荣耀。我们感谢祢赐给亚伯拉罕的应许，藉着耶稣，这

应许延伸到我们所有人，让地上万族得福。在耶稣的降生中，我们看到

祢是持守应许的神。请帮助我们信靠和盼望耶稣的再来，奉耶稣的名祷

告，阿们。

Lesson 3: 神的教导
第三课
shén de jiào dǎo

课堂灵修 Class Devotional
kè táng líng xiū

dàn nǐ suǒ xué xí de   suǒ què xìn de   yào cún zài xīn lǐ   yīn wèi nǐ zhīdào shì gēn shéi xué
但你所学习的，所确信的，要存在心里；因为你知道是跟谁学

de bìngqiě zhīdao shì cóngxiǎo míngbái shèngjīng zhè shèngjīng néng shǐ nǐ yīn xìn jīdū yēsū yǒu dé jiù
的，并且知道是从小明白圣经，这圣经能使你因信基督耶稣，有得救

de zhì huì
的智慧。

— 提摩太后书 3:14-15

Daily Memory Verse

每
日
经
文
背
诵
měi rì jīng wén bèi sòng

zhè dào néng jiàn lì nǐ men   jiào nǐ men hé yí qiè
这道能建立你们，叫你们和一切
chéng shèng de rén tóng dé jī yè
成圣的人同得基业。

— 使徒行传 20:32

圣经金句 Frequently Quoted Verse
shèng jīng jīn jù

jìng wèi yēhéhuá shì zhīshi de kāiduān   yúwàng rén miǎoshì zhìhuì hé xùnhuì
敬畏耶和华是知识的开端；愚妄人藐视智慧和训诲。

— 箴言 1:7

The fear of the Lord is the beginning of knowledge, but fools despise wisdom and instruction.

— Proverbs 1:7

盟约应许 Covenantal Promise

彩虹之约
cǎi hóng zhī yuē

神说："我与你们并你们这里的各样活物所立的永约是有记号的。

我把虹放在云彩中，这就可作我与地立约的记号了。我使云彩盖地的时候，必有虹现在云彩中，我便记念我与你们和各样有血肉的活物所立的约，水就再不泛滥、毁坏一切有血肉的物了。"

— 创世记 9:12-15

The Rainbow Covenant

And God said, 'This is the sign of the covenant I am making between me and you and every living creature with you, a covenant for all generations to come: I have set my rainbow in the clouds, and it will be the sign of the covenant between me and the earth. Whenever I bring clouds over the earth and the rainbow appears in the clouds, I will remember my covenant between me and you and all living creatures of every kind. Never again will the waters become a flood to destroy all life.'"

— Genesis 9:12-15

诗篇集锦 Psalm Reading

我用嘴唇
wǒ yòng zuǐchún

传扬你口中的一切典章。
chuányáng nǐ kǒuzhōng de yíqiè diǎnzhāng

我喜悦你的法度，
wǒ xǐyuè nǐ de fǎdù

如同喜悦一切的财物。
rútóng xǐyuè yíqiè de cáiwù

我要默想你的训词，
wǒ yào mò xiǎng nǐ de xùncí

看重你的道路。
kànzhòng nǐ de dàolù

— 诗篇 119:13-15 —

With my lips

I recount all the laws that come from your mouth.

I rejoice in following your statutes

as one rejoices in great riches.

I meditate on your precepts and

consider your ways.

— Psalm 119:13-15 —

课文预读 Introductory Reading

神藉着圣经向人说话，

是要叫人认识耶稣，

明白祂的心意。

耶稣是整本圣经的中心。

耶稣的话，

是叫人活的灵，

是生命的道。

祂的话是脚前的灯，

能照亮我们前面的路；

祂的话是路上的光，

使我们因信祂有得救的智慧。

神的话语，

没有一句不带着能力，

它的教训是活的，

有属神的权威。

圣经的力量

shén jièzhe shèngjīng xiàng rén shuōhuà,

shì yào jiào rén rènshi yēsū,

míngbái tā de xīnyì.

yēsū shì zhěng běn shèngjīng de zhōngxīn.

yēsū de huà

shì jiào rén huó de líng,

shì shēngmìng de dào.

tā de huà shì jiǎoqián de dēng,

néng zhào liàng wǒmen qiánmiàn de lù;

tā de huà shì lùshàng de guāng,

shǐ wǒmen yīn xìn tā yǒu déjiù de zhìhuì.

shén de huàyǔ,

méiyǒu yíjù bú dàizhe nénglì,

tā de jiàoxùn shì huó de,

yǒu shǔ shén de quánwēi.

预读问题 Pre-reading Questions

1. 神藉着圣经作什么？

2. 为什么说神的话是灯，是光？

3. 神的话有什么样的力量？

参考经文 Reference Verses for the Text

诗40:6-10；赛52:13-53:12；来4:12

圣经*是神的启示，是创造宇宙万物之神所赐的信息，包含了一切关于得救的要道。圣经的**内容**和**体裁**是多样的，有历史、**神学**、哲学、**忠告**、**诫命**和预言；有律法书、历史书、智慧文学、诗歌、先知书、福音书、书信、和启示文学等。旧约主要记载神如何创造天地万物和人类，**始祖**如何**犯罪*堕落**，以及神如何**拣选**以色列民族*成为祂的子民。新约记载救主耶稣基督一生的事迹，教会的成立与发展及使徒的**教导**。

使徒们一致认为耶稣大过亚伯拉罕*，摩西*和大卫*等所有的旧约先知和伟人，**应验**了旧约圣经中所有的先知的预言。比如说，旧约描述了一个受苦的仆人*，将会为神的子民受苦，担当他们的**忧患**，而这一切的预言都在耶稣身上完全实现。除此之外，圣经还记录了耶稣基督完美**无瑕**的**品格**，大能的作为，奇异的神迹和祂死而复活的事实。因此，耶稣基督是神的儿子，是罪人的救主，成为基督徒**信仰**的忠实宣告。

总而言之，圣经是神的话，是活泼有生命的，让我们可以从中学习祂的**训诲**和教导，使我们得盼望，并叫我们因相信神而得生命。

课文特注

* 《圣经》写作的语言是多样的，有希伯来文、亚兰文（亚拉姆语）和希腊文。

* "犯罪"fànzuì：希伯来文原意是"失败""失迷方向"或"失去目标"。

* 以色列民族 yǐsèlièmínzú：People of Israel

* 亚伯拉罕 yàbólāhàn：Abraham

* 摩西 móxī：Moses

* 大卫 dàwèi：David

* "受苦的仆人" shòukǔ de púrén：记录在以赛亚书42:1-7, 49:1-9, 50:4-9, 52:13-53:12，其中以52-53章的这一篇最为人熟知。

shèngjīng* shì shén de qǐshì, shì chuàngzào yǔzhòu wànwù zhī shén suǒ cì de xìnxī, bāohán le yíqiè guānyú déjiù de yāodào. shèngjīng de **nèiróng** hé **tǐcái** shì duōyàng de, yǒu lìshǐ, **shén xué**, zhéxué, **zhōnggào**, **jièmìng** hé yùyán; yǒu lǜfǎshū, lìshǐshū, zhìhuìwénxué, shīgē, xiānzhīshū, fúyīnshū, shūxìn, hé qǐshìwénxué děng. jiùyuē zhǔyào jìzǎi shén rúhé chuàngzào tiāndì wànwù hé rénlèi, **shǐzǔ** rúhé **fànzuì*** **duòluò**, yǐjí shén rúhé **jiǎnxuǎn** <u>yǐsèliè mínzú</u>* chéngwéi tā de zǐmín. xīnyuē jìzǎi jiùzhǔ yēsū jīdū yìshēng de shìjī, jiàohuì de chénglì yǔ fāzhǎn jí shǐtú de jiàodǎo.

shǐtúmen yìzhì rènwéi yēsū dà guò <u>yàbólāhǎn</u>*, <u>móxī</u>* hé <u>dàwèi</u>* děng suǒyǒu de jiùyuē xiānzhī hé wěirén, **yìngyàn** le jiùyuē shèngjīng zhōng suǒyǒu de xiānzhī de yùyán. bǐrú shuō, jiùyuē miáoshù le yígè <u>shòukǔ de púrén</u>*, jiāng huì wèi shén de zǐmín shòukǔ, dāndāng tāmen de **yōuhuàn**, ér zhè yíqiè de yùyán dōu zài yēsū shēnshang wánquán shíxiàn. chúcǐzhīwài, shèngjīng hái jìlù le yēsū jīdū wánměi **wúxiá** de **pǐn gé**, dà néng de zuòwéi, qíyì de shénjì hé tā sǐ ér fùhuó de shìshí. yīncǐ, yēsū jīdū shì shén de érzi, shì zuìrén de jiùzhǔ, chéngwéi jīdūtú **xìnyǎng** de zhōngshí xuāngào.

zǒng'ér yán zhī, shèngjīng shì shén de huà, shì huópō yǒu shēngmìng de, ràng wǒmen kěyǐ cóng zhōng xuéxí tā de **xùnhuì** hé jiàodǎo, shǐ wǒmen dé pànwàng, bìng jiào wǒmen yīn xiāngxìn shén ér dé shēngmìng.

Special Notes on Text

* The Bible was written in a variety of languages, including Hebrew (xībóláiwén), Aramaic (yàlánwén or yàlāmǔyǔ), and Greek (xīlàwén).

* fànzuì (sin or to sin): The original Hebrew word for fànzuì is "to fail" (shībài), "to lose one's way" (shīmí fāngxiàng), or "to lose sight of one's goal" (shīqù mùbiāo).

* yǐsèliè mínzú: People of Israel

* yàbólāhàn: Abraham

* móxī: Moses

* dàwèi: David

* shòukǔ de púrén (the Suffering Servant) is recorded in Isaiah 42:1-7, 49:1-9, 50:4-9, and 52:13-53:12, with chapters 52-53 being the most well-known.

1.	内容	nèi róng	(N)	content
2.	体裁	tǐ cái	(N)	genre
3.	神学	shén xué	(N)	theology
4.	忠告	zhōng gào	(N)	advice
5.	诫命	jiè mìng	(N)	commandment
6.	始祖	shǐ zǔ	(N)	earliest ancestor
7.	犯罪	fàn zuì	(V)	to sin
8.	堕落	duò luò	(V)	to be fallen
9.	拣选	jiǎn xuǎn	(V)	to choose
10.	教导	jiào dǎo	(N)	teaching/guidance
11.	应验	yìng yàn	(V)	to be fulfilled
12.	忧患	yōu huàn	(N)	worry/sorrow
13.	无瑕	wú xiá	(Adj)	flawless
14.	品格	pǐn gé	(N)	moral character
15.	信仰	xìn yǎng	(N)	faith
16.	训悔	xùn huì	(N)	instruction

读后讨论 Post-reading Discussion

1. 圣经的内容有哪些体裁？

2. 圣经的新旧约各记载了什么内容？

3. 圣经有什么功用？有什么目的？

jìng bài zàn měi
敬拜赞美 Worship and Praise

Joy in the Lord

Shout for joy in the Lord,

O you righteous!

Praise befits the upright.

Give thanks to the Lord with the lyre;

make melody to him with the harp of ten strings!

Sing to him a new song;

play skillfully on the strings,

with loud shouts.

For the word of the Lord is upright,

and all his work is done in faithfulness.

— Psalm 33:1-4 —

sòng zàn zhī gē
颂赞之歌

yì rén nǎ
义人哪，

nǐmen yīngdāng kào yēhéhuá huānlè
你们应当靠耶和华欢乐；

zhèngzhí rén de zànměi shì héyí de
正直人的赞美是合宜的。

nǐmen yīngdāng tánqín chēngxiè yēhéhuá
你们应当弹琴称谢耶和华，

yòng shíxiánsè gēsòng tā
用十弦瑟歌颂他。

yīngdāng xiàng tā chàng xīn'gē
应当向他唱新歌，

tán de qiǎomiào shēngyīn hóngliàng
弹得巧妙，声音洪亮。

yīnwèi yēhéhuá de yányǔ zhèngzhí
因为耶和华的言语正直；

fán tā suǒ zuò de jǐn dōu chéngshí
凡他所做的尽都诚实。

— 诗篇 33:1-4 —

主祷文

所以，你们祷告要这样说：

我们在天上的父：

愿人都尊你的名为圣。

愿你的国降临；

愿你的旨意行在地上，如同行在天上。

我们日用的饮食，今日赐给我们。

免我们的债，如同我们免了人的债。

不叫我们遇见试探，救我们脱离凶恶。

因为国度、权柄、荣耀，全是你的，直到永远。

阿们！

—马太福音 6:9-13

Zhǔ Dǎo Wén

bú jiào wǒmen yùjiàn shìtàn, jiù wǒmen tuōlí xiōng'è.
yīnwèi guódù, quánbǐng, róngyào, quán shì nǐ de, zhídào yǒngyuǎn.
āmen!

The Lord's Prayer

And lead us not into temptation, but deliver us from the evil one.
For yours is the kingdom, the power, and the glory, forever.
Amen!

诗文祷告 Prayer Passage

有一件事，我曾求耶和华，我仍要寻求：就是一生一

世住在耶和华的殿中，瞻仰他的荣美，在他的殿里求问。

— 诗篇 27:4

One thing I ask from the Lord, this only do I seek: that I may dwell in the
house of the Lord all the days of my life, to gaze on the beauty of the Lord and to
seek him in his temple.

— Psalm 27:4

祈祷范文 Exemplary Prayer

太22:29；徒17:11；林前2:4-5

神啊，感谢祢的话语和真理。圣经要教给我们的太多了，在信心成

长的过程中，要不断学习。我们有时不明白圣经，也不知道祢的能力，

会质疑祢的话语，对祢的应许感到疑惑。今天求祢再次坚定我们，相信

耶稣是万主之主和万王之王，也是祢应许的弥赛亚。惟愿我们怀着信心

宣告："耶稣是我们一切所需的。"奉祂的名祷告，阿们。

单元简要 Unit Summary
dān yuán jiǎn yào

神是圣经的源头，	shén shì shèngjīng de yuántóu,
圣经是神的话成文字的道。	shèngjīng shì shén de huà chéng wénzì de dào.
正如圣经上所说的，	zhèng rú shèngjīng shàng suǒ shuō de,
上帝为爱祂的人所预备的，	shàngdì wèi ài tā de rén suǒ yùbèi de,
是眼睛未曾见过，耳朵未曾听闻，	shì yǎnjīng wèicéng jiànguò, ěrduǒ wèicéng tīngwén,
人心也未曾想到的。	rén xīn yě wèi céng xiǎng dào de.
我们人活着不是单靠食物，	wǒmen rén huó zhe bú shì dān kào shíwù,
而是要靠神口里所出的一切话。	ér shì yào kào shén kǒu lǐ suǒ chū de yíqiè huà.
圣经教导我们信耶稣基督，	shèngjīng jiàodǎo wǒmen xìn yēsū jīdū,
因祂的名得生命和得救的智慧，	yīn tā de míng dé shēngmìng hé déjiù de zhìhuì,
使我们归正，教导我们学义，	shǐ wǒmen guī zhèng, jiàodǎo wǒmen xué yì,
叫属神的人得以完全，	jiào shǔ shén de rén déyǐ wánquán,
预备行各样的善事。	yùbèi xíng gè yàng de shànshì.

圣经权威
(shèng jīng quán wēi)

字词集解 Word Explanation
zì cí jí jiě

道成肉身 (The Word Became Flesh)
dào chéng ròu shēn

神爱世人，差(chāi)他的独生子耶稣来到世上，是藉(jí)着圣灵感孕(gǎn yùn)，童女(tóng nǚ)马利亚(lì yà)所生，是神的儿子成为人子的样式(yàng shì)，在世上把神表明(biǎo)给人。道成了肉身，就是神的儿子降世(jiàng shì)，成为肉身的人。这"道"是指(zhǐ)耶稣基督说的："道就是神"。

—约1:1，3:16；路1:35

问题跟踪 Follow-up Questions

1. 圣经是如何写成的？

2. 圣经的权威从哪里来？

3. 圣经怎样教导我们？

4. 为什么圣经如此重要？

5. 我们怎样才能记住神的话？

jīng wén huí yìng

经文回应 Scripture Response Reading

cóngqián suǒ xiě de shèngjīng dōu shì wèi jiàoxùn wǒmen xiě de
从 前 所 写 的 圣 经 都 是 为 教 训 我 们 写 的 ，

jiào wǒmen yīn shèngjīng suǒ shēng de rěnnài hé ānwèi kěyǐ dézháo pànwàng
叫 我 们 因 圣 经 所 生 的 忍 耐 和 安 慰 可 以 得 着 盼 望 。

— 罗马书 15:4 —

For everything that was written in the past was written to teach us,
so that through the endurance taught in the Scriptures and the
encouragement they provide we might have hope.

— Romans 15:4 —

故事阅读 Bible Story Reading

yà dāng hé xià wá

亚当和夏娃

(创2:7-3:24)

耶和华神用地上的尘土造人，把生命的气吹进他的鼻孔，那人就成了有生命的活人，名叫亚当。主把那人安置在美丽的伊甸园里，并且告诉他，园中各样树上的果子，他都可以吃，只是那知善恶树的果子，他不可吃。

后来，神用从那人身上所取的肋骨为他造了一个和他相配的帮手，称为女人，名叫夏娃。

Yēhéhuá shén yòng dìshàng de chéntǔ zào rén, bǎ shēngmìng de qì chuī jìn tā de bí kǒng, nà rén jiù chéngle yǒu shēng mìng de huó rén, míng jiào yàdāng. Zhǔ bǎ nà rén ānzhì zài měilì de yīdiànyuán lǐ, bìng qiě gàosu tā, yuánzhōng gèyàng shù shàng de guǒzi, tā dōu kěyǐ chī, zhǐshì nà zhī shàn'è shù de guǒzi, tā bùkě chī.

Hòulái, shén yòng cóng nà rén shēn shàng suǒ qǔ de lèigǔ wèi tā zàole yígè hé tā xiāng pèi de bāngshǒu, chēng wèi nǚrén, míng jiào xià wá.

有一天，蛇对夏娃说："神不准你们吃那辨别善恶树上的果子，是因为你们吃了，就能像神一样知道善恶。"

亚当和夏娃听信蛇的话，就吃了那果子，违背了神的命令。神知道了这事，对他们说："因为你们不遵从我的吩咐，你们必须离开伊甸园。"

于是，亚当和夏娃被赶出伊甸园。

Yǒu yìtiān, shé duì xiàwá shuō: "Shén bù zhǔn nǐmen chī nà biànbié shàn'è shù shàng de guǒzi, shì yīnwèi nǐmen chī le, jiù néng xiàng shén yíyàng zhīdao shàn'è."

Yàdāng hé xiàwá tīngxìn shé de huà, jiù chī le nà guǒzi, wéibèi le shén de mìng lìng. Shén zhīdao le zhè shì, duì tāmen shuō: "Yīnwèi nǐmen bù zūncóng wǒ de fēn fù, nǐmen bìxū líkāi yīdiànyuán."

Yúshì, yàdāng hé xiàwá bèi gǎn chū yīdiànyuán.

救赎恩典

救　赎　恩　典
jiù　shú　ēn　diàn

Unit 3

第三单元
dì　sān　dān　yuán

Learning Objectives

学习目的
xué　xi　mù　dì

In this unit, you will learn to...

- Articulate the fall of humankind in the Bible
- Talk about the prophecy of Christ as the Redeemer
- Understand the key terms of salvation in the Bible
- Describe God's salvation plan in the Bible
- Discuss the theme of redemption in the Bible

shén ài shì rén,　　shènzhì jiāng tā de dúshēngzǐ cì gěi　tāmen,　　jiào yí qiè xìn tā de　　bú zhì miè wáng
神爱世人，甚至将他的独生子赐给他们，叫一切信他的，不致灭亡，

fǎn dé yǒngshēng
反得永生。

—约翰福音 3:16

Unit 3：预备学习
第三单元

关键词汇 Key Terms

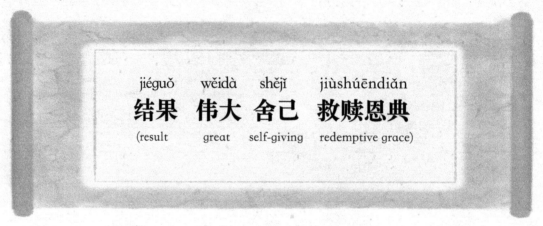

jiéguǒ　　wěidà　　shějǐ　　jiùshúēndiǎn
结果　伟大　舍己　救赎恩典
(result　　great　　self-giving　　redemptive grace)

rè shēn wèn tí
热身问题 Warm-up Questions

1. 你认为"罪"是从哪里来的？罪的结果是什么？

2. 你觉得"舍己"是世界上最伟大的爱吗？

3. 圣经中救赎的"恩典"是什么？

jīng wén xì dú
经文细读 Key Verse Reading

zhǔ shuō　 yīn wèi zài nà xiē　rì zǐ yǐ hòu　 wǒ yào yǔ yǐ sè liè jiā suǒ lì de yuē shì zhè yàng
主说："因为在那些日子以后，我要与<u>以色列</u>家所立的约是这样：

wǒ yào bǎ wǒ de　lǜ fǎ fàng zài tā men de xīn sī lǐ miàn　 xiě zài tā men de xīn shàng wǒ yào zuò tāmen
我要把我的律法放在他们的心思里面，写在他们的心上。我要作他们

de shén　 tāmen yào zuò wǒ de zǐ mín
的神，他们要作我的子民。" 　　　　　　　　　　　　　　—希伯来书 8:10

"This is the covenant I will establish with the people of Israel after that time,

declares the Lord. I will put my laws in their minds and write them on their hearts. I will be

their God and they will be my people. 　　　　　　　　　　　　　　— Hebrews 8:10

Lesson 第一课 1：罪与堕落
zuì yǔ duò luò

课堂灵修 Class Devotional
kè táng líng xiū

yīn wèi shì rén dōu fàn le zuì　　kuī quē le shén de róng yào　rú jīn què méng shén de ēndiǎn　yīn jī
因为世人都犯了罪，亏缺了神的荣耀；如今却蒙神的恩典，因基

dū yē sū de jiù shú　　jiù bái bái de chēng yì
督耶稣的救赎，就白白地称义。

— 罗马书 3:23

Daily Memory Verse

每日经文背诵
měi rì jīng wén bèi sòng

yīn wèi shén chāi tā de　ér zi jiàng shì　　bú shì yào dìng shì rén
因为神差他的儿子降世，不是要定世人

de zuì　　　nǎi shì yào jiào shì rén yīn　tā dé jiù
的罪，乃是要叫世人因他得救。

— 约翰福音 3:17

圣经金句 Frequently Quoted Verse
shèng jīng jīn jù

nǐ yào bǎoshǒu nǐ xīn, shèngguò bǎoshǒu yíqiè　yīnwèi yìshēng de guǒxiào shì yóu xīn fāchū
你要保守你心，胜过保守一切，因为一生的果效是由心发出。

— 箴言 4:23

Above all else, guard your heart, for everything you do flows from it.

— Proverbs 4:23

盟约应许 Covenantal Promise

shén hū zhào mó xī
神呼召摩西

所以你要对以色列人说：“我是耶和华；我要用伸出来的膀臂重重地刑罚埃及人，救赎你们脱离他们的重担，不做他们的苦工。我要以你们为我的百姓，我也要作你们的神。你们要知道我是耶和华——你们的神，是救你们脱离埃及人之重担的。我起誓应许给亚伯拉罕、以撒、雅各的那地，我要把你们领进去，将那地赐给你们为业。我是耶和华。”

— 出埃及记 6:6-8

God's Call to Moses

"Therefore, say to the Israelites: "I am the Lord, and I will bring you out from under the yoke of the Egyptians. I will free you from being slaves to them, and I will redeem you with an outstretched arm and with mighty acts of judgment. I will take you as my own people, and I will be your God. Then you will know that I am the Lord your God, who brought you out from under the yoke of the Egyptians. And I will bring you to the land I swore with uplifted hand to give to Abraham, to Isaac and to Jacob. I will give it to you as a possession. I am the Lord."

— Exodus 6:6-8

shī piān jí jǐn
诗篇集锦 Psalm Reading

He does not treat us as our sins deserve
or repay us according to our iniquities.
For as high as the heavens are above the earth,
so great is his love for those who fear him;
as far as the east is from the west,
so far has he removed our transgressions from us.

— Psalm 103:10-12 —

tā méiyǒu àn wǒmen de zuìguò dài wǒmen
他没有按我们的罪过待我们，
yě méiyǒu zhào wǒmen de zuìniè bàoyìng wǒmen
也没有照我们的罪孽报应我们。
tiān lí dì hé děng de gāo
天离地何等的高，
tā de cí'ài xiàng jìngwèi tā de rén yě shì hé děng de dà
他的慈爱向敬畏他的人也是何等的大！
dōng lí xī yǒu duō yuǎn
东离西有多远，
tā jiào wǒmen de guòfàn lí wǒmen yě yǒu duō yuǎn
他叫我们的过犯离我们也有多远！

—诗篇 103:10-12—

课文预读 Introductory Reading

神用祂的智慧创造天地，

也创造了人和万物。

神爱人，让人管理万物。

神爱人，祝福祂所造的人。

神爱人，人也要爱神。

人却离开了祂，

不愿意听祂的话而得罪了神。

圣经称这个为"罪"，还说：

若是人心中有不好的念头，

就是犯罪了。

所以没有人能说："我没有犯罪"。

罪使人失去了神的祝福，

也使人失去了生命的平安。

圣经如此这样告诉我们：

人人都有一死，罪的结局就是死。

zuì

罪

de

的

jié

结

jú

局

shén yòng tā de zhìhuì chuàngzào tiāndì,

yě chuàngzào le rén hé wànwù.

shén ài rén, ràng rén guǎnlǐ wànwù.

shén ài rén, zhùfú tā suǒ zào de rén.

shén ài rén, rén yě yào ài shén.

rén què lí kāi le tā,

bú yuànyì tīng tā de huà ér dézuì le shén.

shèngjīng chēng zhège wéi "zuì", hái shuō:

ruò shì rén xīnzhōng yǒu bù hǎo de niàntou,

jiù shì fànzuì le.

suǒyǐ méiyǒu rén néng shuō: "wǒ méiyǒu fànzuì".

zuì shǐ rén shīqù le shén de zhùfú,

yě shǐ rén shīqù le shēngmìng de píng'ān.

shèngjīng rúcǐ zhèyàng gàosu wǒmen:

rén rén dōu yǒu yì sǐ, zuì de jiéjú jiù shì sǐ.

预读问题 Pre-reading Questions

1. 神怎么爱人？

2. 人是怎么得罪了神的？

3. 罪的结局是什么？

参考经文 Reference Verses for the Text

创2:1-8，17，3:2-6；罗6:23；来9:27

神创造亚当[*]和夏娃[*]，把他们安置在伊甸园[*]中，有神永远的同在。神告诉亚当他可以随意吃园中各样树上的果子，但是唯独不可吃"分别善恶树[*]"上的果子，因为神说人吃的日子必定死。然而，人**背叛**了神。夏娃听了**魔鬼**的**引诱**，摘下那果子吃了，还拿给亚当吃了。这样，他们因没有**遵命**，犯了罪，**悖逆**了神，被赶出伊甸园，离开了神的面。

所以，人类始祖**违反**神**警告**的**结局**就是与神永远的**隔绝**。而且，因始祖的悖逆，众人成为罪人，人人都生而有罪，这称为原罪。除了原罪，我们人也有本罪。本罪就是人出生之后所犯的罪行。因着原罪和这个被罪恶**败坏**的世界对我们的影响，我们的思想、言语和行为都有可能犯罪。

圣经说：按着定命，人人都有一死，死后且有**审判**。也就是说，人的**灵魂**并未因死亡而**灭绝**。如果按着神公义的审判，人所应得的**惩罚**将是永远地落在**地狱**，无法自救。可是，神爱世人，祂的爱子耶稣基督因圣灵感孕[*]而生，降世为人[*]，成为唯一的无罪者担当我们的罪，为人付上了罪的赎价。这样，人就可以藉着信耶稣基督罪得**赦免**，灵魂得救。

* "亚当和夏娃"yàdāng hé xiàwá：Adam and Eve

* "伊甸园"yī diàn yuán：the Garden of Eden

* "分别善恶树"fēn bié shàn'è shù：the Tree of Knowledge of Good and Evil

* "圣灵感孕"shènglíng gǎn yùn：conceived by the Holy Spirit

* "降世为人"jiàng shì wéi rén：descend to earth as a human

shén chuàngzào <u>yàdāng</u>* hé <u>xiàwá</u>*, bǎ tāmen ānzhì zài <u>yīdiànyuán</u>* zhōng, yǒu shén yǒngyuǎn de tóng zài. shén gàosu <u>yàdāng</u> tā kěyǐ suíyì chī yuánzhōng gè yàng shù shàng de guǒzi, dànshì wéidú bùkě chī "fēnbié shàn è shù*" shàng de guǒzi, yīnwèi shén shuō rén chī de rìzi bìdìng sǐ. rán'ér, rén **bèipàn** le shén. xiàwá tīng le **móguǐ** de **yǐnyòu**, zhāi xià nà guǒzi chī le, hái ná gěi <u>yàdāng</u> chī le. zhèyàng, tāmen yīn méiyǒu **zūnmìng**, fàn le zuì, **bèinì** le shén, bèi gǎn chū yīdiànyuán, lí kāi le shén de miàn.

suǒyǐ, rénlèi shǐzǔ **wéifǎn** shén **jǐnggào** de **jiéjú** jiùshì yǔ shén yǒngyuǎn de **géjué**. érqiě, yīn shǐzǔ de **bèinì**, zhòngrén chéngwéi zuìrén, rén rén dōu shēng ér yǒuzuì, zhè chēng wéi yuánzuì. chú le yuánzuì, wǒmen rén yěyǒu běn zuì. běn zuì jiùshì rén chūshēng zhīhòu suǒ fàn de zuìxíng. yīnzhe yuánzuì hé zhège bèi zuì'è **bàihuài** de shìjiè duì wǒmen de yǐngxiǎng, wǒmen de sīxiǎng, yányǔ hé xíngwéi dōu yǒu kě néng fànzuì.

shèngjīng shuō: ànzhe dìng mìng, rén rén dōu yǒu yìsǐ, sǐ hòu qiě yǒu **shénpàn**. yě jiùshì shuō, rén de **línghún** bìng wèi yīn sǐwáng ér **mièjué**. rúguǒ ànzhe shén gōngyì de shěnpàn, rén suǒ yīng dé de **chéngfá** jiāng shì yǒngyuǎn de luò zài **dìyù**, wúfǎ zìjiù. kěshì, shén ài shìrén, tā de àizǐ yēsū jīdū yīn shènglíng gǎnyùn ér shēng, jiàngshì wéi rén, chéngwéi wéiyī de wú zuì zhě dāndāng wǒmen de zuì, wèirén fù shàng le zuì de shújià. zhèyàng, rén jiù kěyǐ jièzhe xìn yēsū jīdū zuì dé **shèmiǎn**, línghún déjiù.

Special Notes on Text

* yàdāng: Adam

* xiàwá: Eve

* yī diàn yuán: the Garden of Eden

* fēn bié shàn è shù: the Tree of Knowledge and of Good and Evil

* shènglíng gǎn yùn: conceived by the Holy Spirit

* jiàng shì wéi rén: descend to earth as a human

1.	背叛	bèi pàn	(V)	to betray
2.	魔鬼	mó guǐ	(N)	demon, devil
3.	引诱	yǐn yòu	(V)	to tempt, to entice
4.	遵命	zūn mìng	(V)	to obey, to comply
5.	悖逆	bèi nì	(V)	to rebel
6.	违反	wéi fǎn	(V)	to violate
7.	警告	jǐng gào	(N)	warning
8.	结局	jié jú	(N)	ending, result
9.	隔绝	gé jué	(V)	to separate
10.	败坏	bài huài	(N)	depravity
11.	审判	shěn pàn	(N)	judgement
12.	灵魂	líng hún	(N)	soul
13.	灭绝	miè jué	(V)	to die out
14.	惩罚	chéng fá	(N)	punishment
15.	地狱	dì yù	(N)	hell
16.	赦免	shè miǎn	(V)	to remit(a punishment)

读后讨论 Post-reading Discussion

1. 神造人原本就堕落悖逆吗？

2. 我们从哪里能读到人类堕落的历史？

3. 人的初罪或原罪是什么？人类始祖犯了什么罪？

jìng bài zàn měi

敬拜赞美 Worship and Praise

Praise the Lord, O My Soul

Praise the Lord, my soul,
and forget not all his benefits —
who forgives all your sins
and heals all your diseases,
who redeems your life from the pit
and crowns you with love and compassion,
who satisfies your desires with good things
so that your youth is renewed like the eagle's.

— Psalm 103:2-5 —

yē hé huá de ēn diǎn
耶和华的恩典

wǒ de xīn nǎ nǐ yào chēngsòng yēhéhuá
我的心哪，你要称颂耶和华！

bù kě wàng jì tā de yí qiè ēn huì
不可忘记他的一切恩惠！

tā shè miǎn nǐ de yí qiè zuì niè
他赦免你的一切罪孽，

yī zhì nǐ de yí qiè jí bìng
医治你的一切疾病。

tā jiù shú nǐ de mìng tuō lí sǐ wáng
他救赎你的命脱离死亡，

yǐ rén'ài hé cí bēi wéi nǐ de guān miǎn
以仁爱和慈悲为你的冠冕。

tā yòng měi wù shǐ nǐ suǒ yuàn de dé yǐ zhī zú
他用美物使你所愿的得以知足，

yǐ zhì nǐ rú yīng fǎn lǎo huán tóng
以致你如鹰返老还童。

— 诗篇 103:2-5 —

诗篇二十三篇

耶和华是我的牧者，我必不致缺乏。

他使我躺卧在青草地上，领我在可安歇的水边。

他使我的灵魂苏醒，为自己的名引导我走义路。

我虽然行过死荫的幽谷，也不怕遭害，因为你与我同在；

你的杖，你的竿，都安慰我。

在我敌人面前，你为我摆设筵席；

你用油膏了我的头，使我的福杯满溢。

我一生一世必有恩惠慈爱随着我，

我且要住在耶和华的殿中，

直到永远。

——诗篇 23:1-6

shīpiān èrshísān piān

yēhéhuá shì wǒ de mù zhě, wǒ bì búzhì quēfá.

tā shǐ wǒ tǎng wò zài qīngcǎo dìshàng, lǐng wǒ zài kě ānxiē de shuǐ biān.

tā shǐ wǒ de línghún sūxǐng, wèi zìjǐ de míng yǐndǎo wǒ zǒu yì lù.

Psalm 23:1-3

The Lord is my shepherd, I lack nothing.

He makes me lie down in green pastures, he leads me beside quiet waters,

he refreshes my soul. He guides me along the right paths for his name's sake.

诗文祷告 Prayer Passage

神啊，求你按你的慈爱怜恤我！按你丰盛的慈悲涂抹我的过犯！求
你将我的罪孽洗除净尽，并洁除我的罪！因为，我知道我的过犯；我的

罪常在我面前。

— 诗篇 51:1-3

Have mercy on me, O God, according to your unfailing love; according to your great compassion blot out my transgressions. Wash away all my iniquity and cleanse me from my sin. For I know my transgressions, and my sin is always before me.

— Psalm 51:1-3

祈祷范文 Exemplary Prayer

诗51:1，3；罗3:23；提前1:15

主耶稣，我们世人都犯了罪，亏缺了祢的荣耀。我们常常以自我为中
心，得罪了祢，不愿意承认自己就是罪人中的罪魁。求祢赦免我们的罪，洁
净我们自私自利的罪，叫我们转向祢，来到祢的十字架前，寻求与祢和好。

奉祢的名祷告，阿们。

Lesson 第二课 2: 悔改重生

hui gǎi chóng shēng

课堂灵修 Class Devotional
kè táng líng xiū

wǒ gào su nǐ men   yí gè zuì rén huǐ gǎi   zài tiānshàng yě yào zhèyàng wèi tā huānxǐ   jiào bǐ wéi
我告诉你们，一个罪人悔改，在天上也要这样为他欢喜，较比为

jiǔ shí jiǔ gè bú yòng huǐgǎi de yì rén huānxǐ gèng dà
九十九个不用悔改的义人欢喜更大。　　　　　　　　　— 路加福音 15:7

Daily Memory Verse

每日经文背诵
měi rì jīng wén bèi sòng

wǒ lái běn bú shì zhào yì rén huǐ gǎi
我来本不是召义人悔改，

nǎi shì zhào zuì rén huǐ gǎi
乃是召罪人悔改。

— 路加福音 5:32

圣经金句 Frequently Quoted Verse
shèng jīng jīn jù

wǒ men búzhì xiāomiè   shì chū yú yē hé huá zhū bān de cí ài   shì yīn tā de liánmǐn bú zhì
我们不致消灭，是出于耶和华诸般的慈爱；是因他的怜悯不致

duànjué měi zǎochén zhè dōu shì xīn de   nǐ de chéngshí jí qí guǎng dà
断绝。每早晨，这都是新的；你的诚实极其广大！　　　— 耶利米哀歌 3:22-23

Because of the Lord's great love we are not consumed, for his compassions
never fail. They are new every morning; great is your faithfulness.

— Lamentations 3:22-23

盟约应许 Covenantal Promise

xī nài shān zhī yuē
西奈山之约

mó xī   jiāng shí bǎn
耶和华对摩西说："你上山到我这里来，住在这里，我要将石版并我
lǜ fǎ   jiè mìng cì   shǐ   jiào xùn
所写的律法和诫命赐给你，使你可以教训百姓。"

— 出埃及记 24:12

The Sinaitic Covenant

The Lord said to Moses, "Come up to me on the mountain and stay here, and I will give you the tablets of stone with the law and commandments I have written for their instruction."

— Exodus 24:12

shī piān jí jǐn
诗篇集锦 Psalm Reading

Come,

let us bow down in worship,

let us kneel before the Lord our Maker;

for he is our God and

we are the people of his pasture,

the flock under his care.

— Psalm 95:6-7—

lái a
来啊，

wǒmen yào qūshēn jìng bài
我们要屈身敬拜，

zài zào wǒmen de yēhéhuá miànqián guì xià
在造我们的耶和华面前跪下。

yīn wèi tā shì wǒmen de shén
因为他是我们的神；

wǒmen shì tā cǎo chǎng de yáng
我们是他草场的羊，

shì tā shǒuxià de mín
是他手下的民。

— 诗篇 95:6-7—

人得罪了神，　　　　　　　　　　　　rén dézuì le shén,

活在罪中。　　　　　　　　　　　　　huó zài zuì zhōng.

可是神爱世人，　　　　　　　　　　　kěshì shén ài shìrén,

像父亲爱孩子一样，　　　　　　　　　xiàng fùqīn ài háizi yíyàng,

祂不要我们死在罪中。　　　　　　　　tā búyào wǒmen sǐ zài zuì zhōng.

神将祂的独生子耶稣赐给我们。　　　　shén jiāng tā de dúshēngzǐ yēsū cì gěi wǒmen.

耶稣为了爱我们，　　　　　　　　　　yēsū wèi le ài wǒmen,

来到这个世界上，　　　　　　　　　　lái dào zhège shìjiè shàng,

带来了天国的福音，　　　　　　　　　dài lái le tiānguó de fúyīn,

让我们知罪悔改。　　　　　　　　　　ràng wǒmen zhī zuì huǐgǎi.

耶稣为了爱我们，　　　　　　　　　　yēsū wèi le ài wǒmen,

死在十字架上，　　　　　　　　　　　sǐ zài shízìjià shàng,

舍了祂自己的生命，　　　　　　　　　shě le tā zìjǐ de shēngmìng,

为了要赐给我们新生命，　　　　　　　wèi le yào cìgěi wǒmen xīn shēngmìng,

活在神的恩典祝福之中。　　　　　　　huó zài shén de ēndiǎn zhùfú zhī zhōng.

神 的 恩 典
shén de ēn diǎn

预读问题 Pre-reading Questions

1. 耶稣为什么来到世上？

2. 人如何得着新生命？

3. 什么是神的恩典？

参考经文 Reference Verses for the Text

创2:7，太3:8；约3:16；帖前1:9；彼后3:9；约一1:9

神造人时，**永生**原本就如同**呼吸**一样是人生命的一部分。可是，人违背了神的**命令**，死亡就临到了人类。从此，人类再没有其他结局。然而，神为我们**提供**了一条出路，就是藉着信靠耶稣基督得永生。正如圣经上说："神爱世人，甚至将他的独生子**赐给**他们，叫一切信他的，不致灭亡，反得永生。"

人若要得永生就必须先**悔改**。悔改就是人要**承认**内心里的**邪恶**和败坏。这种内心的败坏致使人远离神，**违抗**神的律法，以及神对我们生命的**主宰**。但一个真实悔改的人能认识到自己的罪*，愿意放弃罪恶的生活，全心全意**顺服**神。

同时，悔改不是口头上的承认，而是要求内心和行为上的转变。圣经说：你们要结出果子来，与悔改的心相称。因此，悔改是愿意远离一切已知的罪，放弃那专求自己快乐的生活方式，离弃**偶像**归向神，活在神的**恩典**中，并全心**侍奉**那又真又活的神。

神是信实的，是公义的，我们若认自己的罪，承认耶稣基督是生命之主，并且愿意**跟随**祂，神必要赦免我们的罪，洗净我们的不义，带我们进入那永恒的生命。

课文特注

* "罪"（zuì）在圣经原文里的字义是"射不中"（shè bú zhòng）的意思。圣经认为只要违背了上帝的话就是"错过了目标"（cuò guò le mù biāo），就是犯"罪"。

shén zào rén shí, **yǒngshēng** yuánběn jiù rútóng **hūxī** yíyàng shì rén shēngmìng de yí bù fèn. Kěshì, rén wéibèi le shén de **mìnglìng**, sǐwáng jiù lín dào le rénlèi. cóngcǐ, rénlèi zài méiyǒu qítā jiéjú. rán'ér, shén wèi wǒmen **tígōng** le yì tiáo chūlù, jiùshì jièzhe xìnkào yēsū jīdū dé yǒngshēng. zhèngrú shēngjīng shàng shuō: shén ài shì rén, shènzhì jiāng tā de dúshēngzǐ **cìgěi** tāmen, jiào yíqiè xìn tā de, búzhì mièwáng, fǎn dé yǒngshēng.

rén ruò yào dé yǒngshēng jiù bìxū xiān **huǐgǎi**. huǐgǎi jiùshì rén yào **chéngrèn** nèixīn lǐ de **xié'è** hé bàihuài. zhè zhǒng nèixīn de bàihuài zhìshǐ rén yuǎnlí shén, **wéikàng** shén de lǜfǎ, yǐjí shén duì wǒmen shēngmìng de **zhǔzǎi**. dàn yígè zhēnshí huǐgǎi de rén néng rènshí dào zìjǐ de zuì[*], yuànyì fàngqì zuì'è de shēnghuó, quánxīn quányì **shùnfú** shén.

tóngshí, huǐgǎi búshì kǒutóu shàng de chéngrèn, érshì yāo qiú nèixīn hé xíngwéi shàng de zhuǎnbiàn. shèngjīng shuō: nǐmen yào jiéchū guǒzi lái, yǔ huǐgǎi de xīn xiāngchèn. yīncǐ, huǐgǎi shì yuànyì yuǎnlí yíqiè yǐzhī de zuì, fàngqì nà zhuān qiú zìjǐ kuàilè de shēnghuó fāngshì, líqì **ǒuxiàng** guīxiàng shén, huó zài shén de **ēndiǎn** zhōng, bìng quánxīn **shìfèng** nà yòu zhēn yòu huó de shén.

shén shì xìnshí de, shì gōngyì de, wǒmen ruò rèn zìjǐ de zuì, chéngrèn yēsū jīdū shì shēngmìng zhī zhǔ, bìngqiě yuànyì **gēnsuí** tā, shén bìyào shèmiǎn wǒmen de zuì, xǐ jìng wǒmen de búyì, dài wǒmen jìnrù nà yǒnghéng de shēngmìng.

Special Notes on Text

*   The word "sin" (zuì) in the original text of the Bible means "to miss the mark" (shèbúzhòng). The Bible considers that to disobey God's word is to "miss the mark" (cuòguò le mùbiāo) and to commit "sin".

1.	永生	yǒng shēng	(N)	eternal life
2.	呼吸	hū xī	(V)	to breathe
3.	命令	mìng lìng	(N)	command
4.	提供	tí gōng	(V)	to provide
5.	赐给	cì gěi	(V)	to give, to bestow
6.	悔改	huǐ gǎi	(N)	repentance
7.	承认	chéng rèn	(V)	to admit
8.	邪恶	xié'è	(N)	wickedness, evil
9.	违抗	wéi kàng	(V)	to defy, to disobey
10.	主宰	zhǔ zǎi	(V)	to dominate
11.	顺服	shùn fú	(V)	to be obedient
12.	偶像	ǒu xiàng	(N)	idol
13.	恩典	ēn diǎn	(N)	grace
14.	侍奉	shì fèng	(V)	to serve, to wait on
15.	跟随	gēn suí	(V)	to follow

读后讨论 Post-reading Discussion

1. 什么叫"悔改"?

2. 什么叫"得救"? 人怎样才能得救?

3. 圣经中所说的"永生"是怎样的?

敬拜赞美 Worship and Praise

The Unfailing Love of the LORD

The Lord works righteousness

and justice for all the oppressed.

He made known his ways to Moses,

his deeds to the people of Israel:

The Lord is compassionate and gracious,

slow to anger, abounding in love.

He will not always accuse,

nor will he harbor his anger forever.

— Psalm 103:6-9 —

yē hé huá de cí ài
耶和华的慈爱

yēhéhuá shī xíng gōng yì
耶和华施行公义,

wèi yí qiè shòu qū de rén shēnyuān
为一切受屈的人伸冤。

tā shǐ móxī zhī dào tā de fǎ zé
他使摩西知道他的法则,

jiào yǐ sè liè rén xiǎode tā de zuò wéi
叫以色列人晓得他的作为。

yēhéhuá yǒu liánmǐn yǒu ēndiǎn
耶和华有怜悯, 有恩典,

bù qīng yì fā nù qiě yǒu fēngshèng de cí ài
不轻易发怒, 且有丰盛的慈爱。

tā bù chángjiǔ zé bèi yě bù yǒngyuǎn huái nù
他不长久责备, 也不永远怀怒。

— 诗篇 103:6-9 —

诗篇二十三篇

耶和华是我的牧者，我必不致缺乏。

他使我躺卧在青草地上，领我在可安歇的水边。

他使我的灵魂苏醒，为自己的名引导我走义路。

我虽然行过死荫的幽谷，也不怕遭害，因为你与我同在；

你的杖，你的竿，都安慰我。

在我敌人面前，你为我摆设筵席；

你用油膏了我的头，使我的福杯满溢。

我一生一世必有恩惠慈爱随着我，

我且要住在耶和华的殿中，

直到永远。

— 诗篇 23:1-6

shīpiān èrshísān piān

wǒ suīrán xíngguò sǐyīn de yōugǔ, yě búpà zāohài, yīnwèi nǐ yǔ wǒ tóngzài;

nǐ de zhàng, nǐ de gān, dōu ānwèi wǒ.

zài wǒ dírén miànqián, nǐ wèi wǒ bǎishè yánxí;

Psalm 23:4-5

Even though I walk through the darkest valley, I will fear no evil, for you are with me;

your rod and your staff, they comfort me.

You prepare a table before me in the presence of my enemies.

主啊，求你听我的声音！愿你侧耳听我恳求的声音！主—耶和

华啊，你若究察罪孽，谁能站得住呢？但在你有赦免之恩，要叫人

敬畏你。我等候耶和华，我的心等候；我也仰望他的话。

—诗篇 120:2-5

Lord, hear my voice. Let your ears be attentive to my cry for mercy. If you, Lord, kept a record of sins, Lord, who could stand? But with you there is forgiveness, so that we can, with reverence, serve you. I wait for the Lord, my whole being waits, and in his word I put my hope.

— Psalm 120:2-5

qí dǎo fàn wén

祈祷范文 Exemplary Prayer

结18:31；路5:32；徒3:19，13:38

全能的神啊，祢已将最大的礼物赐给我们，就是祢的儿子，我们的救

主。只要我们认罪悔改，祈求赦免，祢就在耶稣里完全地赦免我们的罪。

求祢感动我们每一个人都能对祢说："主啊，求祢赦免我的罪。"奉耶稣

的名求，阿们！

Lesson 第三课 3: 死里复活

sǐ lǐ fù huó

kè táng líng xiū
课堂灵修 Class Devotional

méiyǒu rén duó wǒde mìng qù shì wǒ zì jǐ shě de   wǒ yǒu quánbǐng shě le yě yǒu quánbǐng
没有人夺我的命去，是我自己舍的。我有权柄舍了，也有权柄

qǔ huí lái   zhè shì wǒ cóng wǒ fù suǒ shòu de mìnglìng
取回来。这是我从我父所受的命令。　　　　　　　　　— 约翰福音 10:18

■— Daily Memory Verse —■

每
日
经
文
背
诵

měi rì jīng wén bèi sòng

wéi yǒu jī dū zài wǒ men hái zuò zuì rén de shí hòu wèi wǒ men sǐ
惟有基督在我们还作罪人的时候为我们死，
shén de ài jiù zài cǐ xiàng wǒmen xiǎn míng le
神的爱就在此向我们显明了。

— 罗马书 5:8

shèng jīng jīn jù
圣经金句 Frequently Quoted Verse

nǐ bú yào hài pà   yīn wèi wǒ yǔ nǐ tóng zài   bú yào jīng huáng yīnwèi wǒ shì nǐ de shén
你不要害怕，因为我与你同在；不要惊惶，因为我是你的神。
wǒ bì jiān gù nǐ   wǒ bì bāngzhù nǐ   wǒ bì yòng wǒ gōngyì de yòushǒu fúchí nǐ
我必坚固你，我必帮助你；我必用我公义的右手扶持你。

— 以赛亚书 41:10

So do not fear, for I am with you; do not be dismayed, for I am your God. I will
strengthen you and help you: I will uphold you with my righteous right hand.

— Isaiah 41:10

盟约应许 Covenantal Promise

摩西之约
（mó xī zhī yuē）

看哪，我今日将祝福与咒诅的话都陈明在你们面前。你们若听从耶和华——你们神的诫命，就是我今日所吩咐你们的，就必蒙福。你们若不听从耶和华——你们神的诫命，偏离我今日所吩咐你们的道，去事奉你们素来所不认识的别神，就必受祸。

— 申命记 11:26-28

The Mosaic Covenant

"See, I am setting before you today a blessing and a curse— the blessing if you obey the commands of the Lord your God that I am giving you today; the curse if you disobey the commands of the Lord your God and turn from the way that I command you today by following other gods, which you have not known."

— Deuteronomy 11:26-28

诗篇集锦 Psalm Reading
（shī piān jí jǐn）

The Lord is my rock,

my fortress and my deliverer;

my God is my rock, in whom I take refuge,

my shield and the horn of my salvation,

my stronghold.

— Psalm 18:2—

耶和华是我的岩石，
（yēhéhuá shì wǒ de yánshí）

我的山寨，我的救主，
（wǒ de shānzhài, wǒ de jiùzhǔ）

我的神，我的磐石，我所投靠的。
（wǒ de shén wǒ de pánshí wǒ suǒ tóukào de）

他是我的盾牌，是拯救我的角，
（tā shì wǒ de dùnpái shì zhěngjiù wǒ de jiǎo）

是我的高台。
（shì wǒ de gāotái）

— 诗篇 18:2—

课文预读 Introductory Reading

世人都犯了罪，　　　　　　　　shìrén dōu fàn le zuì,

可是神爱世人，　　　　　　　　kěshì shén ài shìrén,

将祂的独生爱子赐给他们，　　　jiāng tā de dú shēng ài zǐ cìgěi tāmen,

叫一切信祂的得永生。　　　　　jiào yí qiè xìn tā de dé yǒngshēng.

耶稣基督为了救世人，　　　　　yēsū jīdū wèi le jiù shìrén,

被钉在十字架上，　　　　　　　bèi dìng zài shízìjià shàng,

祂的血洗净了我们的罪，　　　　tā de xuè xǐ jìng le wǒmen de zuì,

因信他，我们的罪得到了赦免。　yīn xìn tā, wǒmen de zuì dé dào le shè miǎn.

耶稣为我们而死，又从死里复活，yēsū wèi wǒmen ér sǐ, yòu cóng sǐ lǐ fùhuó,

成为我们的救主，　　　　　　　chéngwéi wǒmen de jiùzhǔ,

耶稣曾说：复活在我，生命也在我。yēsū céng shuō: fùhuó zài wǒ, shēngmìng yě zài wǒ.

如此完全的福音是何等奇妙的救恩。rúcǐ wánquán de fúyīn shì hé děng qímiào de jiù ēn.

认识我们独一的真神，　　　　　rènshi wǒmen dú yī de zhēnshén,

并且认识祂所差来的耶稣基督，　bìngqiě rènshi tā suǒ chāi lái de yēsū jīdū,

这就是永生。　　　　　　　　　zhè jiù shì yǒngshēng.

复活的救主
fù huó de jiù zhǔ

预读问题 Pre-reading Questions

1. 人的罪怎样得到了赦免？

2. 为什么说耶稣是我们的救主？

3. 什么是永生？

参考经文 Reference Verses for the Text

林前15:3-4，14-17，22；罗10:9-10

在亚当里众人都死了，照样，在基督里众人也都要复活。可见，虽然我们都在亚当里犯了罪，但因着神的儿子一次并永远地**代替**我们**献上**了赎罪祭^{*}，我们可以靠着耶稣的**宝血**洗去我们一切的罪。因着**经历**基督的死，我们和基督同**钉十字架**；因着耶稣的复活，我们**拥有**神儿子复活的生命而向神活着。

基督若没有复活，我们的信便是**徒然**，我们仍在罪里，等待我们的将是永远的灭亡。所以，我们所信的是死而复活的神。正如保罗^{*}所说："我当日所**领受**又**传**给你们的，第一，就是基督照圣经所说，为我们的罪死了，而且**埋葬**了，又照圣经所说，第三天复活了。"

可见，主耶稣基督的复活是**福音**的**核心**。如果耶稣基督没有复活，我们的生命就没有永生的盼望。这福音已经为我们设立，我们若口里认耶稣为主，心里信神叫祂从死里复活，就可**称义**，就必得救。

課文特注

* "赎罪祭"shúzuìjì 是以色列人为了他们的罪向神献上的流过血的祭物，使这一个祭物代替以色列人的罪而死，藉以遮掩他们的罪并得到神的赦免。

* "保罗"bǎoluó：本名为"扫罗"sǎoluó，他是早期教会最具有影响力的传教士之一，基督徒的第一代领导者之一。因为他向非犹太人传播基督的福音，所以被奉为外邦人的使徒。

zài <u>yàdāng</u> lǐ zhòngrén dōu sǐ le, zhàoyàng, zài jīdū lǐ zhòngrén yě dōu yào fùhuó. kějiàn, suīrán wǒmen dōu zài <u>yàdāng</u> lǐ fàn le zuì, dàn yīnzhe shén de érzi yícì bìng yǒngyuǎn de **dàitì** wǒmen **xiànshàng** le shúzuìjì*, wǒmen kěyǐ kàozhe yēsū de **bǎoxuè** xǐ qù wǒmen yíqiè de zuì. yīnzhe **jīnglì** jīdū de sǐ, wǒmen hé jīdū tóng **dìng shízìjià**; yīnzhe yēsū de fùhuó, wǒmen **yǒngyǒu** shén érzi fùhuó de shēngmìng ér xiàng shén huózhe.

jīdū ruò méiyǒu fùhuó, wǒmen de xìn biàn shì **túrán**, wǒmen réng zài zuì lǐ, děngdài wǒmen de jiāng shì yǒngyuǎn de mièwáng. suǒyǐ, wǒmen suǒxìn de shì sǐ ér fùhuó de shén. zhèngrú <u>bǎoluó</u>* suǒ shuō: "wǒ dāngrì suǒ **lǐngshòu** yòu **chuán** gěi nǐmen de, dì yī, jiùshì jīdū zhào shèngjīng suǒ shuō, wèi wǒmen de zuì sǐ le, érqiě **máizàng** le, yòu zhào shèngjīng suǒ shuō, dì sān tiān fùhuó le".

Kějiàn, zhǔ yēsū jīdū de fùhuó shì **fúyīn** de **héxīn**. rúguǒ yēsū jīdū méiyǒu fùhuó, wǒmen de shēngmìng jiù méiyǒu yǒngshēng de pànwàng. zhè fúyīn yǐjīng wèi wǒmen shèlì, wǒmen ruò kǒu lǐ rèn yēsū wéi zhǔ, xīnlǐ xìn shén jiào tā cóng sǐ lǐ fùhuó, jiù kě **chēngyì**, jiù bì dé jiù.

Special Notes on Text

* shúzuìjì (the Atonement Sacrifice): a blood sacrifice (liúguòxuè de jìwù) that the Israelites offered to God for their sins, so that this one sacrifice (jìwù) would die in place of the Israelites' sins, thereby covering their sins and receiving God's forgiveness.

* bǎoluó (Paul): Originally named "Saul" (sǎoluó), he was one of the most influential missionaries (chuánjiàoshì) of the early church (jiàohuì) and one of the first-generation leaders of the Christians (jīdūtú). Because he preached the Gospel of Christ to non-Jews (fēi yóutàirén), he was regarded as an apostle of the Gentiles (wàibāngrén de shǐtú).

1.	代替	dài tì	(V)	to take the place of
2.	献上	xiàn shàng	(V)	to offer
3.	宝血	bǎo xuè	(N)	precious blood
4.	经历	jīng lì	(V)	to experience
5.	钉	dìng	(V)	to nail
6.	十字架	shí zì jià	(N)	the cross
7.	拥有	yǒng yǒu	(V)	to have
8.	徒然	tú rán	(Adj)	in vain
9.	领受	lǐng shòu	(V)	to receive
10.	传	chuán	(V)	to spread
11.	埋葬	mái zàng	(V)	to bury
12.	福音	fú yīn	(N)	the Gospel
13.	核心	hé xīn	(N)	core
14.	称义	chēng yì	(V)	to be justified

读后讨论 Post-reading Discussion

1. 基督耶稣受死流血是为了什么？

2. 耶稣从死里复活显明了什么？（罗1:4）

3. 耶稣被钉十字架，使信祂的得到什么？

jìng bài zàn měi

敬拜赞美 Worship and Praise

God's Faithfulness

I will sing of the Lord's great love forever;

with my mouth I will make your faithfulness known

through all generations.

I will declare that

your love stands firm forever,

that you have established

your faithfulness in heaven itself.

You said,

I have made a covenant with my chosen one,

I have sworn to David my servant,

I will establish your line forever

and make your throne firm

through all generations.

— Psalm 89: 1-4 —

yē hé huá de xìn shí

耶和华的信实

wǒ yào gēchàng yēhéhuá de cí'ài,

我要歌唱耶和华的慈爱，

zhídào yǒngyuǎn;

直到永远；

wǒ yào yòng kǒu jiāng nǐ de xìnshí chuán yǔ wàndài.

我要用口将你的信实传与万代。

yīn wǒ céng shuō: nǐ de cíbēi bì jiànlì dào yǒngyuǎn;

因我曾说：你的慈悲必建立到永远；

nǐ de xìnshí bì jiānlì zài tiānshàng.

你的信实必坚立在天上。

wǒ yǔ wǒ suǒ jiǎnxuǎn de rén lì le yuē,

我与我所拣选的人立了约，

xiàng wǒ de púrén dàwèi qǐ le shì:

向我的仆人大卫起了誓：

wǒ yào jiànlì nǐ de hòuyì, zhídào yǒngyuǎn;

我要建立你的后裔，直到永远；

yào jiànlì nǐ de bǎozuò, zhídào wàndài.

要建立你的宝座，直到万代。

— 诗篇 89:1-4 —

诗篇二十三篇

耶和华是我的牧者，我必不致缺乏。

他使我躺卧在青草地上，领我在可安歇的水边。

他使我的灵魂苏醒，为自己的名引导我走义路。

我虽然行过死荫的幽谷，也不怕遭害，因为你与我同在；

你的杖，你的竿，都安慰我。

在我敌人面前，你为我摆设筵席；

你用油膏了我的头，使我的福杯满溢。

我一生一世必有恩惠慈爱随着我，

我且要住在耶和华的殿中，

直到永远。

— 诗篇 23:1-6

shīpiān èrshísān piān

nǐ yòng yóu gāo le wǒ de tóu, shǐ wǒ de fú bēi mǎn yì.

wǒ yìshēng yíshì bì yǒu ēnhuì cí'ài suízhe wǒ,

wǒ qiě yào zhù zài yēhéhuá de diànzhōng,

zhídào yǒngyuǎn.

Psalm 23:5-6

You anoint my head with oil; my cup overflows.

Surely your goodness and love will follow me all the days of my life,

and I will dwell in the house of the Lord

forever.

神啊，求你为我造清洁(zào qīng jié)的心，使我里面重新有正直的灵(chóng xīn zhèng zhí líng)。不要丢弃(diū qì)我，使我离开你的面；不要从我收(shōu)回你的圣灵。求你使我仍得救恩之乐(réng dé jiù ēn zhī lè)，赐(cì)我乐意的灵扶持(fú chí)我。

— 诗篇 51:10-12

Create in me a pure heart, O God, and renew a steadfast spirit within me. Do not cast me from your presence or take your Holy Spirit from me. Restore to me the joy of your salvation and grant me a willing spirit, to sustain me.

— Psalm 51:10-12

qí dǎo fàn wén
祈祷范文 Exemplary Prayer

诗119:105；来9:26，10:12

复活(fù huó)的主啊，我们赞美(zàn měi)祢死而复活的大爱和大能，祢是我们最终(zuì zhōng)的大祭司(jì sī)，永远(yǒng yuǎn)的赎罪祭(shú zuì jì)。祢的宝血(bǎo xuè)，只一次(yí)的完美牺牲(xī shēng)使我们的罪得赦免(dé shè miǎn)，从罪中得自由(zì yóu)。祢(shǐ)的复活使我们在黑暗(hēi àn)里看见了大光(guāng)。求祢照亮(zhào liàng)我们脚(jiǎo)前的路(lù)，帮助我们向他人发出(fā chū)祢的亮光，分享(fēn xiǎng)祢救恩(jiù ēn)的好消息(xiāo xī)。奉祢的名祈(qí)求(qiú)，阿们。

103

单元简要 Unit Summary
dān yuán jiǎn yào

十架救恩
shí jià jiù ēn

神创造了人，

并祝福祂所造的人。

神爱人，祂要人也爱祂。

人却不听神的话，

离开了神，得罪了神。

可是，神爱世人，

甚至将祂的独生子耶稣赐给我们。

耶稣离开天堂来到这个世界，

为要赐给我们新生命。

耶稣舍了自己的生命，

被钉十字架，死而复活，

带给我们永生的救恩。

shén chuàngzào le rén,

bìng zhùfú tā suǒ zào de rén.

shén ài rén, tā yào rén yě ài tā.

rén què bù tīng shén de huà,

lí kāi le shén, dé zuì le shén.

kěshì, shén ài shìrén,

shènzhì jiāng tā de dúshēngzǐ yēsū cìgěi wǒmen.

yēsū líkāi tiāntáng lái dào zhège shìjiè,

wèi yào cìgěi wǒmen xīn shēngmìng.

yēsū shě le zìjǐ de shēngmìng,

bèi dìng shízìjià, sǐ ér fùhuó,

dài gěi wǒmen yǒngshēng de jiù ēn.

字词集解 Word Explanation
zì cí jí jiě

以马内利 (Immanuel)
yǐ mǎ nèi lì

"以马内利"的意思是"神与我们同在"。在耶稣降生前七百多年，先知
yǔ 　　　　　　　　　　　　　　　　　jiàng shēng

以赛亚曾预言神会给人一个兆头，即一个婴孩要藉着童女降生，祂的名字
céng yù yán　　　　　yí zhào tou　jí　　yīng hái　　tóng nǚ

是"以马内利"—神要与祂的子民同在。耶稣的降生应验了这个应许。
zǐ mín　　　　　　　　　　yìng yàn　　yīng xǔ

—赛7:14；太1:20-25

问题跟踪 Follow-up Questions

1. "罪"这个词是什么意思?

2. 人人都有原罪吗? 人人都犯有本罪吗?

3. 为什么只有耶稣才能担当人的罪?

4. 我们靠自己能自救吗?

5. 信主耶稣的人为什么还要认罪悔改?

jīng wén huí yìng
经文回应 Scripture Response Reading

zhè fúyīn shì shén cóngqián jiè zhòng xiānzhī zài shèngjīng shàng suǒ yīngxǔ de
这福音是神从前借众先知在圣经上所应许的,

lùn dào tā érzi　　wǒ zhǔ yēsū jīdū
论到他儿子—我主耶稣基督。

àn ròutǐ shuō　shì cóng dàwèi hòuyì shēng de　àn shèngshàn de líng shuō
按肉体说,是从大卫后裔生的;按圣善的灵说,

yīn cóng sǐ lǐ fùhuó　yǐ dànéng xiǎnmíng shì shén de érzi
因从死里复活,以大能显明是神的儿子。

— 罗马书 1:2-4 —

The gospel he promised beforehand through his prophets in the Holy Scriptures regarding his Son, who as to his earthly life was a descendant of David, and who through the Spirit of holiness was appointed the Son of God in power by his resurrection from the dead: Jesus Christ our Lord.

— Romans 1:2-4 —

yē sū fù huó
耶稣复活
（太27:57-28:10）

耶稣在十字架上断气以后，到了晚上有一个财主来了。他名叫约瑟，也是耶稣的门徒。他把耶稣的身体领了去，用干净细麻布裹好，安放在他自己的新坟墓里。约瑟又用一块大石头挡住坟墓的门，然后才离开。

过了安息日是星期日的时候，抹大拉的马利亚和另一个马利亚来看坟墓。忽然，主的使者从天上降下来，把挡住坟墓的石头推开，坐在上面。

Yēsū zài shízìjià shàng duànqì yǐhòu, dào le wǎnshàng yǒu yígè cáizhǔ lái le. Tā míng jiào yuēsè, yě shì yēsū de méntú. Tā bǎ yēsū de shēntǐ lǐng le qù, yòng gānjìng xì má bù guǒ hǎo, ānfàng zài tā zìjǐ de xīn fénmù lǐ. Yuēsè yòu yòng yí kuài dà shítou dǎngzhù fén mù de mén, ránhòu cái líkāi.

Guò le ān xí rì shì xīng qī rì de shí hòu, mǒdàlā de mǎlìyà hé lìng yí gè mǎlìyà lái kàn fénmù. Hūrán, zhǔ de shǐzhě cóng tiānshàng jiàng xiàlái, bǎ dǎngzhù fén mù de shítou tuī kāi, zuò zài shàngmiàn.

天使对两个女人说："不要害怕，我知道你们是在找那位被钉十字架的耶稣。祂不在这里，正如祂从前所说的，祂已经复活了。你们来看，这是安放祂的地方。快去把这消息告诉祂的门徒，祂已经从死里复活了。祂要比你们先到加利利去。在那里，你们会见到祂！"

她们两个听了立刻离开了坟地，又惊又喜，跑去告诉耶稣的门徒。

Tiānshǐ duì liǎng gè nǚrén shuō: "búyào hàipà, wǒ zhīdao nǐmen shì zài zhǎo nà wèi bèi dīng shízìjià de yēsū. Tā búzài zhè lǐ, zhèngrú tā cóngqián suǒ shuō de, tā yǐjīng fùhuó le. Nǐmen lái kàn, zhè shì ānfàng tā de dì fāng. Kuài qù bǎ zhè xiāoxi gàosu tā de mén tú, tā yǐjīng cóng sǐ lǐ fùhuó le. Tā yào bǐ nǐmen xiān dào jiālìlì qù. Zài nàlǐ, nǐmen huì jiàn dào tā!"

Tāmen liǎnggè tīng le lìkè líkāi le fén dì, yòu jīng yòu xǐ, pǎo qù gàosu yēsū de méntú.

因信称义

因 信 称 义

yīn xīn chēng yì
因 信 称 义
Unit 4
dì sì dān yuán
第四单元

Learning Objectives

xué xí mù dì
学习目的

In this unit, you will learn to...

- Understand the essential terms for Christian faith
- Articulate what the Christian faith is
- Make statements about faith and righteousness
- Explain why Jesus is important to the Christian faith
- Discuss what it means to be a Christian

yīn wèi   rén xīn lǐ xiāng xìn jiù kě yǐ chēng yì   kǒu lǐ chéng rèn jiù kě yǐ dé jiù
因为，人心里相信就可以称义，口里承认就可以得救。

— 罗马书 10:10

Unit 4: 预备学习
第四单元 yù bèi xué xí

guān jiàn cí huì
关键词汇 Key Terms

xìnxīn	jiěshì	shànxíng	gōngdé	láiyuán
信心	解释	善行	功德	来源
(faith	explain	good deeds	merits	source)

rè shēn wèn tí
热身问题 Warm-up Questions

1. 圣经里是怎么解释"信心"的？

2. 我们人必须拥有"善行"和"功德"吗？

3. 人信心的来源是什么？

jīng wén xì dú
经文细读 Key Verse Reading

wǒmen jì yīn xìn chēng yì   jiù jiè zhe wǒmen de zhǔ yēsū jīdū dé yǔ shén xiāng hé
我们既因信称义，就藉着我们的主耶稣基督得与神相和。

—罗马书 5:1

Therefore, since we have been justified by faith, we have peace with God through our Lord Jesus Christ.

— Romans 5:1

108

Lesson 1
第一课

lǎo wǒ xīn wǒ
老我新我

kè táng líng xiū
课堂灵修 Class Devotional

zuògōng de dé gōng jià bú suàn ēndiǎn nǎi shì gāi dé de wéiyǒu bú zuògōng de zhǐ xìn chēng zuì
做工的得工价，不算恩典，乃是该得的；惟有不做工的，只信称罪

rén wéi yì de shén tā de xìn jiùsuàn wéi yì
人为义的神，他的信就算为义。

— 罗马书 4: 4-5

Daily Memory Verse

měi rì jīng wén bèi sòng
每日经文背诵

yē sū bèi jiāo gěi rén shì wèi wǒmen de guò fàn
耶稣被交给人，是为我们的过犯，

fù huó shì wèi jiào wǒmen chēng yì
复活是为叫我们称义。

— 罗马书 4:25

shèng jīng jīn jù
圣经金句 Frequently Quoted Verse

yīnwèi fán shìjiè shàng de shì jiù xiàng ròutǐ de qíngyù yǎnmù dì qíngyù bìng jīnshēng
因为，凡世界上的事，就像肉体的情欲、眼目的情欲，并今生

de jiāo'ào dōu búshì cóng fù lái de nǎi shì cóng shìjiè lái de
的骄傲，都不是从父来的，乃是从世界来的。

— 约一 2:16

For everything in the world—the lust of the flesh, the lust of the eyes, and the pride
of life—comes not from the Father but from the world.

— 1 John 2:16

盟约应许 Covenantal Promise

神呼召亚伯兰
shén hū zhào yà bó lán

耶和华对亚伯兰说:"你要离开本地、本族、父家,往我所要指示你的地去。我必叫你成为大国。我必赐福给你,叫你的名为大;你也要叫别人得福。为你祝福的,我必赐福与他;那咒诅你的,我必咒诅他。地上的万族都要因你得福。"

— 创世记 12:1-3

The Call of Abram

The Lord had said to Abram, 'Go from your country, your people and your father's household to the land I will show you. I will make you into a great nation, and I will bless you; I will make your name great, and you will be a blessing. I will bless those who bless you, and whoever curses you I will curse; and all peoples on earth will be blessed through you.'

—.Genesis 12:1-3

诗篇集锦 Psalm Reading
shī piān jí jǐn

I lift up my eyes to the mountains—
where does my help come from?
My help comes from the Lord,
the Maker of heaven and earth.

— Psalm 121:1-2 —

我要向山举目;
wǒ yào xiàngshān jǔmù

我的帮助从何而来?
wǒ de bāngzhù cóng hé ér lái

我的帮助从造天地的耶和华而来。
wǒ de bāngzhù cóng zào tiāndì de yēhéhuá ér lái

— 诗篇 121:1-2 —

课文预读 Introductory Reading

神造人，将智慧和能力赐给人，

为的是让人爱神，也爱人。

但是人忘记了这位真神，

不求天上的事而思念地上的事，

得不到真正的平安和喜乐。

耶稣基督为我们舍命受死，

从死里复活，

胜过了罪恶，胜过了死亡，

带我们出黑暗入光明。

这位得胜的主，复活的主，

将新生命赐给我们，

让我们来到神的恩典面前，

在基督里成为新造的人，

活在祂所完成的救恩里，

靠着圣灵活出新生的样式。

新^{xīn}造^{zào}的^{de}人^{rén}

shén zào rén, jiāng zhìhuì hé nénglì cìgěi rén,

wèi de shì ràng rén ài shén, yě ài rén.

dànshì rén wàngjì le zhè wèi zhēnshén,

bù qiú tiānshàng de shì ér sī niàn dìshàng de shì,

dé bù dào zhēnzhèng de píng'ān hé xǐlè.

yēsū jīdū wèi wǒmen shěmìng shòu sǐ,

cóng sǐ lǐ fùhuó,

shèngguò le zuì'è, shèngguò le sǐwáng,

dài wǒmen chū hēi'àn rù guāngmíng.

zhè wèi déshèng de zhǔ, fùhuó de zhǔ,

jiāng xīn shēngmìng cìgěi wǒmen,

ràng wǒmen lái dào shén de ēndiǎn miànqián,

zài jīdū lǐ chéngwéi xīn zào de rén,

huó zài tā suǒ wánchéng de jiù ēn lǐ,

kàozhe shènglíng huó chū xīn shēng de yàngshì.

^{yù dú wèn tí}

预读问题 Pre-reading Questions

1. 耶稣怎样让我们从旧人变新人？

2. 我们为什么要成为新造的人？

3. 我们怎么才能成为新造的人？

^{cān kǎo jīng wén}

参考经文 Reference Verses for the Text

创2-3；赛53:6，64:6；罗3:10，6:23；

弗4:23-24；西3:9-10

神把人安置在伊甸园中，并与他们同在。亚当和夏娃犯罪背叛神后，一切都改变了。人失去了与神的**完美**关系，开始**惧怕**神。

所以人虽然知道神的存在，但却会远离神，不**荣耀**祂，也不感谢祂，就如经上所记："没有义人，连一个也没有。"罪的工价乃是死，可是神爱世人，差下祂的儿子耶稣基督*来到我们中间，死在十字架上，使我们众人的**罪孽**都归在祂身上，让远离神的人靠着祂的血与神**和好**。耶稣基督又从死里复活，**战胜**了死亡，让人在生命里因着信心从无**指望**到有指望。

正因如此，我们已经"脱去旧人和旧人的**行为**，穿上了新人"，在基督里*成为一个新造的人。这新人是照着神的**形像**所造，有真理的**仁义**和**圣洁**，能在认识神的事情和**知识**上渐渐被**更新**，拥有一个新的生命。也就是说，主的血让我们旧人变新人，如同脱下**污秽**的衣服，换上圣洁的衣服，将我们的**心志**改换一新，能活出新人的**样式**来。

课文特注

* "耶稣基督"yēsū jīdū："耶稣"是人名，"基督"是身份。在当时的犹太人中"耶稣"是个普通的人名，今日的西班牙或南美洲男人，仍有不少用"耶稣"为自己名字的。

* "在基督里"是指因信靠基督，凡事顺服圣灵，生命得与基督联合的状态。耶稣基督用葡萄树与枝子来描述这种紧密的联合关系。(约15:4；弗1:4；林后5:17，12:1-10)

shén bǎ rén ānzhì zài <u>yīdiànyuán</u> zhōng, bìng yǔ tāmen
tóngzài. <u>yàdāng</u> hé <u>xiàwá</u> fànzuì bèipàn shén hòu, yíqiè dōu
gǎibiàn le, rén shīqù le yǔ shén de **wánměi** guānxì, kāishǐ **jùpà**
shén.

suǒyǐ rén suīrán zhīdào shén de cúnzài, dàn què huì
yuǎnlí shén, bù **róngyào** tā, yě bù gǎnxiè tā, jiù rú jīng shàng
suǒ jì: méiyǒu yìrén, lián yígè yě méiyǒu. zuì de gōngjià nǎi
shì sǐ, kěshì shén ài shìrén, chāi xià tā de érzi yēsū jīdū* lái dào
wǒmen zhōngjiān, sǐ zài shízìjià shàng, shǐ wǒmen zhòngrén
de **zuìniè** dōu guī zài tā shēnshang, ràng yuǎnlí shén de rén
kàozhe tā de xuè yǔ shén **héhǎo**. yēsū jīdū yòu cóng sǐ lǐ fùhuó,
zhànshèng le sǐwáng, ràng rén zài shēngmìng lǐ yīnzhe xìnxīn
cóng wú **zhǐwàng** dào yǒu zhǐwàng.

zhèng yīn rúcǐ, wǒmen yǐjīng "tuō qù jiùrén hé jiùrén
de **xíngwéi**, chuān shàng le xīnrén", zài jīdū lǐ* chéngwéi yígè
xīnzào de rén. zhè xīnrén shì zhàozhe shén de **xíngxiàng** suǒ
zào, yǒu zhēnlǐ de **rényì** hé **shèngjié**, néng zài rènshi shén de
shìqíng hé **zhīshi** shàng jiànjiàn bèi **gēngxīn**, yōngyǒu yígè xīn
de shēngmìng. yě jiùshì shuō, zhǔ de xuè ràng wǒmen jiùrén
biàn xīnrén, rútóng tuō xià **wūhuì** de yīfu, huàn shàng shèngjié
de yīfu, jiāng wǒmen de **xīnzhì** gǎihuàn yì xīn, néng huó chū
xīnrén de **yàngshì** lái.

Special Notes on Text

* yēsū jīdū (Jesus Christ): "Jesus" is the name of a person and "Christ" (jīdū) is the identity. Among the Jews (yóutàirén) of that time, "Jesus" was a common personal name, and there are still many men in Spain or South America today who use "Jesus" as their name.

* zài jīdū lǐ (In Christ) refers to the state in which a person's life is united to Christ by trusting in Him and submitting to the Holy Spirit in all things. Jesus Christ used the term vine (pútáoshù) and branch (zhīzi) to describe this close union. (Jn 15:4; Eph 1:4; 2 Cor 5:17, 12:1-10)

1.	完美	wán měi	(Adj)	perfect
2.	惧怕	jù pà	(V)	to fear
3.	荣耀	róng yào	(V/N)	to honor; glory
4.	罪孽	zuì niè	(N)	sin, iniquity
5.	和好	hé hǎo	(V)	to reconcile
6.	战胜	zhàn shèng	(V)	to conquer, to overcome
7.	指望	zhǐ wàng	(N)	anticipatory hope
8.	行为	xíng wéi	(N)	deeds
9.	形象	xíng xiàng	(N)	image
10.	仁义	rén yì	(N)	benevolence and righteousness
11.	圣洁	shèng jié	(N/Adj)	holiness; holy
12.	知识	zhī shi	(N)	knowledge
13.	更新	gēng xīn	(V)	to renew
14.	污秽	wū huì	(Adj)	filthy
15.	心志	xīn zhì	(N)	heart posture (attitude)
16.	样式	yàng shì	(N)	style, pattern

读后讨论 Post-reading Discussion

1. 为什么圣经说世界上一个义人也没有?

2. "在基督里成为新造的人"是什么意思?

3. 人可以自救吗?

敬拜赞美 Worship and Praise

shén ēn dài bèi nì de zǐ mín
神恩待悖逆的子民

Steadfast Love of the LORD

Praise the Lord.

Give thanks to the Lord, for he is good;

his love endures forever.

Who can proclaim the mighty acts

of the Lord or fully declare his praise?

Blessed are those who act justly,

who always do what is right.

— Psalm 106:1-3 —

nǐmen yào zànměi yēhéhuá
你们要赞美耶和华!

yào chēngxiè yēhéhuá yīn tā běn wéi shàn
要称谢耶和华,因他本为善;

tā de cí'ài yǒngyuǎn cháng cún
他的慈爱永远长存!

shéi néng chuánshuō yēhéhuá de dànéng
谁能传说耶和华的大能?

shéi néng biǎomíng tā yí qiè de měidé
谁能表明他一切的美德?

fán zūnshǒu gōngpíng chángxíng gōngyì de
凡遵守公平、常行公义的,

zhè rén biàn wèi yǒu fú
这人便为有福!

— 诗篇 106:1-3 —

使徒信经

我信上帝，全能的父，创造天地的主。

我信我主耶稣基督，上帝的独生子；

因着圣灵感孕，从童贞女马利亚所生；

在本丢彼拉多手下受难，被钉在十字架上、受死，埋葬；

降在阴间；第三天从死里复活；

他升天，坐在全能父上帝的右边；

将来必从那里降临，审判活人、死人。

我信圣灵；

我信圣而公之教会；我信圣徒相通；

我信罪得赦免；

我信身体复活；

我信永生。阿们！

— The Apostles' Creed

Shǐ Tú Xìn Jīng

wǒ xìn shàngdì, quánnéng de fù, chuàngzào tiāndì de zhǔ.

wǒ xìn wǒ zhǔ yēsū jīdū, shàngdì de dúshēngzǐ;

yīnzhe shènglíng gǎnyùn, cóng tóngzhēnnǚ mǎlìyà suǒ shēng;

The Apostles' Creed

I believe in God, the Father Almighty, Creator of heaven and earth.

I believe in Jesus Christ, his only Son, our Lord,

who was conceived by the Holy Spirit, born of the Virgin Mary.

bǎo yòu　　　　　tóu kào　　　　　　céng
神啊，求你保佑我，因为我投靠你。我的心哪，你曾对耶

和华说：你是我的主；我的好处不在你以外。

— 诗篇 16:1-2

Keep me safe, my God, for in you I take refuge. I say to the Lord, "You are my Lord; apart from you I have no good thing."

— Psalm 16:1-2

qí dǎo fàn wén
祈祷范文 Exemplary Prayer

约11:25-26；林后5:17；多3:5

dé zháo xīn　　　　　shèng líng
主啊，感谢祢为我死，也为我复活，好叫我得着新的生命。圣灵

jìn rù　　　　　　shǐ　　　　xiāng xìn　　　　　zào
啊，求祢进入我们的心，使我们因为相信耶稣基督而成为新造的人。主

xù　　　　　　　　bú duàn
啊，祢知道我们的需要，求祢来用祢的赦免不断更新我们。我们也为祢

bāng zhù　　　　　　　　　　lè yì cān yù
新造的人感谢祢，求祢帮助我们看见祢的工作，又叫我们乐意参与祢更

新的工作。奉耶稣的名祷告，阿们。

Lesson 2: 诚命吩咐
第二课 | jiè mìng fēn fù

课堂灵修 Class Devotional

rén fēi yǒu xìn   jiù bù néng dé shén de xǐ yuè   yīn wèi dào shén miànqián lái de rén bìxū xìn yǒu shén
人非有信，就不能得神的喜悦；因为到神面前来的人必须信有神，

qiě xìn tā shǎngcì nà xúnqiú tā de rén
且信他赏赐那寻求他的人。

— 希伯来书 11:6

Daily Memory Verse

每
日
经
文
背
诵

měi rì jīng wén bèi sòng

xìn jiù shì suǒ wàng zhī shì de shí dǐ
信就是所望之事的实底，

shì wèi jiàn zhī shì de què jù
是未见之事的确据。

— 希伯来书 11:1

圣经金句 Frequently Quoted Verse

nǐmen suǒ yùjiàn de shìtàn   wúfēi shì rén suǒ néng shòu de   shén shì xìnshí de   bì bú jiào
你们所遇见的试探，无非是人所能受的。神是信实的，必不叫

nǐmen shòu shìtàn guòyú suǒ néng shòu de zài shòu shìtàn de shíhòu   zǒngyào gěi nǐmen kāi yì tiáo chū
你们受试探过于所能受的；在受试探的时候，总要给你们开一条出

lù   jiào nǐmen néng rěnshòu dé zhù
路，叫你们能忍受得住。

— 哥林多前书 10:13

No temptation has overtaken you except what is common to mankind. And God is faithful; he will not let you be tempted beyond what you can bear. But when you are tempted, he will also provide a way out so that you can endure it.

— 1 Corinthians 10:13

méng yuē yīng xǔ 盟约应许 Covenantal Promise

shén yǔ yà bó lán lì yuē 神与亚伯兰立约

yú lǐng
于是领他走到外边，说："你向天观看，数算众星，能数得过来吗？"

hòu yì jiāng rú cǐ yà bó lán
又对他说："你的后裔将要如此。"亚伯兰信耶和华，耶和华就以此为他

yì céng jiā lè dǐ wú ěr
的义。耶和华又对他说："我是耶和华，曾领你出了迦勒底的吾珥，为要

jiāng cì
将这地赐你为业。"

— 创世记 15:5-7

The LORD's Covenant with Abram

He took him outside and said, "Look up at the sky and count the stars—if indeed you can count them." Then he said to him, "So shall your offspring be." Abram believed the Lord, and he credited it to him as righteousness. He also said to him, "I am the Lord, who brought you out of Ur of the Chaldeans to give you this land to take possession of it."

— Genesis 15:5-7

shī piān jí jǐn 诗篇集锦 Psalm Reading

When I consider your heavens,

the work of your fingers,

the moon and the stars,

which you have set in place,

what is mankind that you are mindful of them,

human beings that you care for them?

— Psalm 8:3-4 —

wǒ guānkàn nǐ zhǐtou suǒ zào de tiān
我观看你指头所造的天，

bìng nǐ suǒ chénshè de yuèliàng xīngxiù
并你所陈设的月亮星宿，

biàn shuō rén suàn shénme
便说：人算什么，

nǐ jìng gù niàn tā
你竟顾念他！

shìrén suàn shénme nǐ jìng juàn gù tā
世人算什么，你竟眷顾他！

— 诗篇 8:3-4 —

爱神要爱神的话，

因为信道是从听道来的，

听道是从基督的话来的。

圣经中父神给我们的命令，

就是叫我们信祂儿子基督耶稣的名，

且照祂所赐给我们的命令彼此相爱。

天父的这两个命令，

一个是"信"，一个是"爱"。

耶稣在被钉十字架前的最后一晚，

设立了圣餐，

亲自为门徒洗脚，

然后对他们说：

我怎样爱你们，你们也要怎样相爱。

赐下了一条新命令，

为祂的门徒留下了爱的榜样。

耶 sū 稣 的 de 命 mìng 令 lìng (yē)

ài shén yào ài shén de huà,

yīn wéi xìn dào shì cóng tīng dào lái de,

tīng dào shì cóng jīdū de huà lái de.

shèngjīng zhōng fùshén gěi wǒmen de mìnglìng,

jiù shì jiào wǒmen xìn tā érzi jīdū yēsū de míng,

qiě zhào tā suǒ cìgěi wǒmen de mìnglìng bǐcǐ xiāng'ài.

tiānfù de zhè liǎng gè mìnglìng,

yí gè shì "xìn", yí gè shì "ài".

yēsū zài bèi dìng shízìjià qián de zuìhòu yì wǎn,

shè lì le shèng cān,

qīnzì wèi méntú xǐ jiǎo,

ránhòu duì tāmen shuō:

wǒ zěnyàng ài nǐmen, nǐmen yě yào zěnyàng xiāng'ài.

cì xià le yì tiáo xīn mìnglìng,

wèi tā de méntú liú xià le ài de bǎngyàng.

1. 父神给我们什么命令？

2. 耶稣什么时候给祂门徒赐下了新命令？

3. 耶稣的新命令是什么？

太28:19；可16:15；徒1:8；
罗3:22-24，4:11，10:10；约一3:18，23，4:7-8

神的义，因信耶稣基督加给一切**相信**的人，因为圣经上说：人心里相信就可以称义，口里承认就可以得救。人人都犯了罪，**亏缺**了神的荣耀却**蒙**神的恩典，因基督耶稣的救赎白白地称义。也就是说，我们是因着相信耶稣基督而称义。

接受耶稣基督就是与神**建立**关系，有新生命，成为神的儿女，也就是"基督徒[*]"。因耶稣的死为我们的罪付上了**代价**，神就使耶稣的义成为我们的义—祂使我们称义。这样，基督徒成为"信心之父"<u>亚伯拉罕</u>[*]**属灵**的**后裔**，相信耶稣拯救的应许，相信神所应许的必能**成就**。

但信心若没有行为就是死的，所以信主之人还要**遵守**神的命令。神最大的命令就是爱神并且爱人如己。信主之人不仅要爱神，还要照祂所赐的命令**彼此**相爱。耶稣曾告诉祂的<u>门徒</u>[*]："我赐给你们一条新命令，乃是叫你们彼此相爱；我怎样爱你们，你们也要怎样相爱。"所以基督徒应当彼此相爱，"因为爱是从神来的，凡有爱心的，都是由神而生，并且认识神。"我们若遵守神的命令，就常在祂的爱里，如基督遵守了父神的命令，常在父神的爱里一样。

不仅如此，我们还要将基督的爱传到普天下去，将基督的福音传给万民听。正如耶稣离开世界以前**吩咐**门徒的那样："你们要去，使万民作我的门徒，**奉**父、子、圣灵的名给他们**施洗**。""但圣灵降临在你们身上，你们就必得着能力，并要在<u>耶路撒冷</u>，<u>犹太</u>全地，和<u>撒马利亚</u>，直到地极，作我的**见证**。"

课文特注

* "基督徒"jīdūtú：在圣经新约里出现过三次，基督徒是基督的门徒、跟随者。门徒第一次被称为基督徒是从<u>安提阿</u>起首，意为"基督的人"或"基督的支持者"（徒11:26，26:2；彼前4:16）。圣经中基督徒通常称之为门徒、信徒、圣徒。

* "亚伯拉罕"yà bó lā hàn：旧约圣经里的<u>亚伯兰</u>（yàbólán）是犹太人和阿拉伯人的始祖，上帝与<u>亚伯兰</u>立约的同时将他的名字改为"<u>亚伯拉罕</u>"，意思是"多国之父"。

* "门徒"méntú：指学生或学徒。耶稣那时候，门徒是跟着拉比（lābǐ）走，拉比就是老师。拉比到哪里去，门徒就往哪里去；拉比做什么，门徒就做什么。也就是说，门徒就是跟从者。

shén de yì, yīn xìn yēsū jīdū jiā gěi yíqiè **xiāngxìn** de rén, yīnwèi shèngjīng shàng shuō rén xīnlǐ xiāngxìn jiù kěyǐ chēngyì, kǒulǐ chéngrèn jiù kěyǐ dé jiù. rénrén dōu fàn le zuì, **kuīquē** le shén de róngyào què **méng** shén de ēndiǎn, yīn jīdū yēsū de jiùshú, báibái de chēngyì. yě jiùshì shuō, wǒmen shì yīnzhe xiāngxìn yēsū jīdū ér chēngyì.

jiēshòu yēsū jīdū jiùshì yǔ shén **jiànlì** guānxì, yǒu xīn shēngmìng, chéngwéi shén de ér nǚ, yě jiùshì "jīdūtú*". yīn yēsū de sǐ wèi wǒmen de zuì fù shàng le **dàijià**, shén jiù shǐ yēsū de yì chéngwéi wǒmen de yì——tā shǐ wǒmen chēngyì. zhèyàng, jīdūtú chéngwéi "xìnxīn zhī fù" yàbólāhàn* **shǔlíng** de **hòuyì**, xiāngxìn yēsū zhěngjiù de yīngxǔ, xiāngxìn shén suǒ yīngxǔ de bì néng **chéngjiù**.

dàn xìnxīn ruò méiyǒu xíngwéi jiùshì sǐ de, suǒyǐ xìn zhǔ zhī rén hái yào **zūnshǒu** shén de mìnglìng. shén zuìdà de mìnglìng jiùshì ài shén bìngqiě ài rén rú jǐ. xìn zhǔ zhī rén bùjǐn yào ài shén, hái yào zhào tā suǒ cì de mìnglìng **bǐcǐ** xiāng'ài. yēsū céng gàosu tā de méntú*: "wǒ cìgěi nǐmen yìtiáo xīn mìnglìng, nǎi shì jiào nǐmen bǐcǐ xiāng'ài; wǒ zěnyàng ài nǐmen, nǐmen yě yào zěnyàng xiāng'ài." suǒyǐ jīdūtú yīngdāng bǐcǐ xiāng'ài, "yīnwèi ài shì cóng shén ér lái de. fán yǒu àixīn de, dōu shì yóu shén ér shēng, bìngqiě rènshi shén. wǒmen ruò zūnshǒu shén de mìnglìng, jiù cháng zài tā de ài lǐ, rú jīdū zūnshǒu le fùshén de mìnglìng, cháng zài fùshén de ài lǐ yíyàng.

bùjǐn rúcǐ, wǒmen hái yào jiāng jīdū de ài chuán dào pǔ tiān xià qù, jiāng jīdū de fúyīn chuán gěi wànmín tīng. zhèngrú yēsū líkāi shìjiè yǐqián **fēnfù** méntú de nàyàng: nǐmen yào qù, shǐ wànmín zuò wǒ de méntú, **fèng** fù, zǐ, shènglíng de míng gěi tāmen **shīxǐ**. "dàn shènglíng jiànglín zài nǐmen shēnshang, nǐmen jiù bì dézháo nénglì, bìng yào zài yēlùsālěng, yóutài quán dì, hé sāmǎlìyǎ, zhídào dì jí, zuò wǒ de **jiànzhèng**."

Special Notes on Text

* jīdūtú (Christian): It appears three times in the New Testament. Christians are disciples (méntú) and followers (gēnsuízhě) of Christ. The first time that the disciples were called Christians was in Antioch (ān tí ā), meaning "people of Christ" (jīdū de rén) or "supporters of Christ" (jīdū de zhīchízhě) (Acts 11:26, 26:28; 1 Pet. 4:16). Christians in the Bible are commonly called disciples (méntú), believers (xìntú), and saints (shèngtú).

* yàbólāhàn (Abraham): Abram (yàbólán) of the Old Testament was the patriarch (shǐzǔ) of the Jews (yóutàirén) and Arabs (ālābórén). God made a covenant (lìyuē) with Abram and changed his name to Abraham, meaning "father of many nations" (duōguózhīfù).

* méntú (Disciple) refers to a student or apprentice (xuétú). At the time of Jesus, the disciples followed the teacher/ rabbi (lābǐ): wherever the rabbi went, the disciples went; whatever the rabbi did, the disciples did. In other words, a disciple is a follower (gēnsuízhě).

課文詞彙 Vocabulary

1.	相信	xiāng xìn	(V)	to believe
2	亏缺	kuī quē	(V)	to fall short of; to be lacking
3.	蒙	méng	(V)	to receive; to be covered by
4.	接受	jiē shòu	(V)	to accept
5.	建立	jiàn lì	(V)	to establish, to build
6.	代价	dài jià	(N)	cost, price
7.	属灵	shǔ líng	(Adj)	spiritual
8.	后裔	hòu yì	(N)	descendant
9.	成就	chéng jiù	(V)	to accomplish
10.	遵守	zūn shǒu	(V)	to comply with
11.	彼此	bǐ cǐ	(Pr)	each other
12.	吩咐	fēn fù	(V)	to instruct
13.	奉（…的名）	fèng	(V)	(to offer) in the name of
14.	施洗	shī xǐ	(V)	to baptize
15.	见证	jiàn zhèng	(N)	witness

123

读后讨论 Post-reading Discussion

1. 基督徒怎么"称义"？

2. 什么样的信心是没有用的？

3. 基督徒是眼见为信？还是先信后见？

jìng bài zàn měi
敬拜赞美 Worship and Praise

Splendor of God's Holiness

Ascribe to the Lord,

you heavenly beings,

ascribe to the Lord glory and strength.

Ascribe to the Lord the glory due his name;

worship the Lord

in the splendor of his holiness.

— Psalm 29:1-2 —

yē hé huá de wēi shēng
耶和华的威声

shén de zhòng zi a
神的众子啊，

nǐmen yào jiāng róngyào nénglì
你们要将荣耀、能力

guī gěi yēhéhuá
归给耶和华，

guī gěi yēhéhuá
归给耶和华！

yào jiāng yēhéhuá de míng suǒ dāng dé de róngyào guī gěi tā
要将耶和华的名所当得的荣耀归给他，

yǐ shèngjié de zhuāngshì jìngbài yēhéhuá
以圣洁的妆饰敬拜耶和华。

— 诗篇 29:1-2 —

使徒信经

我信上帝，全能的父，创造天地的主。

我信我主耶稣基督，上帝的独生子；

因着圣灵感孕，从童贞女马利亚所生；

在本丢彼拉多手下受难，被钉在十字架上，受死，埋葬；

降在阴间；第三天从死里复活；

他升天，坐在全能父上帝的右边；

将来必从那里降临，审判活人，死人。

我信圣灵；

我信圣而公之教会；我信圣徒相通；

我信罪得赦免；

我信身体复活；

我信永生。阿们！

— The Apostles' Creed

Shǐ Tú Xìn Jīng

zài **běndiūbǐlāduō** shǒuxià shòu nàn, bèi dìng zài shízìjià shàng, shòu sǐ, mái zàng;

jiàng zài yīnjiān; dì sān tiān cóng sǐ lǐ fùhuó;

tā shēngtiān, zuò zài quánnéng fù shàngdì de yòubiān;

jiānglái bì cóng nàlǐ jiànglín, shěnpàn huó rén, sǐ rén

The Apostles' Creed

He suffered under Pontius Pilate, was crucified, died, and was buried;

he descended to hell; on the third day he rose again from the dead;

he ascended to heaven and is seated at the right hand of God the Father Almighty;

From there he will come to judge the living and the dead.

耶和华啊，谦卑人的心愿，你早已知道。你必预备他们的

心，也必侧耳听他们的祈求，为要给孤儿和受欺压的人伸冤，使

强横的人不再威吓他们。

—— 诗篇 10:17-18

You, Lord, hear the desire of the afflicated; you encourage them. and you listen to their cry, defending the fatherless and the opressed, so that mere earthly mortals will never again strike.

—— Psalm 10:17-18

罗8:1；弗1:3；希10:10

主耶稣，感谢祢为了我们将你的生命献上为祭。恩慈的神啊，感谢祢

赐给我们在基督里的义。我们愿意做祢的儿女，每天凭信心将自己交在祢

的手中。称义单单靠信心，但信心从不单独出现。求祢的圣灵加给我们力

量，引导我们的言行举止，为要得着那永世里属灵的福乐，因为我们知道

祢会把属灵的爱赏赐给那求告祢名的人。奉耶稣的名祷告，阿们。

Lesson 第三课 3：福音盼望

课堂灵修 Class Devotional
kè táng líng xiū

yīnwèi shén de yì zhèngzài zhè fúyīn shàng xiǎnmíng chūlái zhè yì shì běn yú xìn　　yǐ zhì yú xìn

因为神的义正在这福音上显明出来；这义是本于信，以至于信。

rú jīngshàng suǒ jì　　yì rén bì yīn xìn dé shēng

如经上所记："义人必因信得生。"　　　　　　　　　　—罗马书 1:17

Daily Memory Verse

每日经文背诵
měi rì jīng wén bèi sòng

nǐ men dé jiù　shì běn hū ēn　　　　yě yīn zhe xìn　　zhè bìng bú

你们得救是本乎恩，也因着信，这并不

shì chū yú zì jǐ　　　　nǎi shì shén suǒ cì de

是出于自己，乃是神所赐的。

—以弗所书 2:8

圣经金句 Frequently Quoted Verse
shèng jīng jīn jù

wǒmen xiǎode wànshì dōu hùxiāng xiàolì　jiào ài shén de rén dé yì chu　　jiù shì àn tā zhǐ yì

我们晓得万事都互相效力，叫爱神的人得益处，就是按他旨意

bèi zhào de rén

被召的人。　　　　　　　　　　　　　　　　　　　　—罗马书 8:28

And we know that in all things God works for the good of those who love

him, who have been called according to his purpose.　　　　— Romans 8:28

亚伯拉罕之约
yà bó lā hàn zhī yuē

我与你立约：你要作多国的父。从此以后，你的名不再叫亚伯兰，
yǔ   yà bó lán

要叫亚伯拉罕，因为我已立你作多国的父。我必使你的后裔极其繁多；
yà bó lā hàn   bì shǐ   hòu yì jí qí fán

国度从你而立，君王从你而出。我要与你并你世世代代的后裔坚立我的
dù ér jūn   shì shì dài dài   jiān

约，作永远的约，是要作你和你后裔的神。   — 创世记 17:4-7
yǒng

The Abrahamic Covenant

As for me, this is my covenant with you: You will be the father of many nations. No longer will you be called Abram; your name will be Abraham, for I have made you a father of many nations. I will make you very fruitful; I will make nations of you, and kings will come from you. I will establish my covenant as an everlasting covenant between me and you and your descendants after you for the generations to come, to be your God and the God of your descendants after you.

— Genesis 17:4-7

诗篇集锦 Psalm Reading
shī piān jí jǐn

Yes, my soul, find rest in God;

my hope comes from him.

Truly he is my rock and my salvation;

he is my fortress; I will not be shaken.

My salvation and my honor depend on God;

he is my mighty rock, my refuge.

— Psalm 62:5-7 —

wǒ de xīn nǎ nǐ dāng mòmò wúshēng zhuān děnghòu shén
我的心哪，你当默默无声，专等候神，

yīnwèi wǒ de pànwàng shì cóng tā ér lái
因为我的盼望是从他而来。

wéidú tā shì wǒ de pánshí wǒ de zhěngjiù
惟独他是我的磐石，我的拯救；

tā shì wǒ de gāotái wǒ bì bú dòngyáo
他是我的高台，我必不动摇。

wǒ de zhěngjiù wǒ de róngyào dōu zàihu shén
我的拯救、我的荣耀都在乎神；

wǒ lì liàng de pánshí wǒ de bìnànsuǒ dōu zàihu shén
我力量的磐石、我的避难所都在乎神。

— 诗篇 62:5-7 —

课文预读 Introductory Reading

相信神的话是基督徒信心的来源。

耶稣说祂是道路、真理和生命，

若不藉着祂，没有人能到父那里去。

我们信靠祂，

祂就指引我们往天国的道路，

将真理启示给我们，

也要将生命赐给我们。

耶稣离开世界以前，

吩咐祂的门徒去传福音给万民听。

叫人认罪悔改得救恩。

这福音是天国来的好消息，

是耶稣基督为我们而死，

为我们复活，作我们君王的好消息。

福音是圣经的核心，

是我们盼望的根基和善行的基础。

办
bàn
法
fǎ
与
yǔ
救
jiù
法
fǎ

xiāngxìn shén de huà shì jīdūtú xìnxīn de láiyuán.

yēsū shuō tā shì dàolù, zhēnlǐ hé shēngmìng,

ruò bú jiè zhe tā, méiyǒu rén néng dào fù nàlǐ qù.

wǒmen xìn kào tā,

tā jiù zhǐyǐn wǒmen wǎng tiānguó de dàolù,

jiāng zhēnlǐ qǐshì gěi wǒmen,

yě yào jiāng shēngmìng cìgěi wǒmen.

yēsū líkāi shìjiè yǐ qián,

fēnfù tā de méntú qù chuán fúyīn gěi wànmín tīng.

jiào rén rènzuì huǐgǎi dé jiù ēn.

zhè fúyīn shì tiānguó lái de hǎo xiāoxi,

shì yēsū jīdū wèi wǒmen ér sǐ,

wèi wǒmen fùhuó, zuò wǒmen jūnwáng de hǎo xiāoxi.

fúyīn shì shèngjīng de héxīn,

shì wǒmen pànwàng de gēnjī hé shànxíng de jīchǔ.

预读问题 Pre-reading Questions

1. 耶稣赐给我们什么？

2. 圣灵的工作是什么？

3. 我们怎么可以得到真正的平安喜乐？

参考经文 Reference Verses for the Text

路19:10；约11:25；罗1:16-17；林前1:17；
弗3:17-19；彼前1:24-25

福音*就是好**消息**。圣经里说：人子*来，为要寻找、拯救失丧的人。因此，福音这好消息是耶稣的故事（祂的生命、死亡、复活和升天），是<u>以色列</u>故事的实现，它使上帝的子民从罪和死亡中得到救赎。我们因信耶稣基督为罪人的救主而得救。正如<u>保罗</u>说："我不以福音为**耻**；这福音是神的大能，要救所有相信的。"复活的主已经**得胜**了，我们藉此可以得到永生的盼望。

我们如果心里**确信**耶稣基督已经从死里复活，生命就有**平安**。因为相信我们死去的生命将如同一粒**种子**，虽然种子**腐烂**了，但是却长出了一个新的生命。因此，我们应当常在耶稣基督里面，让复活的主也常在我们里面，并且在**破碎**中经历神的同在，这样，生命就**充满**平安、**喜乐**和盼望。

所有的人，如经上所说："尽都如**草**，他的**荣美**都像草上的花；草必**枯干**，花必**凋谢**，惟有主的道永远长存。"所传给我们的福音就是这道。我们人的生命真的如同花草，但因着基督在我们里面，我们的盼望便有根有基，这就是基督徒信心的**根基**。

课文特注

* "福音"fúyīn：这个词希腊文的原意是"佳音"（jiāyīn）或"好消息"（hǎoxiāoxi）。在圣经中福音有特殊的含义：耶稣基督降世救人的事迹、讲论、受难、复活、升天和再来，显明了祂是独一的救主，以及由此而带给世人永生的"祝福佳音"。所以圣经中提到传讲基督的事工、道理、教导和救恩时，常常说成是"传福音"、"宣讲福音"或者是"传扬福音"。

* "人子"rénzǐ：旧约中先知但以理、以西结都曾用"人子"自称，表明自己卑微的身份。福音书中耶稣这样自称，表面上类同古时先知的谦称，实际上却含有耶稣自称是神所差来的弥赛亚的身份之意。耶稣自称"人子"，既表明了祂具有百分之百的人性，也表明祂是道成肉身，降世为人的救主。

fúyīn* jiùshì hǎo **xiāoxi**. shèngjīng lǐ shuō: rénzǐ* lái, wèi yào xúnzhǎo, zhěngjiù shī sàng de rén. yīncǐ, fúyīn zhè hǎo xiāoxi shì yēsū de gùshi (tā de shēngmìng, sǐwáng, fùhuó hé shēngtiān), shì <u>yǐsèliè</u> gùshi de shíxiàn, tā shǐ shàngdì de zǐmín cóng zuì hé sǐwáng zhōng dédào jiùshú. wǒmen yīn xìn yēsū jīdū wéi zuìrén de jiùzhǔ ér déjiù. zhèngrú <u>bǎoluó</u> shuō: "wǒ bù yǐ fúyīn wéi **chǐ**; zhè fúyīn shì shén de dà néng, yào jiù suǒyǒu xiāngxìn de." fùhuó de zhǔ yǐjīng **déshèng** le, wǒmen jiè cǐ kěyǐ dédào yǒngshēng de pànwàng.

wǒmen rúguǒ xīnlǐ **quèxìn** yēsū jīdū yǐjīng cóng sǐ lǐ fùhuó, shēngmìng jiù yǒu **píng'ān**. yīnwèi xiāngxìn wǒmen sǐ qù de shēngmìng jiàng rútóng yí lì **zhǒngzi**, suīrán zhǒng zi **fǔlàn** le, dànshì què zhǎng chū le yí gè xīn de shēng mìng. yīncǐ, wǒmen yīngdāng cháng zài yēsū jīdū lǐmiàn, ràng fùhuó de zhǔ yě cháng zài wǒmen lǐmiàn, bìngqiě zài **pòsuì** zhōng jīnglì shén de tóngzài, zhèyàng, shēngmìng jiù **chōngmǎn** píng'ān, **xǐlè** hé pànwàng.

suǒyǒu de rén, rú jīng shàng suǒ shuō: "jìn dōu rú **cǎo**, tā de róngměi dōu xiàng cǎo shàng de huā; cǎo bì **kūgān**, huā bì **diāoxiè**, wéiyǒu zhǔ de dào yǒngyuǎn cháng cún." suǒ chuán gěi wǒmen de fúyīn jiùshì zhè dào. wǒmen rén de shēngmìng zhēn de rútóng huācǎo, dàn yīnzhe jīdū zài wǒmen lǐmiàn, wǒmen de pànwàng biàn yǒu gēn yǒu jī, zhè jiùshì jīdūtú xìnxīn de **gēnjī**.

Special Notes on Text

* fúyīn (Gospel): The original Greek word means "good news" (jiāyīn, hǎoxiāoxi). It has a special meaning in Scripture: the coming, preaching, crucifixion, resurrection, ascension and return of Jesus Christ, revealing Him as the only Savior and the "blessed good news" (zhùfú jiāyīn) thereby bringing eternal life to the world. Therefore, when the Bible refers to the preaching of Christ's ministry (chuánjiǎng jīdū de shìgōng), truth, teaching and salvation, it is often referred to as "preaching the gospel" (chuánfúyīn), "proclaiming the gospel" (xuānjiǎng fúyīn or chuányáng fúyīn).

* rénzǐ (Son of Man): The Old Testament prophets Daniel (dànyǐlǐ) and Ezekiel (yǐxìjié) both used the term "Son of Man" to indicate their humble status. The Gospel's reference to Jesus as "Son of Man" is, on the surface, similar to the humble title of the ancient prophets, but in fact it implies Jesus' claim to be the Messiah (mísàiyà) sent by God. By calling himself "the Son of Man," Jesus is showing that he is both completely (lit. "one hundred percent") human (bǎifēnzhībǎi de rénxìng) and that he is the incarnate Savior (dàochéng ròushēn) who came into the world as a human being (jiàngshìwéirén).

1.	消息	xiāo xi	(N)	news, message
2.	耻	chǐ	(N)	shame, disgrace
3.	得胜	dé shèng	(V)	to win a victory
4.	确信	què xìn	(V)	to be sure of
5.	平安	píng'ān	(N)	peace
6.	种子	zhǒng zi	(N)	seed
7.	腐烂	fǔ làn	(V)	to rot, to decay
8.	破碎	pò suì	(N)	brokenness
9.	充满	chōng mǎn	(V)	to be filled with
10.	喜乐	xǐ lè	(N)	joy
11.	草	cǎo	(N)	grass
12.	荣美	róng měi	(N)	splendor
13.	枯干	kū gān	(V)	to dry up
14.	凋谢	diāo xiè	(V)	wither and fall
15.	根基	gēn jī	(N)	foundation

1. 人得救到底是"因信"还是"因行"？

2. 为什么我们的善行不能作为我们在神面前的义？

3. 没有行为的信心是什么样的信心？

jìng bài zàn měi
敬拜赞美 Worship and Praise

Great Is the LORD

One generation commends your works to another;
they tell of your mighty acts.
They speak of the glorious splendor of your majesty—
and I will meditate on your wonderful works.
They tell of the power of your awesome works—
and I will proclaim your great deeds.
They celebrate your abundant goodness
and joyfully sing of your righteousness.

— Psalm 145:4-7 —

chēngsòng de shèngshī
称颂的圣诗

zhè dài yào duì nà dài sòngzàn nǐ de zuòwéi
这代要对那代颂赞你的作为，

yě yào chuányáng nǐ de dànéng
也要传扬你的大能。

wǒ yào mòniàn nǐ wēiyán de zūnróng
我要默念你威严的尊荣

hé nǐ qímiào de zuòwéi
和你奇妙的作为。

rén yào chuánshuō nǐ kě wèi zhī shì de nénglì
人要传说你可畏之事的能力；

wǒ yě yào chuányáng nǐ de dàdé
我也要传扬你的大德。

tāmen jìniàn nǐ de dà ēn jiù yào chuán chū lái
他们记念你的大恩就要传出来，

bìng yào gēchàng nǐ de gōngyì
并要歌唱你的公义。

— 诗篇 145:4-7 —

使徒信经

我信上帝，全能的父，创造天地的主。

我信我主耶稣基督，上帝的独生子；

因着圣灵感孕，从童贞女马利亚所生；

在本丢彼拉多手下受难，被钉在十字架上，受死、埋葬；

降在阴间；第三天从死里复活；

他升天，坐在全能父上帝的右边；

将来必从那里降临，审判活人、死人。

我信圣灵；

我信圣而公之教会；我信圣徒相通；

我信罪得赦免；

我信身体复活；

我信永生。阿们！

— The Apostles' Creed

Shǐ Tú Xìn Jīng

wǒ xìn shènglíng;

wǒ xìn shèng ér gōng zhī jiàohuì; wǒ xìn shèng tú xiāng tōng;

wǒ xìn zuì dé shè miǎn;

wǒ xìn shēn tǐ fù huó;

wǒ xìn yǒng shēng. āmen!

The Apostles' Creed

I believe in the Holy Spirit,

the holy Catholic Church, the communion of saints,

the forgiveness of sins,

the resurrection of the body,

and life everlasting. Amen!

主啊，你本为良善，乐意饶恕人，有丰盛的慈爱赐给凡求告你的人。耶和华啊，求你留心听我的祷告，垂听我恳求的声音。我在患难之日要求告你，因为你必应允我。

—— 诗篇 86:5-7

You, Lord, are forgving and good, abounding in love to all who call to you. Hear my prayer, Lord, listen to my cry for mercy. When I am in distress, I call to you, because you answer me.

— Psalm 86:5-7

qí dǎo fàn wén
祈祷范文 Exemplary Prayer

弗2:8；雅1:22；彼后1:5-7

父啊，因着祢的恩典和怜悯，祢不仅赐给我们一位救主，也赐给我们为着救恩和生命信靠祂所需的信心。为着祢的道我们感谢祢，请帮助我们不仅听道，也要行道。求主激励我们在信心之上加上德行、知识、节制、忍耐、虔敬、和爱众人的心，阿们。

单元简要 Unit Summary
dān yuán jiǎn yào

信心是一种接受，
接受神及祂所赐的恩典。
信心是一种承认，
承认神是有主权的神，
是我们生命的主宰。
信心也是一种信服，
相信圣经所启示的真理，
信而顺服，听从神的话。
信心还是一种委身，
把我们自己交托给神，
悔改归向神，
信靠祂而得救。

信 靠 得 救
xìn kào dé jiù

xìnxīn shì yì zhǒng jiēshòu,

jiēshòu shén jí tā suǒ cì de ēndiǎn.

xìnxīn shì yì zhǒng chéngrèn,

chéngrèn shén shì yǒu zhǔquán de shén,

shì wǒmen shēngmìng de zhǔzǎi.

xìnxīn yěshì yì zhǒng xìnfú,

xiāngxìn shèngjīng suǒ qǐshì de zhēnlǐ,

xìn ér shùnfú, tīngcóng shén de huà.

xìnxīn háishì yì zhǒng wěishēn,

bǎ wǒmen zìjǐ jiāotuō gěi shén,

huǐgǎi guī xiàng shén,

xìnkào tā ér déjiù.

字词集解 Word Explanation
zì cí jí jiě

因信称义 (Justified by Faith)
yīn xìn chēng yì

始祖亚当、夏娃犯罪，世人都成为罪人。罪的工价就是死，死后且
shǐ zǔ yàdāng xiàwá fànzuì   jià

有审判，可是神爱世人，愿万人得救，设立了救法，差祂的独生子耶稣
shěn pàn   dé jiù shè lì   chāi dú

降世，替罪人死在十字架上，流出宝血，叫一切信他的，罪得赦免，被
jiàng shì tì   shí zì jià   liú chū bǎo xuè   dé shè miǎn

神称为义人。信的人称义，不是因遵行律法，而是因信靠基督耶稣，是
bèi   zūn xíng lù fǎ   xìn kào

"因信称义"。

— 赛53:11；加2:16；罗3:22-26；4:13

问题跟踪 Follow-up Questions

1. 什么是"因信称义"？圣经里是怎么解释的？

2. 称义使罪人得以免罪。称义的人被谁免罪呢？

3. 基督徒真正的信心应该是什么样的？

4. 基督徒做善行是为了什么？

5. 既然人得救是"本乎恩，也因着信"，那我们为什么还要行善呢？（弗2:8）

经文回应 Scripture Response Reading

因一人的悖逆，众人成为罪人；照样，
因一人的顺从，众人也成为义了。

— 罗马书 5:19 —

For just as through the disobedience of the one man the many were made sinners, so also through the obedience of the one man the many will be made righteous.

— Romans 5:19 —

yà bó lán méng shén hū zhào
亚伯兰蒙神呼召
（创12:1-21:3）

有一天，耶和华对挪亚的后裔亚伯兰说："你要离开你的故乡、亲族，和你父亲的家，到我指示你的地方去。"亚伯兰听了上帝的吩咐，带着他的妻子撒莱和他拥有的财物，就离开了他的本家到迦南地去。

后来，当亚伯兰到迦南的时候，耶和华对他说："我要将这地赐给你和你的后裔，直到永远。"于是，亚伯兰就和撒莱在迦南住下了。

Yǒu yìtiān, yēhéhuá duì nuóyà de hòu yì yàbólán shuō :"Nǐ yào lí kāi nǐ de gù xiāng, qīn zú, hé nǐ fùqīn de jiā, dào wo zhǐshì nǐ de dìfāng qù. Yàbólán tīng le shàngdì de fēnfù, dàizhe tā de qīzi sā lái hé tā yōngyǒu de cáiwù, jiù líkāi le tā de běnjiā dào jiā nán dì qù.

Hòulái, dāng yàbólán dào jiā nán de shíhòu, yēhéhuá duì tā shuō: "Wǒ yào jiāng zhè dì cìgěi nǐ hé nǐ de hòuyì, zhídào yǒng yuǎn." Yúshì, yàbólán jiù hé sālái zài jiā nán zhù xià le.

由于亚伯兰信耶和华，耶和华就认他为义人。有一天，耶和华向他显现，对他说："我要和你立约，你要做多国之父。从此以后，你的名字不再叫亚伯兰，要叫亚伯拉罕；你的妻子撒莱要改名叫撒拉，因为她要做多国之母；我还要赐给你们一个儿子，你要给他取名叫以撒。"

亚伯拉罕年老的时候，孩子果然在神应许的日期出生。他们就按照神所吩咐的，将他起名"以撒"。

Yóuyú yàbólán xìn yēhéhuá, yēhé huá jiù rèn tā wèi yì rén. Yǒu yì tiān, yēhé huá xiàng tā xiǎnxiàn, duì tā shuō :"Wǒ yào hé nǐ lìyuē, nǐ yào zuò duōguó zhī fù. Cóngcǐ yǐ hòu, nǐ de míngzi bú zài jiào yàbólán, yào jiào yàbólāhǎn; nǐ de qīzi sālái yào gǎimíng jiào sālā, yīnwèi tā yào zuò duō guó zhī mǔ; wǒ háiyào cìgěi nǐmen yígè érzi, nǐ yào gěi tā qǔ míng jiào yǐsā."

Yàbólāhǎn nián lǎo de shí hòu, háizi guǒrán zài shén yīngxǔ de rìqī chūshēng. Tāmen jiù ànzhào shén suǒ fēnfù de, jiāng tā qǐmíng "yǐ sā".

神的荣耀

shén de róng yào
神 的 荣 耀

Unit 5

dì wǔ dān yuán
第五单元

Learning Objectives

xué xí mù dì
学习目的

In this unit, you will learn to...

- Articulate God's grace and His forgiveness
- Make statements about God's glory through His love
- Understand how sanctification differs from justification
- Talk about why Christians should worship and praise God
- Discuss what it means to live for Christ and His Kingdom

ā men sòng zàn róng yào zhì huì gǎn xiè zūn guì quán bǐng dà lì dōu guī yǔ wǒmen de shén zhí dào
阿们！颂赞、荣耀、智慧、感谢、尊贵、权柄、大力都归与我们的神，直到

yǒngyǒng yuǎnyuǎn ā men
永永远远。阿们！

—启示录 7:12

关键词汇 Key Terms
guān jiàn cí huì

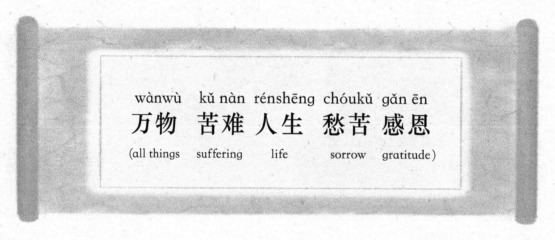

wànwù kǔ nàn rénshēng chóukǔ gǎn ēn

万物 苦难 人生 愁苦 感恩

(all things suffering life sorrow gratitude)

热身问题 Warm-up Questions
rè shēn wèn tí

1. 世界上的万物是从哪里来的？

2. 人生为什么有"苦难"和"愁苦"？

3. "感恩"是什么意思？我们怎样才能懂得"感恩"？

经文细读 Key Verse Reading
jīng wén xì dú

nà wéi āmen de wéi chéngxìn zhēnshí jiànzhèng de zài shén chuàngzào wànwù zhī shàng wéi yuánshǒu de shuō
那为阿们的，为诚信真实见证的，在神创造万物之上为元首的，说…

— 启示录 3:14

These are words of the Amen, the faithful and true witness, the ruler of God's creation...

— Revelation 3:14

课堂灵修 Class Devotional
kè táng líng xiū

ài zǐ shì nà bù néng kànjiàn zhī shén de xiàng shì shǒu shēng de zài yíqiè bèi zào de yǐ xiān

爱子是那不能看见之神的像，是首生的，在一切被造的以先。

— 歌罗西书 1:15

Daily Memory Verse

每日经文背诵
měi rì jīng wén bèi sòng

yē hé huá bì zuò quán dì de wáng nà rì yē hé huá bì wéi

耶和华必作全地的王。那日耶和华必为

dú yī wú èr de tā de míng yě shì dú yī wú èr de

独一无二的，他的名也是独一无二的。

— 撒迦利亚书 14:9

圣经金句 Frequently Quoted Verse
shèng jīng jīn jù

yīn wèi wǒ shēnxìn wúlùn shì sǐ shì shēng shì tiānshǐ shì zhǎngquán de shì yǒu néng de

因为我深信无论是死，是生，是天使，是掌权的，是有能的，

shì xiànzài de shì shì jiānglái de shì shì gāo chù de shì dī chù de shì bié de shòu zào zhī

是现在的事，是将来的事，是高处的，是低处的，是别的受造之

wù dōu bù néng jiào wǒmen yǔ shén de ài géjué

物，都不能叫我们与神的爱隔绝。

— 罗马书 8:38-39

For I am convinced that neither death nor life, neither angels nor demons, neither the present nor the future, nor any powers, neither height nor depth, nor anything else in all creation, will be able to separate us from the love of God.

— Romans 8:38-39

盟约应许 Covenantal Promise

dà wèi zhī yuē
大卫之约

现在，你要告诉我仆人大卫，说万军之耶和华如此说："我从羊圈中将你召来，叫你不再跟从羊群，立你作我民以色列的君。"你的家和你的国必在我面前永远坚立。你的国位也必坚定，直到永远。

— 撒母耳记下 7:8，16

The Davidic Covenant

Now then, tell my servant David, "This is what the Lord Almighty says: I took you from the pasture, from tending the flock, and appointed you ruler over my people Israel." Your house and your kingdom will endure forever before me; your throne will be established forever.

— 2 Samuel 7:8, 16

诗篇集锦 Psalm Reading

The Lord reigns,

he is robed in majesty;

the Lord is robed in majesty and

armed with strength;

indeed, the world is established,

firm and secure.

Your throne was established long ago;

you are from all eternity

— Psalm 93:1-2 —

yē hé huá zuò wáng
耶和华作王！

tā yǐ wēi yán wéi yī chuān shàng
他以威严为衣穿上；

yē hé huá yǐ néng lì wéi yī
耶和华以能力为衣，

yǐ néng lì shù yāo
以能力束腰，

shì jiè jiù jiān dìng　bù dé dòng yáo
世界就坚定，不得动摇。

nǐ de bǎozuò cóng tài chū lì dìng
你的宝座从太初立定；

nǐ cóng gèn gǔ jiù yǒu
你从亘古就有。

— 诗篇 93:1-2 —

142

课文预读 Introductory Reading

神创造了宇宙万物，

是万有的根源。

神是创造者，不是被造的。

神首生的爱子基督耶稣，

是祂本体的真像，

是在一切被造的以先。

万有都是藉着基督造的，

又是为祂造的。

神照着自己的形象造男造女，

赐福给他们，称他们为人，

差派他们为祂的荣耀去管理万物。

人是神最宝贵的受造物。

基督用祂带有能力的话语掌管世界，

用祂权能的命令托住万有。

我们一切被祂造的都要感谢和敬畏祂。

神
shén

的
de

形
xíng

象
xiàng

shén chuàngzào le yǔzhòu wànwù,

shì wàn yǒu de gēnyuán.

shén shì chuàngzàozhě, bú shì bèi zào de.

shén shǒu shēng de ài zǐ jīdū yēsū,

shì tā běntǐ de zhēn xiàng,

shì zài yí qiè bèi zào de yǐ xiān.

wàn yǒu dōu shì jiè zhe jīdū zào de,

yòu shì wèi tā zào de.

shén zhào zhe zìjǐ de xíngxiàng zào nán zào nǚ,

cì fú gěi tāmen, chēng tāmen wéi rén,

chāi pài tāmen wèi tā de róngyào qù guǎnlǐ wànwù.

rén shì shén zuì bǎoguì de shòu zào wù.

jīdū yòng tā dài yǒu nénglì de huà yǔ zhǎngguǎn shìjiè,

yòng tā quán néng de mìnglìng tuō zhù wàn yǒu.

wǒmen yí qiè bèi tā zào de dōu yào gǎnxiè hé jìngwèi tā.

预读问题 Pre-reading Questions

1. 世界上的万物是从哪里来的？

2. 我们人是怎么被造的？

3. 神为什么造人？

参考经文 Reference Verses for the Text

> 创1:1；诗24:1，119:91；赛40:26，66:22；但2:21；
>
> 罗8:14-17；西1:15-17；提前1:17；提后2:12；
>
> 来1:3；彼后3:13；启21:6-7

自有永有、三位一体的独一真神是**宇宙**万物的创造者和万有的根源。祂是开始，也是**终结**。神起初创造天地，又照着自己的形象创造了人类作为祂最宝贵的受造物，**接纳**成为祂的儿女，并**差派**他们为祂的荣耀去**看顾**和管理万物。因此，"地和其中所充满的，世界和住在其间的，都属耶和华。"神要藉着祂所造之物来**彰显**祂的荣耀和尊贵。

神藉着祂的话语创造万有，祂的话语就是道。祂是智慧的本体，生命的源头。"无论是天上的，地上的，万有都靠祂而立，又为祂所造。"祂是首生的爱子，是那不能看见之神的像，是神荣耀所发的**光辉**。基督用祂权能的命令**托住**万有。

神不但创造了宇宙，而且日复一日，年复一年地**支撑**和**维护**宇宙，**掌管**一切，永远作王。经上说，神将**星宿**"按数目领出，祂一一称其名。因祂的权能，又因祂的大能大力，连一个都不缺"。天地因此按照神的**安排**存到今日。

神又在基督里将保惠师赐给万人，藉着圣灵的能力，人必能战胜罪恶，**忍耐**到底，成为圣洁，进入神应许的新天和新地，和祂一同作王。所以，我们一切被祂造的都要**称颂**主耶和华。"但愿尊贵、荣耀归与那不能**朽坏**、不能看见、永世的君王—独一的神，直到永永远远！阿们*！"

课文特注

* "阿们"（āmen）常有两个意思：1）作动词用，意思是"但愿如此"或"诚心所愿"。"阿们"常用在祷告结束时，是最常见的用法。2）作名词用，意思是"实在的，真实的神"（林后1:20；启3:14）。旧约共用阿们二十多次，新约使用阿们有五十多次。在此课文中，"阿们"的意思可是"愿为如此"，也可是"这句话就是事实！原来神就是这样；以后神也是这样！"

zìyǒuyǒngyǒu, sānwèiyìtǐ de dúyī zhēnshén shì **yǔzhòu** wànwù de chuàngzàozhě hé wànyǒu de gēnyuán. tā shì kāishǐ, yěshì **zhōngjié**. shén qǐchū chuàngzào tiāndì, yòu zhàozhe zìjǐ de xíngxiàng chuàngzào le rénlèi zuòwéi tā zuì bǎoguì de shòuzàowù, **jiē'nà** chéngwéi tā de ér nǚ, bìng **chāipài** tāmen wèi tā de róngyào qù **kàngù** hé guǎnlǐ wànwù. yīncǐ, dì hé qízhōng suǒ chōngmǎn de, shìjiè hé zhù zài qíjiān de, dōu shǔ yēhéhuá. shén yào jièzhe tā suǒ zào zhī wù lái **zhāngxiǎn** tā de róngyào hé zūn guì.

shén jièzhe tā de huà yǔ chuàngzào wànyǒu, tā de huà yǔ jiùshì dào. tā shì zhìhuì de běntǐ, shēngmìng de yuántóu. wúlùn shì tiānshàng de, dìshàng de, wànyǒu dōu kào tā ér lì, yòu wèi tā suǒ zào. tā shì shǒu shēng de àizǐ, shì nà bù néng kànjiàn zhī shén de xiàng, shì shén róngyào suǒ fā de **guānghuī**. jīdū yòng tā quánnéng de mìnglìng **tuōzhù** wànyǒu.

shén búdàn chuàngzào le yǔzhòu, érqiě rì fù yí rì, nián fù yī nián de **zhīchēng** hé **wéihù** yǔzhòu, **zhǎngguǎn** yíqiè, yǒngyuǎn zuò wáng. jīng shàng shuō, shén jiāng **xīngxiù** "àn shùmù lǐng chū, tā yīyī chēng qí míng. yīn tā de quánnéng, yòu yīn tā de dà néng dàlì, lián yígè dōu bù quē". tiāndì yīncǐ ànzhào shén de **ānpái** cún dào jīnrì.

shén yòu zài jīdū lǐ jiāng bǎohuìshī cìgěi wànrén, jièzhe shènglíng de nénglì, rén bì néng zhànshèng zuì'è, **rěnnài** dàodǐ, chéngwéi shèngjié, jìnrù shén yīngxǔ de xīntiān hé xīndì, hé tā yītóng zuò wáng. suǒyǐ, wǒmen yíqiè bèi tā zào de dōu yào **chēngsòng** zhǔ yēhéhuá. "dànyuàn zūnguì, róngyào guīyǔ nà bù néng **xiǔhuài**, bù néng kànjiàn, yǒngshì de jūnwáng--dú yī de shén, zhídào yǒngyǒng yuǎnyuǎn! Āmen*!"

1.	宇宙	yǔ zhòu	(N)	universe, cosmos
2.	终结	zhōng jié	(N)	end, finality
3.	接纳	jiē nà	(V)	to admit (into), to adopt
4.	差派	chāi pài	(V)	to send, to dispatch
5.	看顾	kàn gù	(V)	to look after
6.	彰显	zhāng xiǎn	(V)	to manifest
7.	光辉	guāng huī	(N)	splendor, radiance
8.	托住	tuō zhù	(V)	to support, to hold up
9.	支撑	zhī chēng	(V)	to sustain
10.	维护	wéi hù	(V)	to maintain, to protect
11.	掌管	zhǎng guǎn	(V)	to control, to be in charge of
12.	星宿	xīng xiù	(N)	constellation
13.	安排	ān pái	(N)	arrangement
14.	忍耐	rěn nài	(V)	to endure
15.	称颂	chēng sòng	(V)	to pay tribute to (in order to glorify)
16.	朽坏	xiǔ huài	(V)	to decay

1. 神为什么要造万物?

2. 人是怎样被造的?

3. 为什么说人是神最宝贵的创造?

jìng bài zàn měi
敬拜赞美 Worship and Praise

Kingdom of God

The Lord has established his throne in heaven,

and his kingdom rules over all.

Praise the Lord, you his angels,

you mighty ones

who do his bidding,

who obey his word.

Praise the Lord, all his heavenly hosts,

you his servants who do his will.

Praise the Lord, all his works

everywhere in his dominion.

Praise the Lord, my soul.

— Psalm 103:19-22 —

yē hé huá de quán bǐng
耶和华的权柄

yēhéhuá zài tiānshàng lìdìng bǎozuò
耶和华在天上立定宝座;

tā de quánbǐng tǒngguǎn wàn yǒu
他的权柄统管万有。

tīngcóng tā mìnglìng　chéngquán tā zhǐyì
听从他命令、成全他旨意、

yǒu dà néng de tiānshǐ　dōu yào chēngsòng yēhéhuá
有大能的天使,都要称颂耶和华!

nǐmen zuò tā de zhū jūn
你们作他的诸军,

zuò tā de púyì　xíng tā suǒ xǐyuè de
作他的仆役,行他所喜悦的,

dōu yào chēngsòng yēhéhuá
都要称颂耶和华!

nǐmen yí qiè bèi tā zào de
你们一切被他造的,

zài tā suǒ zhìlǐ de gè chù
在他所治理的各处,

dōu yào chēngsòng yēhéhuá
都要称颂耶和华!

— 诗篇 103:19-22 —

登山宝训（八福）

虚心的人有福了！因为天国是他们的。

哀恸的人有福了！因为他们必得安慰。

温柔的人有福了！因为他们必承受地土。

饥渴慕义的人有福了！因为他们必得饱足。

怜恤人的人有福了！因为他们必蒙怜恤。

清心的人有福了！因为他们必得见神。

使人和睦的人有福了！因为他们必称为神的儿子。

为义受逼迫的人有福了！因为天国是他们的。

— 马太福音 5:3-10

Dēng Shān Bǎo Xùn (Bā Fú)

xūxīn de rén yǒu fú le! yīnwèi tiānguó shì tāmen de.

āitòng de rén yǒu fú le! yīnwèi tāmen bì dé ānwèi.

Sermon on the Mount (The Beatitudes)

Blessed are the poor in spirit, for theirs is the kingdom of heaven.

Blessed are those who mourn, for they will be comforted.

神啊，求你听我的呼求，侧耳听我的祷告！我心里发昏的

时候，我要从地极求告你。求你领我到那比我更高的磐石！因

为你作过我的避难所，作过我的坚固台，脱离仇敌。

—— 诗篇 61:1-3

Hear my cry, O God; listen to my prayer. From the ends of the earth I call to you, I call as my heart grows faint; lead me to the rock that is higher than I. For you have been my refuge, a strong tower against the foe.

— Psalm 61:1-3

创1:26；罗8:17；林前15:28

创造主和救赎主啊，我们感谢祢！祢把祢的形象赐给我们，叫我们

成为尊贵。我们赞美祢！祢使我们藉着信心成为祢的儿女和后嗣。祢是

全地的王，在万物之上，为万物之主。求祢帮助我们以智慧看顾祢的创

造、又凡事活出祢的慈爱和公义来。求祢引导我们，天天效法耶稣而

活。阿们！

Lesson 2: 全然成圣
第二课
quán rán chéng shèng

课堂灵修 Class Devotional
kè táng líng xiū

神的应许，不论有多少，在基督都是'是'的。所以藉着他也都是实在
shén de yīngxǔ bú lùn yǒu duō shǎo zài jī dū dōu shì shì de suǒ yǐ jiè zhe tā yě dōu shì shí zài

的，叫神因我们得荣耀。
de jiào shén yīn wǒmen dé róngyào

—哥林多后书 1:20

Daily Memory Verse

每
日
经
文
背
诵
měi rì jīng wén bèi sòng

在各样善事上成全你们，叫你们遵行他的旨意，
zài gè yàng shànshì shàng chéngquán nǐmen jiào nǐ men zūnxíng tā de zhǐ yì

又藉着耶稣基督在你们心里行他所喜悦的事。
yòu jiè zhe yē sū jī dū zài nǐ men xīn lǐ xíng tā suǒ xǐ yuè de shì

愿荣耀归给他，直到永永远远。阿们！
yuàn róngyào guī gěi tā zhí dào yǒngyǒng yuǎnyuǎn ā men

—希伯来书 13:21

圣经金句 Frequently Quoted Verse
shèng jīng jīn jù

不要效法这个世界，只要心意更新而变化，叫你们察验何为
búyào xiàofǎ zhè ge shì jiè zhǐ yào xīnyì gēngxīn ér biànhuà jiào nǐmen chá yàn hé wéi

神的善良、纯全、可喜悦的旨意。
shén de shànliáng chúnquán kě xǐ yuè de zhǐ yì

—罗马书 12:2

Do not conform to the pattern of this world, but be transformed by the renewing of your mind. Then you will be able to test and approve what God's will is—his good, pleasing and perfect will.

— Romans 12:2

盟约应许 Covenantal Promise

shén duì dà wèi de yīng xǔ

神对大卫的应许

yì xiàng　xiǎo yù

当时，你在异象中晓谕你的圣民，说：我已把救助之力加在那有能

jǔ　　　　　jiǎn xuǎn　　xún dé　　pú　　wèi

者的身上；我高举那从民中所拣选的。我寻得我的仆人大卫，用我的圣

gāo　　　　　　　　jiān lì　　bǎng bì　　gù　　　　　　zhǎng zǐ

膏膏他。我的手必使他坚立；我的膀臂也必坚固他。我也要立他长子，

jūn　　　cún liú　cí

为世上最高的君王。我要为他存留我的慈爱，直到永远；我与他立的约

yì　　　　　　　　bǎo zuò

必要坚定。我也要使他的后裔存到永远，使他的宝座如天之久。

—— 诗篇 89:19-21，27-29

God's Promise to David

Once you spoke in a vision, to your faithful people you said: 'I have bestowed strength on a warrior; I have raised up a young man from among the people. I have found David my servant; with my sacred oil I have anointed him. My hand will sustain him; surely my arm will strengthen him.' And I will appoint him to be my firstborn, the most exalted of the kings of the earth. I will maintain my love to him forever, and my covenant with him will never fail. I will establish his line forever, his throne as long as the heavens endure.

—— Psalm 89:19-21, 27-29

shī piān jí jǐn

诗篇集锦 Psalm Reading

Give thanks to the Lord, for he is good.

His love endures forever.

Give thanks to the God of gods.

His love endures forever.

Give thanks to the Lord of lords:

His love endures forever.

—— Psalm 136:1-3 ——

nǐmen yào chēngxiè yēhéhuá

你们要称谢耶和华，

yīn tā běn wéi shàn tā de cí'ài yǒngyuǎn cháng cún

因他本为善；他的慈爱永远长存。

nǐmen yào chēngxiè wàn shén zhī shén

你们要称谢万神之神，

yīn tā de cí'ài yǒngyuǎn cháng cún

因他的慈爱永远长存。

nǐmen yào chēngxiè wàn zhǔ zhī zhǔ

你们要称谢万主之主，

yīn tā de cí'ài yǒngyuǎn cháng cún

因他的慈爱永远长存。

—— 诗篇 136:1-3 ——

课文预读 Introductory Reading

信徒要在主里成为圣洁，

因为神是圣洁的。

非圣洁，没有人能见主。

神要把信徒从罪中分别出来归于祂，

使信徒藉着神的话，

藉着耶稣的宝血和圣灵的感动，

对神的顺服和对圣洁的追求，

成为完全、圣洁的果子。

成圣是被建立的，

是神在人身上的工作，

是人按照圣经的真理而活，

做光做盐，让神使用；

荣神益人，成为神的产业；

在神的恩典里活出不一样的生命，

在神面前作一个完全人。

神 (shén)
的 (de)
圣 (shèng)
洁 (jié)

xìntú yào zài zhǔ lǐ chéngwéi shèngjié,

yīnwèi shén shì shèngjié de.

fēi shèngjié, méiyǒu rén néng jiàn zhǔ.

shén yào bǎ xìntú cóng zuì zhōng fēnbié chūlái guīyú tā,

shǐ xìntú jiè zhe shén de huà,

jiè zhe yēsū de bǎoxuè hé shènglíng de gǎndòng,

duì shén de shùnfú hé duì shèngjié de zhuīqiú,

chéngwéi wánquán, shèngjié de guǒzi.

chéngshèng shì bèi jiànlì de,

shì shén zài rén shēnshang de gōngzuò,

shì rén ànzhào shèngjīng de zhēnlǐ ér huó,

zuò guāng zuò yán, ràng shén shǐyòng;

róng shén yì rén, chéngwéi shén de chǎnyè;

zài shén de ēndiǎn lǐ huó chū bù yíyàng de shēngmìng,

zài shén miànqián zuò yígè wánquán rén.

预读问题 Pre-reading Questions

1. 人为什么要成为圣洁？

2. 神的信徒怎样才能"分别为圣"？

3. 对于基督徒来说，"成圣"是什么意思？

参考经文 Reference Verses for the Text

利19:2；约1:1-5，10:10，17:17-19；
林前6:11；彼前1:16

道太初与神同在，凡被造的，没有一样不是藉着祂造的。生命在祂里头，这生命就是人的光。耶稣说："我来了，是要叫羊得生命，并且得的更**丰盛**。"神**命定**基督，差祂到世间，使祂把神的光照在**黑暗**里，把信徒从罪恶中**分别**为圣**归与**神。

神说：你们要圣洁，因为我是圣洁的。因此，人因信称义之后，也应该因信过圣洁的生活。人非圣洁不能见主面，所以圣洁是神对信徒的旨意。但人**成圣***不是靠自己的能力。如保罗所说，基督徒奉主耶稣基督的名，与世界分别，藉着圣灵得胜世界，因为他们是属神的，是主特别的**产业**。人藉着神的话，耶稣的宝血和圣灵的感动，就有力量顺服神，**追求**成为完全、圣洁的果子。

换句话说，基督徒得以成圣乃是**倚靠**神在他们里面动的工，就是圣灵在信祂的人里面作洁净，感动和教导的工作，使他们改变，越来越有耶稣基督的形象，使他们**配得**上神给的身份。没有主耶稣的舍命**流血**，我们就不可能分别为圣。没有圣灵的**引导**，我们就不能过圣洁的生活。主的道就是真理，祂叫我们因真理成圣。既然我们已经分别为圣，我们就应该像祂一样，被祂的圣洁、公义充满，在光明中与祂共行。

这样，我们虽活在世界上，却不属它，乃是在光中与神同行，真正成为属神的子民，蒙神的**保守，脱离凶恶**，归一切荣耀与神，直到主再来之时便得以靠真理**全然**成圣。

课文特注

* "成圣"chéngshèng：即成为圣洁。圣经中数百次提到"成圣"，有时译为"圣"、"圣洁"、"成为圣"或者"成为圣洁"，都是指"分别出来"、"为神分别"、"从罪恶中分别"和"分别过圣洁生活"的意思。

dào tàichū yǔ shén tóngzài, fán bèi zào de, méiyǒu yíyàng
búshì jièzhe tā zào de. shēngmìng zài tā lǐtou, zhè shēngmìng jiùshì
rén de guāng. yēsū shuō: wǒ lái le, shì yào jiào yáng dé shēngmìng,
bìngqiě dé de gèng **fēngshèng**." shén **mìngdìng** jīdū, chāi tā dào
shìjiān, shǐ tā bǎ shén de guāng zhào zài **hēi'àn** lǐ, bǎ xìntú cóng
zuì'è zhōng **fēnbié** wéi shèng **guīyǔ** shén.

shén shuō: nǐmen yào shèngjié, yīnwèi wǒ shì shèngjié de.
yīncǐ, rén yīnxìnchēngyì zhīhòu, yě yīnggāi yīn xìn guò shèngjié de
shēnghuó. rén fēi shèngjié bù néng jiàn zhǔ miàn, suǒyǐ shèngjié
shì shén duì xìntú de zhǐyì. dàn rén **chéngshèng*** búshì kào zìjǐ de
nénglì. rú <u>bǎoluó</u> suǒ shuō, jīdūtú fèng zhǔ yēsū jīdū de míng, yǔ
shìjiè fēnbié, jièzhe shènglíng déshèng shìjiè, yīnwèi tāmen shì shǔ
shén de, shì zhǔ tèbié de **chǎnyè**. rén jièzhe shén de huà, yēsū
de bǎoxuè hé shènglíng de gǎndòng, jiù yǒu lìliàng shùnfú shén,
zhuīqiú chéngwéi wánquán, shèngjié de guǒzi.

huànjùhuàshuō, jīdūtú déyǐ chéngshèng nǎi shì **yǐkào** shén zài
tāmen lǐmiàn dòng de gōng, jiùshì shènglíng zài xìn tā de rén lǐmiàn
zuò jiéjìng, gǎndòng hé jiàodǎo de gōngzuò, shǐ tāmen gǎibiàn,
yuè lái yuè yǒu yēsū jīdū de xíngxiàng, shǐ tāmen **pèidé** shàng shén
gěi de shēnfèn. méiyǒu zhǔ yēsū de shěmìng **liúxuè**, wǒmen jiù
bù kěnéng fēnbié wéi shèng. méiyǒu shènglíng de **yǐndǎo**, wǒmen
jiù bù néng guò shèngjié de shēnghuó. zhǔ de dào jiùshì zhēnlǐ, tā
jiào wǒmen yīn zhēnlǐ chéngshèng. jìrán wǒmen yǐjīng fēnbié wéi
shèng, wǒmen jiù yīnggāi xiàng tā yíyàng, bèi tā de shèngjié, gōng
yì chōngmǎn, zài guāngmíng zhōng yǔ tā gòng xíng.

zhèyàng, wǒmen suī huó zài shìjiè shàng, què bù shǔ tā, nǎi
shì zài guāng zhōng yǔ shén tóngxíng, zhēnzhèng chéngwéi shǔ
shén de zǐmín, méng shén de **bǎoshǒu, tuōlí xiōng'è**, guī yíqiè
róngyào yǔ shén, zhídào zhǔ zàilái zhī shí biàn dé yǐ kào zhēnlǐ
quánrán chéngshèng.

*   chéngshèng
(Sanctification) means "to
become holy" (chéngwéi
shèngjié). "Sanctification"
is mentioned hundreds
of times in the Bible,
sometimes translated as
"holy" (shèng), "holiness"
(shèngjié), and "to become
sanctified" (chéngwéi
shèng), which all mean
"to be set apart" (fēnbié
chūlái), "to be set apart
for God" (wèi shén
fēnbié), "to separate from
sin" (cóng zuì'è zhōng
fēnbié) and "to live a holy
life separately" (fēnbié
guò shèngjié shēnghuó).

1.	丰盛	fēng shèng	(Adj)	rich, abundant
2.	命定	mìng dìng	(V)	to ordain
3.	黑暗	hēi àn	(N)	darkness
4.	分别	fēn bié	(V)	to differentiate
5.	归与	guī yǔ	(V)	to be attributed to
6.	成圣	chéng shèng	(V)	to be sanctified
7.	产业	chǎn yè	(N)	estate, property
8.	追求	zhuī qiú	(N)	pursuit
9.	倚靠	yǐ kào	(V)	to lean on
10.	配得	pèi dé	(V)	to be worthy of
11.	流血	liú xuè	(N)	bloodshed
12.	引导	yǐn dǎo	(N)	guidance
13.	保守	bǎo shǒu	(N)	preservation, protection
14.	脱离	tuō lí	(V)	to break away
15.	凶恶	xiōng è	(N)	evil, malevolence
16.	全然	quán rán	(Adv)	completely, entirely

读后讨论 Post-reading Discussion

1. "称义"和"成圣"一样不一样？

2. 你认为"称义"在先还是"成圣"在先？

3. 作一名基督徒意味着什么？

jìng bài zàn měi
敬拜赞美 Worship and Praise

Sing to the Lord a New Song

Sing to the Lord a new song;
sing to the Lord, all the earth.
Sing to the Lord, praise his name;
proclaim his salvation day after day.
Declare his glory among the nations,
his marvelous deeds among all peoples.
For great is the Lord and most worthy of praise;
he is to be feared above all gods.
For all the gods of the nations are idols,
but the Lord made the heavens.
Splendor and majesty are before him;
strength and glory are in his sanctuary.

— Psalm 96:1-6 —

zuì gāo de jūn wáng
最高的君王

nǐmen yào xiàng yēhéhuá chàng xīn gē
你们要向耶和华唱新歌！
quán dì dōu yào xiàng yēhéhuá gēchàng
全地都要向耶和华歌唱！
yào xiàng yēhéhuá gēchàng chēngsòng tā de míng
要向耶和华歌唱，称颂他的名！
tiāntiān chuányáng tā de jiù ēn
天天传扬他的救恩！
zài lièbāng zhōng shùshuō tā de róngyào
在列邦中述说他的荣耀！
zài wànmín zhōng shùshuō tā de qíshì
在万民中述说他的奇事！
yīn yēhéhuá wéi dà dāng shòu jí dà de zànměi
因耶和华为大，当受极大的赞美；
tā zài wàn shén zhī shàng dāng shòu jìngwèi
他在万神之上，当受敬畏。
wài bāng de shén dōu shǔ xū wú
外邦的神都属虚无；
wéidú yēhéhuá chuàngzào zhūtiān
惟独耶和华创造诸天。
yǒu zūnróng hé wēiyán zài tā miànqián
有尊荣和威严在他面前；
yǒu nénglì yǔ huáměi zài tā shèngsuǒ
有能力与华美在他圣所。

— 诗篇 96:1-6 —

156

登山宝训（八福）

"虚心的人有福了！因为天国是他们的。

哀恸的人有福了！因为他们必得安慰。

温柔的人有福了！因为他们必承受地土。

饥渴慕义的人有福了！因为他们必得饱足。

怜恤人的人有福了！因为他们必蒙怜恤。

清心的人有福了！因为他们必得见神。

使人和睦的人有福了！因为他们必称为神的儿子。

为义受逼迫的人有福了！因为天国是他们的。

— 马太福音 5:3-10

Dēng Shān Bǎo Xùn (Bā Fú)

wēnróu de rén yǒu fú le! yīnwèi tāmen bì chéngshòu dìtǔ.

jī kě mù yì de rén yǒu fú le! yīnwèi tāmen bì dé bǎozú.

liánxù rén de rén yǒu fú le! yīnwèi tāmen bì méng liánxù.

Sermon on the Mount (The Beatitudes)

Blessed are the meek, for they will inherit the earth.
Blessed are those who hunger and thirst for righteousness,
for they will be filled.
Blessed are the merciful, for they will be shown mercy.

　　　　　　　　　　　　zuǐ chún　　　　　　　　chuán yáng zàn měi
主啊，求你使我嘴唇张开，我的口便传扬赞美你的话！你

本不喜爱祭物，若喜爱，我就献上；燔祭，你也不喜悦。神所
　　　jì　　　xiàn fán jì　　yuè

要的祭就是忧伤的灵；神啊，忧伤痛悔的心，你必不轻看。
　yōu shāng　　　　　　tòng huǐ　　　qīng

— 诗篇 51:15-17

Open my lips, Lord, and my mouth will declare your praise. You do not delight in sacrifice, or I would bring it; you do not take pleasure in burnt offerings. My sacrifice, O God, is a broken spirit; a broken and contrite heart you, God, will not despise.

— Psalm 51:15-17

qí dǎo fàn wén
祈祷范文 Exemplary Prayer

出30:25；40:10；箴19:21；徒20:32

　　　　　zhǎng guǎn　　　xū　　shǔ suàn zì jǐ　　　　　　zhì huì
主啊，我们不能掌管明天，需要学习数算自己的日子，以得到智慧
　　　　　　　　　　　　rèn dìng　　　　　　　　chéng jiù　jiù shú
的心。求祢帮助我们知道并认定祢在基督里为我们所成就的救赎。求祢
jiào dǎo　　　　　jì huà　jiāo tuō bǎi　　　　hé hū　zhǐ yì
教导我们把自己所有的计划都交托摆上，叫它们能合乎祢的旨意。主
　　méng gāo mǒ chéng shèng　jié jìng　　xīn sī　yì niàn
啊，在祢面前我们已蒙膏抹成圣。求祢洁净我们的心思、意念、和心
xìn kào　jiāng　　wán quán xiàn　　　　yì　qì jù
灵，帮助我们信靠祢，将我们自己完全献上，给祢做义的器具。奉耶稣

的名祷告，阿们。

Lesson 第三课 3: 国度权柄

课堂灵修 Class Devotional
kè táng líng xiū

tā ài wǒmen　yòng zì jǐ de xuè shǐ wǒmen tuō lí zuì è　yòu shǐ wǒmen chéngwéi guómín zuò
他爱我们，用自己的血使我们脱离罪恶，又使我们成为国民，作

tā fù shén de jì　sī　dàn yuàn róngyào quánnéng dōu guī gěi tā zhídào yǒngyǒng yuǎnyuǎn āmen
他父神的祭司。但愿荣耀、权能都归给他，直到永永远远。阿们！

— 启示录 1:5-6

Daily Memory Verse
每日经文背诵
měi rì jīng wén bèi sòng

guó dù　quánbǐng　hé tiān xià zhū guó de dà quán bì cì gěi
国度、权柄，和天下诸国的大权必赐给

zhì gāo zhě de shèng mín　tā de guó shì yǒngyuǎn de
至高者的圣民。他的国是永远的；

yí qiè zhǎngquán de dōu bì shì fèng tā shǔncóng tā
一切掌权的都必事奉他，顺从他。

— 但以理书 7:27

圣经金句 Frequently Quoted Verse
shèng jīng jīn jù

nǐmen yào xiān qiú tā de guó hé tā de yì　zhèxiē dōngxi dōu yào jiā gěi nǐmen le
你们要先求他的国和他的义，这些东西都要加给你们了。

suǒ yǐ　búyào wèi míngtiān yōulù　yīnwèi míngtiān zì yǒu míngtiān de yōulù　yì tiān de nán chù
所以，不要为明天忧虑，因为明天自有明天的忧虑；一天的难处

yì tiān dāng jiù gòu le
一天当就够了。

— 马太福音 6:33-34

But seek first his kingdom and his righteousness, and all these things will be given to you as well. Therefore do not worry about tomorrow, for tomorrow will wory about itself. Each day has enough trouble of its own. — Matthew 6:33-34

盟约应许 Covenantal Promise

更美之约的大祭司

主又说：那些日子以后，我与以色列家所立的约乃是这样：我要

将我的律法放在他们里面，写在他们心上；我要作他们的神；他们要作

我的子民。他们不用各人教导自己的乡邻和自己的弟兄，说：你该认识

主；因为他们从最小的到至大的，都必认识我。我要宽恕他们的不义，

不再记念他们的罪愆。

—— 希伯来书 8:10-12

The High Priest of a New Covenant

This is the covenant I will establish with the people of Israel after that time, declares the Lord. I will put my laws in their minds and write them on their hearts. I will be their God, and they will be my people. No longer will they teach their neighbor, or say to one another, 'Know the Lord,' because they will all know me, from the least of them to the greatest. For I will forgive their wickedness and will remember their sins no more.

— Hebrews 8:10-12

诗篇集锦 Psalm Reading

The Lord has done it this very day

let us rejoice today and be glad.

Lord, save us!

Lord, grant us success!

Blessed is he who comes in the name of the Lord.

From the house of the Lord we bless you.

— Psalm 118:24-26 —

这是耶和华所定的日子，

我们在其中要高兴欢喜！

耶和华啊，求你拯救！

耶和华啊，求你使我们亨通！

奉耶和华名来的是应当称颂的！

我们从耶和华的殿中为你们祝福！

—— 诗篇 118:24-26 ——

耶稣来到世上，

为世人的罪被钉在十字架上，

死后第三天复活，

四十天之后升天。

耶稣升天时，

有天使告诉祂的门徒说：

祂怎么往天上去，还要怎样再回来。

耶稣第一次来，过着人的生活，

体会了我们的软弱，担当了我们的罪。

耶稣第二次再来的时候是要作王，

是要在荣耀中降临。

当耶稣再来的时候，

我们都要站在祂面前，

见证人子在祂的国度中来临，

向众人显明父的荣耀。

基督升天再来
jī dū shēng tiān zài lái

yēsū lái dào shìshàng,

wèi shìrén de zuì bèi dīng zài shízìjià shàng,

sǐ hòu dì sān tiān fùhuó,

sìshí tiān zhī hòu shēng tiān.

yēsū shēng tiān shí,

yǒu tiānshǐ gàosu tā de méntú shuō:

tā zěnme wǎng tiānshàng qù, háiyào zěnyàng zài huílái.

yēsū dì yī cì lái, guò zhe rén de shēnghuó,

tǐhuì le wǒmen de ruǎnruò, dāndāng le wǒmen de zuì.

yēsū dì èr cì zài lái de shíhòu shì yào zuò wáng,

shì yào zài róngyào zhōng jiànglín.

dāng yēsū zài lái de shíhòu

wǒmen dōu yào zhàn zài tā miànqián,

jiànzhèng rénzǐ zài tā de guódù zhòng lái lín,

xiàng zhòngrén xiǎnmíng fù de róngyào.

yù dú wèn tí

预读问题 Pre-reading Questions

1. 耶稣第一次是怎么来到世上的？

2. 主耶稣复活升天后会再回来吗？

3. 耶稣第二次来临的时候会是什么样子的？

cān kǎo jīng wén

参考经文 Reference Verses for the Text

诗19:1-3；93:2，103:19；结36:26；但4:34-35；

太6:9-13，28:18-19；约14:3；来1:3；启21:1-5

圣经说神的**宝座**从太初就**立定**，祂的权柄**统管**万有。神是天地的主宰，**国度**的君王，祂是万王之王，万主之主。在祂那里有生命的源头，在祂的光中必得见生命的光。

神的爱子是"神荣耀所发的光辉，是神本体的真像，常用祂的权能的命令托住万有"。祂已经从死里复活，完成了救赎的工作，使人与神和好，脱离罪恶，得**享**永生。主耶稣在升天前吩咐门徒说："天上地上所有的权柄都赐给我了。所以，你们要去，使万民作我的门徒。"祂又说祂要回到父那里去，为我们预备地方，预备好了还要再来接我们。如今祂已经坐在天上至高者神的右边，承受那万名之上的名。

主的宝贵应许是基督徒信心的**凭据**。耶稣升天以前应许赐下保惠师的圣灵，圣灵凭自己的**意旨**行事，有能力更新和保守所跟从神的人。圣灵要赐给信徒们一个新心，感动他们，叫他们**效法**基督，跟随听从神的**呼召**。在圣灵的能力下信徒就能活出全新的生命，在神圣洁的国度里作工，荣耀**赞美**祂，并向不信的世界作见证。

等到耶稣再来的那日，万物都要被神更新，信徒将被提到天国里，至高的神要永远**亲自**与我们同在。在那里将不再有**痛苦**和死亡。万民都要合而为一，万国都要**歌颂**基督的圣名，一同高唱哈利路亚*，共**赴羔羊**的**筵席**。因为国度、权柄、荣耀，全是祂的，直到永永远远。

课文特注

* "哈利路亚"hā lì lù yà：是"赞美耶"（Hall-Lu-Yah）这希伯来人崇拜仪式中的宣召的音译，意思是"来赞美耶和华"。世界各国的基督徒，不论说何种语言，都通用这一赞美颂词。

shèngjīng shuō shén de **bǎozuò** cóng tàichū jiù **lìdìng**, tā de quánbǐng **tǒngguǎn** wàn yǒu. shén shì tiāndì de zhǔzǎi, **guódù** de jūnwáng, tā shì wàn wáng zhī wáng, wàn zhǔ zhī zhǔ. zài tā nàli yǒu shēngmìng de yuántóu, zài tā de guāng zhōng bì dé jiàn shēngmìng de guāng.

shén de **àizǐ** shì shén róngyào suǒ fā de guānghuī, shì shén běntǐ de zhēn xiàng, cháng yòng tā de quánnéng de mìnglìng tuō zhù wànyǒu. tā yǐjīng cóng sǐ lǐ fùhuó, wánchéng le jiùshú de gōngzuò, shǐ rén yǔ shén héhǎo, tuōlí zuì'è, dé **xiǎng** yǒngshēng. zhǔ yēsū zài shēngtiān qián fēnfù méntú shuō: tiānshàng dìshàng suǒyǒu de quánbǐng dōu cì gěi wǒ le. suǒyǐ, nǐmen yào qù shǐ wànmín zuò wǒ de méntú. tā yòu shuō tā yào huí dào fù nàlǐ qù, wèi wǒmen yùbèi dìfāng, yùbèi hǎo le hái yào zàilái jiē wǒmen. rújīn tā yǐjīng zuò zài tiānshàng zhìgāozhě shén de yòubiān, chéngshòu nà wàn míng zhī shàng de míng.

zhǔ de bǎoguì yīngxǔ shì jīdūtú xìnxīn de **píngjù**. yēsū shēngtiān yǐqián yīngxǔ cì xià bǎohuìshī de shènglíng, shènglíng píng zìjǐ de **yìzhǐ** xíngshì, yǒu nénglì gēngxīn hé bǎoshǒu suǒyǒu gēncóng shén de rén. shènglíng yào cìgěi xìntúmen yígè xīn xīn, gǎndòng tāmen, jiào tāmen **xiàofǎ** jīdū, gēnsuí tīngcóng shén de **hūzhào**. zài shènglíng de nénglì xià xìntú jiù néng huó chū quánxīn de shēngmìng, zài shén shèngjié de guódù lǐ zuògōng, róngyào **zànměi** tā, bìng xiàng bú xìn de shìjiè zuò jiànzhèng.

děngdào yēsū zàilái de nà rì, wànwù dōu yào bèi shén gēngxīn, xìntú jiāng bèi tí dào tiān guó lǐ, zhìgāo de shén yào yǒngyuǎn **qīnzì** yǔ wǒmen tóngzài. zài nàlǐ jiāng bú zài yǒu **tòngkǔ** hé sǐwáng. wànmín dōu yào hé ér wéi yī, wànguó dū yào **gēsòng** jīdū de shèngmíng, yītóng gāo chàng hālìlùyà*, gòng **fù gāoyáng** de **yánxí**. yīnwèi guódù, quánbǐng, róngyào, quán shì tā de, zhídào yǒngyǒng yuǎnyuǎn.

Special Notes on Text

* hālìlùyà (Hallelujah) is the transliteration of the Hebrew call to worship (xībóláirén chóngbài yíshì zhōng de xuānzhào), "Praise the Lord" (Hall-Lu-Yah, zànměi yé), which means "Come and Praise the Lord" (lái zànměi yēhéhuá). Christians all over the world use this eulogy (zànměi sòngcí) no matter what language they speak.

1. 宝座　　bǎo zuò　　(N)　　throne

2. 立定　　lì dìng　　(V)　　to stand firm

3. 统管　　tǒng guǎn　　(V)　　to govern, to rule

4. 国度　　guó dù　　(N)　　nation, kingdom

5. 享　　xiǎng　　(V)　　to share the joy of

6. 凭据　　píng jù　　(N)　　evidence

7. 意旨　　yì zhǐ　　(N)　　intention, will

8. 效法　　xiào fǎ　　(V)　　to imitate

9. 呼召　　hū zhào　　(N)　　calling

10. 赞美　　zàn měi　　(V)　　to praise

11. 亲自　　qīn zì　　(Adv)　　personally

12. 痛苦　　tòng kǔ　　(N)　　pain, suffering

13. 歌颂　　gē sòng　　(V)　　to extol

14. 赴　　fù　　(V)　　to go, to attend

15. 羔羊　　gāo yáng　　(N)　　lamb

16. 筵席　　yán xí　　(N)　　feast, banquet

读后讨论 Post-reading Discussion

1. 神的国是什么样的国？（可4:26-29）

2. 天国对上帝的儿女意味着什么？

3. 我们在世上怎么寻求神的国？

敬拜赞美 Worship and Praise

Your Face Shine Upon Us

May God be gracious to us and bless us
and make his face shine on us—
so that your ways may be known on earth,
your salvation among all nations.
May the peoples praise you, God;
may all the peoples praise you.
May the nations be glad and sing for joy,
for you rule the peoples with equity
and guide the nations of the earth.
May the peoples praise you, God;
may all the peoples praise you.

— Psalm 67:1-5 —

gǎn ēn de shī
感恩的诗

yuàn shén liánmǐn wǒmen   cì fú yǔ wǒmen
愿神怜悯我们，赐福与我们，

yòng liǎn guāng zhào wǒmen
用脸光照我们，

hǎo jiào shì jiè dé zhī nǐ de dào lù
好叫世界得知你的道路，

wàn guó dé zhī nǐ de jiù ēn
万国得知你的救恩。

shén a   yuàn lièbāng chēngzàn nǐ
神啊，愿列邦称赞你！

yuàn wànmín dōu chēngzàn nǐ
愿万民都称赞你！

yuàn wànguó dōu kuàilè huānhū
愿万国都快乐欢呼；

yīnwèi nǐ bì àn gōngzhèng shěnpàn wànmín
因为你必按公正审判万民，

yǐndǎo shìshàng de wànguó
引导世上的万国。

shén a   yuàn lièbāng chēngzàn nǐ
神啊，愿列邦称赞你！

yuàn wànmín dōu chēngzàn nǐ
愿万民都称赞你！

— 诗篇 67:1-5 —

登山宝训（八福）

"虚心的人有福了！因为天国是他们的。

哀恸的人有福了！因为他们必得安慰。

温柔的人有福了！因为他们必承受地土。

饥渴慕义的人有福了！因为他们必得饱足。

怜恤人的人有福了！因为他们必蒙怜恤。

清心的人有福了！因为他们必得见神。

使人和睦的人有福了！因为他们必称为神的儿子。

为义受逼迫的人有福了！因为天国是他们的。

—— 马太福音 5:3-10

Dēng Shān Bǎo Xùn (Bā Fú)

qīngxīn de rén yǒu fú le! yīnwèi tāmen bì dé jiàn shén.
shǐ rén hémù de rén yǒu fú le! yīnwèi tāmen bì chēngwéi shén de érzi.
wèi yì shòu bīpò de rén yǒu fú le! yīn wèi tiānguó shì tāmen de.

Sermon on the Mount (The Beatitudes)

Blessed are the pure in heart, for they will see God.
Blessed are the peacemakers, for they will be called children of God.
Blessed are those who are persecuted because of righteousness,
for theirs is the kingdom of heaven.

诗文祷告 Prayer Passage

shī wén dǎo gào

神啊，我的心切慕你，如鹿切慕溪水。我的心渴想神，就

是永生神；我几时得朝见神呢？我昼夜以眼泪当饮食；人不住

地对我说：你的神在哪里呢？

—诗篇 42:1-3

As the deer pants for streams of water, so my soul pants for you, my God.
My soul thirsts for God, for the living God. When can I go and meet with God?
My tears have been my food day and night, while people say to me all day long,
"Where is your God?"

— Psalm 42:1-3

祈祷范文 Exemplary Prayer

qí dǎo fàn wén

诗72:8；路17:20-21；启7:9

我们在天上的父，祢的名何其圣洁！万国都要同声向基督歌颂祂的

救恩。愿祢的国降临，愿祢的旨意行在地上，如同行在天上。感谢祢启

示我们，该怎样在地上活在祢的国。求祢领我们更亲近祢，尊崇祢，在

我们一切所行中显明祢奇妙的爱。耶稣，天上地下，祢都掌权。求祢赐给

我们信心，叫我们在敬拜和赞美祢时，看到祢的权柄，看得见祢的荣耀

和威严。奉耶稣名祈求，阿们。

167

Unit Wrap-up 5: zōng hé tí yào 综合提要

dān yuán jiǎn yào 单元简要 Unit Summary

神是无始无终的，

祂无所不知，无所不在、无所不能。

祂是无限的、永恒的和不变的。

祂用权柄统管万有，

是知识和智慧的泉源，

我们要敬拜祂。

祂在生命的宝座上，

赐下恩惠和荣耀，

我们要感谢祂。

祂是日头和盾牌，

赐平安在我们心里作主，

我们要赞美祂。

祂是天地国度的主宰，

能力和喜乐在祂圣所，

尊荣和威严都归祂！

jìng 敬 bài 拜 zàn 赞 měi 美

shén shì wú shǐ wú zhōng de,

tā wúsuǒbùzhī, wúsuǒbúzài, wúsuǒbùnéng.

tā shì wúxiàn de, yǒnghéng de hé búbiàn de.

tā yòng quánbǐng tǒngguǎn wàn yǒu,

shì zhīshi hé zhìhuì de quányuán,

wǒmen yào jìngbài tā.

tā zài shēngmìng de bǎozuò shàng,

cì xià ēnhuì hé róngyào,

wǒmen yào gǎnxiè tā.

tā shì rìtóu hé dùnpái,

cì píng'ān zài wǒmen xīn lǐ zuò zhǔ,

wǒmen yào zànměi tā.

tā shì tiān dì guódù de zhǔzǎi,

nénglì hé xǐlè zài tā shèngsuǒ,

zūnróng hé wēiyán dōu guī tā!

zì cí jí jiě 字词集解 Word Explanation

quán rán chéng shèng 全然成圣 (Total Sanctification)

"成圣"即"成为圣洁"，是神对信徒的旨意，是由圣父、圣子、圣灵三位 jí shèng jié xìn tú zhǐ yì yóu

一体的神而作成的，要把信徒"从罪恶中分别出来归与神"。信徒得以成圣是 zuì è fēn bié guī yǔ dé yǐ

藉着神的话，藉着耶稣的宝血、圣灵的感动和神的造就，也藉着信徒自己对 jiè zhe bǎo xuě gǎn dòng zào jiù

神的顺服和对圣洁的追求而成为完全、圣洁的果子。 shùn fú zhuī qiú wán quán

—利20:7-8；约17:17；希2:11；10:14

问题跟踪 Follow-up Questions

1. 重生就可让人脱离人生苦难及一切罪吗？

2. 我们人为什么要感恩？

3. 为什么信主的人没有立即成圣？

4. 神的国度已经来临了吗？

5. 什么是基督徒至大的幸福？

圣文回应 Scripture Response Reading

shēn zāi shén fēngfù de zhìhuì hé zhīshì tā de pànduàn hé qí nán cè
深哉，神丰富的智慧和知识！他的判断何其难测！

tā de zōngjì hé qí nán xún shéi zhīdào zhǔ de xīn shéi zuò guò tā de móushì ne
他的踪迹何其难寻！谁知道主的心？谁作过他的谋士呢？

shéi shì xiān gěi le tā shǐ tā hòulái chánghuán ne
谁是先给了他，使他后来偿还呢？

yīnwèi wàn yǒu dōu shì běn yú tā yǐ kào tā guī yú tā
因为万有都是本于他，倚靠他，归于他。

yuàn róngyào guīgěi tā zhídào yǒngyuǎn āmen
愿荣耀归给他，直到永远。阿们！

— 罗马书 11:33-36 —

Oh, the depth of the riches of the wisdom and knowledge of God! How unsearchable his judgments, and his paths beyond tracing out! "Who has known the mind of the Lord? Or who has been his counselor?" "Who has ever given to God, that God should repay them?" For from him and through him and for him are all things. To him be the glory forever! Amen."

— Romans 11:33-36 —

làng zǐ huí tóu
浪子回头
（路15:11-32）

一个人有两个儿子。一天，小儿子对父亲说："爸爸，请你现在就把我应得的产业分给我。"父亲就把家产分给他们两兄弟。

没过几天，小儿子卖掉了分得的产业，带着钱离家往远方去了。他到了外边，整天花天酒地，钱很快就花光了。那地方又发生大饥荒，他就一贫如洗，只好替人去放猪。他肚子饿到恨不得吃猪所吃的豆荚，可是连这些也没有人给他。

Yí gè rén yǒu liǎng gè érzi. Yì tiān, xiǎo érzi duì fùqīn shuō: "Bàba, qǐng nǐ xiànzài jiù bǎ wǒ yīngdé de chǎnyè fēn gěi wǒ." Fùqīn jiù bǎ jiā chǎn fēn gěi tāmen liǎng xiōngdì.

Méi guò jǐ tiān, xiǎo érzi mài diào le fēn dé de chǎnyè, dài zhe qián lí jiā wǎng yuǎnfāng qù le. Tā dào le wàibian, zhěngtiān huātiānjiǔdì, qián hěn kuài jiù huā guāng le. Nà dìfāng yòu fāshēng dà jī huāng, tā jiù yìpínrúxǐ, zhǐhǎo tì rén qù fàng zhū. Tā dùzi è dào hènbude chī zhū suǒ chī de dòujiá, kěshì lián zhèxiē yě méi yǒu rén gěi tā.

他终于醒悟过来，心想：我为什么在这里等死呢？我要回去找父亲，告诉他我得罪了天，也得罪了他，不配作他的儿子。于是，他动身回父亲那里去。

小儿子还在远处时，父亲老远就看见了他，激动地跑过去，紧抱着他，亲他，并吩咐仆人快去给他换上最好的衣服，给他戴上戒指，穿上鞋，宰一只肥牛让大家一同欢宴庆祝，因为他说他这个儿子是死而复活，失而复得的。

Tā zhōngyú xǐngwù guòlái, xīn xiǎng: Wǒ wèi shéme zài zhèlǐ děng sǐ ne? Wǒ yào huíqù zhǎo fù qīn, gàosu tā wǒ dézuì le tiān, yě dézuì le tā, bú pèi zuò tā de érzi. Yúshi, tā dòngshēn huí fùqīn nàlǐ qù.

Xiǎo érzi hái zài yuǎn chù shí, fùqīn lǎo yuǎn jiù kànjiàn le tā, jīdòng de pǎo guòqù, jǐn bàozhe tā, qīn tā, bìng fēnfù púrén kuài qù gěi tā huàn shàng zuì hǎo de yīfu, gěi tā dài shàng jièzhǐ, chuān shàng xié, zǎi yì zhí féi niú ràng dàjiā yītóng huānyàn qìng zhù, yīnwèi tā shuō tā zhège érzi shì sǐ ér fù huó, shī ér fù dé de.

Index of Scripture References 经文引用索引表

English Translations for Themed Text 主题课文英文翻译

Pre-Unit 预备单元: The Word of God 神的话语

Unit Summary 单元简要: The Word of God 神的话

The word of God is written in a book.
This book is the Bible.
The Bible tells us that
God made heaven and earth and all things.
The Bible tells us about
God's salvation and His love.
The Bible is a book about the meaning of life.
It is a book full of wisdom.

Unit 1 第一单元: The One True God 独一真神

Lesson 1: I Am Who I Am 自有永有

The Bible tells us that there is only one true God. God said: "I am the first and the last, and there is no true God besides me."

The Bible also reveals to us the name of this God, which is called "Jehovah/Yahweh". This name appears thousands of times in the Bible, which means "self-existence", that is to say, God is self-existent and the only source of existence. Therefore, God reveals Himself in the Bible as the one and only true God who exists forever.

There are many other names for God in the Bible, such as God, Lord, Almighty, Creator and Shepherd. But the most common name people use to address God in the Bible is "God" or "Jehovah/Yahweh".

Lesson 2: The Word Became Flesh 道成肉身

In the beginning, the Word already existed, the Word was with God, the Word was God, and through Him all things were made. In Him was life, and that life was the light of humankind. The world was made through Him, but the world did not know Him.

This Word is Jesus Christ, the only begotten and beloved Son of God. In order to love us, God gave us His only begotten Son, Jesus Christ, who became flesh, in human form, and made His dwelling among us. The angel at the birth of Jesus proclaimed: "Today in the town of David, a Savior has been born to you, the Lord Christ." The name of Jesus, the Son of God, tells us that He is our Savior and He came to us so that we are able to receive life.

Jesus said: "I am the way, the truth, and the life; no one comes to the Father except through me." If we trust in Jesus, we will have the life and truth of Jesus in us, and more than that, we will have the most beautiful hope. One day, we will go to the Heavenly Father through Jesus.

Therefore, Jesus Christ is the true God, the "King of kings and Lord of lords". When the Lord Jesus returns, the kingdoms of the world will become the Kingdom of God, and He will reign forever and ever.

Lesson 3: The Work of the Holy Spirit 圣灵运行

The Bible tells us that God is a God who exists from eternity to eternity. He is an omnipotent, omniscient, and omnipresent God. There is only one God, in three persons: the Father, the Son, and the Holy Spirit. The Son is begotten of the Father, and the Holy Spirit comes from the Father. We also know from the Bible that God is spirit: infinite, eternal, and unchanging.

Christ is God, and His origin has existed from the beginning. That is why Paul said, "The beloved Son is the image of the invisible God, the firstborn over all creation." Jesus also said, "I and the Father are one." So, "If anyone acknowledges Jesus as the Son of God, God lives in him, and they in God."

The "Counselor/Comforter" that Jesus promised to give us is the Spirit of truth from the Father and the Spirit of Christ. The Holy Spirit dwells in the hearts of those who trust in Jesus. It moves, reveals itself to, and comforts the hearts of people, giving peace and joy, wisdom and hope. "If the Spirit of God lives in our hearts, we are not of the flesh, but of the Holy Spirit."

Therefore, the Father is God, the Son is God, and the Holy Spirit is God, the "Trinity", equally worshipped, equally honored, and equal in power.

Unit 1 Wrap-Up 综合提要

Unit Summary 单元简要: The Trinity 三位一体

God exists.
He is not a part of the universe.
He is the Creator of the universe.
We are to worship God.
Because He is the true God, God of love,
who created all things, and who is trustworthy.
We are to thank God,
For He has given us life and love,
For He has given us the Bible, the Holy Spirit,
and Jesus, our Savior,
for the forgiveness of our sins,
so that we may have wisdom and strength
and know that we are the children of God.

Unit 2 第二单元: Scripture Alone 唯独圣经

Lesson 1: God's Revelation 神的默示

The Bible is a very unique book. The entire book was written by dozens of authors. These authors varied in status and age, from priests, kings, and prophets to shepherds, fishermen, and farmers. They also differed in the context of the times and places where they wrote. Some wrote in the wilderness of Sinai, some in the Temple of Jerusalem, some by the riverside of Babylon, and some in a Roman prison. More than 1,000 years passed between the writing of the first book of Genesis and the last book of Revelation, but the content of the entire Bible is coherent and makes a complete book.

Because of this, we say that the Bible is inspired by God and written by the Holy Spirit through human hands. "To inspire" means to be breathed into. God breathed His word into humanity, that is, God implied through the Holy Spirit what humanity should say and write. This means that the Bible comes from God, is God's word, is His revelation to humankind, and is unchanging.

Therefore, the Bible is a divine book, a truth revealed by God, but it is also a human book, a fact recorded by man. The Bible is thus a special revelation of God's miraculous and wonderful Word written in words, and is both God's book and man's book. Although it is written in human language, it has the authority of God.

Lesson 2: God's Promise 神的应许

"No prophecy of Scripture came about by the prophet's own interpretation of things. For prophecy never had its origin in the human will, but prophets, though human, spoke from God as they were carried along by the Holy Spirit." God is also a covenant God, and He not only revealed His own words to the authors of the Bible but also made a covenant with His people. Therefore, the covenant was one of the ways God revealed himself.

The Old Testament of the Bible records the story before the coming of the Lord Jesus, a prophecy of a Messiah who came to redeem Israel and become the future hope and salvation of humankind. The New Testament records the story after the Lord Jesus' coming, including the post-birth accounts and the apostolic letters, telling us that Jesus is the Messiah revealed in the Old Testament. In other words, Jesus Christ is the center of all Scripture, for He not only fulfilled the Old Testament covenant between God and His people, but He also made a new covenant with humanity Himself. No matter how many promises God has made, they are "Yes" in Christ.

Jesus Christ said what no one dared to say: "I am the way, truth, and life; no one comes to the Father except through me." "I am the gate; whoever enters through me will be saved." He also said: "Anyone who has seen me has seen the Father." "The Son of Man came to seek and to save the lost, and also to give His life as a ransom for many." All

His words reveal to us that He is Our Savior, able to save us from sin and destruction. Therefore, Jesus Christ is the greatest promise and the greatest miracle that God has ever given us.

Lesson 3: God's Teaching 神的教导

The Bible is the revelation of God, the message given by God who created all things in the universe, and contains all the essential teaching for salvation. The content and genre of the Bible are diverse, including history, theology, philosophy, advice, commandments, and prophecies. There are books of law, history, wisdom literature, poetry, prophets, gospels, epistles, and apocalyptic literature. The Old Testament is the account of how God created the heavens and the earth and humankind, how our earliest ancestors sinned and fell, and how God chose the nation of Israel to be His people. The New Testament records the life of the Savior Jesus Christ, the founding and development of the church, and the teachings of the apostles.

The apostles all agreed that Jesus was greater than all the prophets and great men of the Old Testament, such as Abraham, Moses, and David. He fulfilled all the prophecies of the prophets of the Old Testament. For example, the Old Testament describes a suffering servant who would suffer for the people of God and bear their sorrows, and all these prophecies were fully fulfilled in Jesus. In addition, the Bible records the flawless character of Jesus Christ, His mighty deeds, His miraculous signs, and the fact that He died and rose again. Thus, Jesus Christ is the Son of God and the Savior of sinners, and becomes the true declaration of our Christian faith.

In conclusion, the Bible is the word of God, which is living and active, so that we may learn from it His teaching and instruction, so that we may have hope, and that we may have life through faith in God.

Unit 2 Wrap-Up 综合提要

Unit Summary 单元简要: Biblical Authority 圣经权威

God is the source of the Bible.
The Bible is the Word of God in writing.
As the Bible says,
what God has prepared for those who love Him
is what no eye has seen, nor ear has heard,
and what no human mind has conceived.
We do not live on food alone but on every word that comes from the mouth of God.
The Bible teaches us to believe in Jesus Christ,
to have life and wisdom for salvation in Him,
to correct us, to train us in righteousness,
so that the servant of God may be complete
and thoroughly equipped for every good work.

Unit 3 第三单元: Saving Grace 救赎恩典

Lesson 1: The Fall of Man 罪与堕落

God created Adam and Eve and placed them in the Garden of Eden with God's eternal presence. God told Adam that he was free to eat the fruit from every tree in the garden, but not from the "tree of knowledge of good and evil", for God said that the day he ate of it he would certainly die. But humanity betrayed God. Eve listened to the temptation of the devil, and took the fruit and ate it, and gave it to Adam to eat. Thus, they sinned, rebelled against God, and were driven out of the Garden of Eden, and away from the face of God.

Therefore, the result of the ancestors of humankind violating God's warning was eternal separation from God. Moreover, because of the rebellion of the ancestors, all people became sinners, and all were born with sin. This is called original sin. In addition to original sin, we humans also have our actual sin. This sin is the sin committed by a person after his or her birth. Because of original sin and the influence of this sin-corrupted world on us, we can sin in our thoughts, words, and deeds.

The Bible says: everyone is destined to die once, and there will be judgment after death. In other words, the human soul does not perish due to death. If God's righteous judgment were to take place, the punishment that man deserves would be eternal damnation, unable to save himself. However, God loves the world, and His beloved Son, Jesus Christ, was conceived by the Holy Spirit, came into the world, became the only sinless one to bear our sins, and pay the ransom for our sin. In this way, through faith in Jesus Christ, people can receive the forgiveness of sins and the salvation of their souls.

Lesson 2: Repentance and Rebirth 悔改重生

When God created humankind, eternal life was originally as much a part of human life as breathing. However, humankind disobeyed God's command, and death came to humankind. Since then, there has been no other ending for humankind. However, God has provided a way out for us, that is, eternal life through faith in Jesus Christ. As the Bible says, "God so loved the world that He gave His only begotten Son, that whoever believes in Him shall not perish but have everlasting life."

If one is to have eternal life, he or she must first repent. Repentance means that people must admit the evil and corruption in their hearts. This inner corruption causes people to turn away from God and disobey His law and His sovereignty over our lives. But a truly repentant person is able to recognize his or her sin and is willing to give up a life of sin and obey God with all of his or her heart.

At the same time, repentance is not a verbal confession, but requires a change of heart and behavior. The Bible says, "You shall bear fruit in keeping with repentance." Therefore, repentance means being willing to stay away from all known sins, to give up the lifestyle that is devoted to one's own pleasure, to turn away from idols to God, to live in His grace, and to serve the true and living God with all one's heart.

God is faithful and righteous, and if we confess our sins, acknowledge Jesus Christ as the Lord of life, and are willing to follow Him, God will forgive our sins, cleanse us from unrighteousness, and bring us into that eternal life.

Lesson 3: The Resurrection 死里复活

As in Adam all die, so in Christ all will be made alive. It can be seen that although we have all sinned in Adam, we can have all our sins washed away by the precious blood of Jesus, through the atoning sacrifice of the Son of God once and forever in our place. By experiencing the death of Christ, we were crucified with Him; by the resurrection of Jesus, we have the resurrection life of the Son of God and live our lives for God.

If Christ has not been raised, our faith is in vain, and we are still in our sins, and what awaits us will be eternal destruction. Therefore, what we believe in is the God who died and rose again. As Paul said, "For what I received I passed on to you as of first importance: Christ died for our sins according to the Scriptures, and that he was buried, that he was raised on the third day according to the Scriptures."

It is evident that the resurrection of the Lord Jesus Christ is the core of the gospel. If Jesus Christ had not been resurrected, there would be no hope of eternal life in our lives. This gospel has been established for us, and if we declare with our mouths Jesus as Lord, and believe in our hearts that God raised Him from the dead, we are justified and will be saved.

Unit 3 Wrap-Up 综合提要

Unit Summary 单元简要: Cross of Saving Grace 十架救恩

God created humankind,
and blesses those He has created.
God loves people, and He wants them to love Him.
But people did not listen to God,

turned away from Him and sinned against Him.
But God so loved the world that
He even gave His one and only Son, Jesus, to us.
Jesus left heaven and came to this world,
to give us new life.
Jesus gave up His life,
was crucified, died and rose again
to bring us eternal salvation.

Unit 4 第四单元: Justification by Faith 因信称义

Lesson 1: The Old & New Self 老我新我

God placed humankind in the Garden of Eden and was with them. After Adam and Eve sinned and rebelled against God, everything changed, and humanity lost its perfect relationship with God and began to be afraid of Him.

Therefore, although people know the existence of God, they will turn away from Him, neither glorifying Him nor thanking Him, as it is written in the Scripture, "There is no one righteous, not even one." The wages of sin is death, but God loved the world and sent His Son Jesus Christ to come to us and to die on the cross, and has laid on Him the iniquity of us all, so that those who were far away from God can be reconciled to Him by His blood. Jesus Christ also rose from the dead and conquered death, by faith bringing people from hopelessness to anticipatory hope in life.

Because of this, we "have put off the old self and our former way of life, and have put on the new self", and have become a new creation in Christ. This new self is created in the image of God in true righteousness and holiness, and can be gradually renewed in its knowledge of God and have a new life. In other words, the blood of the Lord transforms us from the old to the new, just as we take off our filthy clothes and put on the holy ones, made new in the attitude of our minds, so that we can live as a new creation.

Lesson 2: God's Commandments 诫命吩咐

The righteousness of God is given through faith in Jesus Christ to all who believe, for the Scripture says that: "it is with our heart that we believe and are justified, and it is with our mouth that we profess our faith and are saved." "All have sinned and fall short of the glory of God, and all are justified freely by His grace through the redemption that came by Christ Jesus." In other words, we are justified by believing in Jesus Christ.

To accept Jesus Christ is to establish a relationship with God, to have new life, and to become a child of God, that

is, a "Christian." Because Jesus' death paid the price for our sins, God made Jesus' righteousness our righteousness—He justified us. In this way, Christians become the spiritual descendants of Abraham, the "father of faith," believing in Jesus' promise of salvation and that God's promise would be fulfilled.

But faith, if not accompanied by action, is dead, so those who believe in the Lord must also obey God's commands. God's greatest command is to love God and to love your neighbor as yourself. Believers are not only to love God, but also to love one another according to the command He has given. Jesus once told His disciples, "A new commandment I give you, that you love one another; as I have loved you, so you also must love one another." So Christians should love one another, "for love is from God, and whoever has love is born of God and knows God". If we keep God's commands, we are always in His love, just as Christ kept the commands of God the Father and was always in His love.

Not only that, but we are to spread the love of Christ to all the world, and to proclaim the gospel of Christ to the whole creation. Just as Jesus told His disciples before He left the world: "Go and make disciples of all nations, baptizing them in the name of the Father and of the Son and of the Holy Spirit." "But you will receive power when the Holy Spirit comes upon you, and you will be my witnesses in Jerusalem, and in all Judea, and Samaria, and to the ends of the earth."

Lesson 3: The Hope of the Gospel 福音盼望

The Gospel is good news. The Bible says, "The Son of Man came to seek and to save the lost." Therefore, the good news of the Gospel is the story of Jesus (his life, death, resurrection and ascension) as the realization of the story of Israel, which leads to salvation from sin and death. We are saved through faith in Jesus Christ, the Savior of sinners. As Paul said: "I am not ashamed of the gospel; it is the power of God that brings salvation to everyone who believes." The risen Lord has won the victory, by which we can have the hope of eternal life.

If we believe in our hearts that Jesus Christ has risen from the dead, we will then have peace in our lives. For we believe that our death in life will be like a seed, though the seed decays (in the ground), it will grow into new life. Therefore, we should always be in Jesus Christ, and let the risen Lord always be in us, experiencing God's presence in our brokenness, so that life is full of peace, joy, and hope.

All people, as said in the Bible, are like grass, "and all their glory and beauty are like the flowers of the field; the grass withers and the flowers fall, but the word of the Lord endures forever." This is the gospel that has been preached to us. Our human lives are really like flowers and grass, but because Christ is in us, our hope is rooted and grounded, which is the foundation of Christian faith.

Unit 4 Wrap-Up 综合提要
Unit Summary 单元简要: Salvation through Trust 信靠得救

Faith is an acceptance,
accepting God and the grace He has bestowed upon us.
Faith is an acknowledgment,
acknowledging that God is a sovereign God,
who rules over our lives.
Faith is also a conviction,
believing in the truth as revealed in the Bible,
and trusting and obeying God's Word.
And faith is a commitment,
submitting ourselves to God,
repenting and turning to Him,
and trusting in Him for salvation.

Unit 5 第五单元: The Glory of God 神的荣耀
Lesson 1: The Creation of the Universe 宇宙创造

The one true God, who is self-existent and eternal and triune, is the Creator of all things in the universe and the source of all things. He is the beginning and the end. God created the heavens and the earth in the beginning, and in His own image created human beings as His most precious creatures, accepting them as His children, and sending them (by giving them the task) to look after and rule over all things for His glory. Therefore, "the earth belongs to the LORD, and everything in it, the world and all who live in it." God wants to manifest His glory and honor through the things He has made.

God created all things through His word, and His word is the Word. He is the essence of wisdom and the source of life. By Him all things stand, "whether in heaven or on earth, and for Him all things were made." He is the firstborn beloved son over all creation, the image of the invisible God, the radiance of His glory. Christ holds all things together by the command of His power.

God not only created the universe, but also sustains and maintains it day after day, year after year, takes charge of everything and reigns as the king forever. It is said that God "brought out the starry host by number, and calls forth each of them by name one by one. Because of His great power and mighty strength, not one of them is missing." Thus the heavens and the earth have sustained to this day according to God's arrangement.

God also gave the Comforter to all people in Christ, and by the power of the Holy Spirit, people will overcome sin, endure to the end, become holy, and enter into the new heaven and the new earth promised by God, and reign with Him. Therefore, all we who are made by Him shall praise the Lord Jehovah. "To the King of all ages, immortal, invisible, the only God, be honor and glory for ever and ever! Amen!"

Lesson 2: Complete Sanctification 全然成圣

"The Word was in the beginning with God, and there was nothing created that was not created through Him. The life is in Him, and that life is the light of men." Jesus said, "I have come that the sheep may have life, and have it more abundantly." God ordained Christ and sent Him into the world that He would shine the light of God in the darkness and differentiate (consecrate) believers from their sins to God.

God said, "You must be holy, for I am holy." Therefore, after a person is justified by faith, he or she should also live a holy life by faith. People who are not holy cannot see the face of the Lord, so holiness is the will of God for believers. But people are not sanctified by their own abilities. As Paul said, Christians are set apart from the world in the name of the Lord Jesus Christ, and overcome the world through the Holy Spirit, because they belong to God, and are the special inheritance of the Lord. Through the word of God, the precious blood of Jesus, and the touch of the Holy Spirit, people have the power to obey God and to pursue becoming the fruit of perfection and holiness.

In other words, Christians are sanctified by the work of God in them, that is, the Holy Spirit works in those who believe in Him to purify, move, and teach, so that they are changed and become more and more like Jesus Christ, making them worthy of the identity given by God. Without the death and bloodshed of the Lord Jesus, we cannot be set apart as holy. Without the guidance of the Holy Spirit, we cannot live a holy life. The word of the Lord is truth, and He sanctifies us by the truth. Since we have been set apart, we should be like Him, filled with His holiness and righteousness, and walk with Him in the light.

In this way, though we live in the world, we do not belong to it, but walk with God in the light, and truly become a people of God, protected by God, free from evil, to the glory of God, until the Lord's return, when we will be completely sanctified by the truth.

Lesson 3: Kingdom Power 国度权柄

The Bible says that God's throne has been established from the beginning of time and that His kingdom rules over all. God is the ruler of heaven and earth, the King of the kingdom, and He is the King of kings and Lord of lords. In

Him is the source of life, and in His light is the light for life.

The beloved Son of God is "the radiance of the glory of God, the exact representation of His being, holding all things together by the command of His power." He has risen from the dead, completed the work of redemption, reconciling man to God, and freeing them from sin to eternal life. Jesus commanded His disciples before ascending to heaven, saying: "All authority in heaven and on earth has been given to me. Therefore, go and make disciples of all nations." He also said that He would go back to the Father to prepare a place for us, and when He is ready He will come back and take us to be with Him. Now He is seated at the right hand of God, the Most High in heaven, and bears the name that is above every name.

The precious promise of the Lord is the evidence of Christian faith. Jesus promised before His ascension to heaven to give the Holy Spirit of the Comforter, who acts according to His will and has the ability to renew and keep all those who follow God. The Holy Spirit will give believers a new heart, and move them to imitate Christ and follow and obey God's call. In the power of the Holy Spirit believers will be able to live a new life, work in the holy kingdom of God, glorify and praise Him, and testify to the unbelieving world.

On the day of Jesus' return, all things will be renewed by God, and believers will be lifted up into the kingdom of heaven, where the Most High God will be with us forever. There will be no more suffering and death. The peoples will become one, and all the nations will sing praises to the holy name of Christ, and sing hallelujahs together to the feast of the Lamb. For His is the kingdom, and the power, and the glory, forever and ever.

Unit 5 Wrap-Up 综合提要

Unit Summary 单元简要: Worship and Praise 敬拜赞美

God is without beginning and without end.
He is omniscient, omnipresent, and omnipotent.
He is infinite, eternal, and unchanging.
He rules over all things with authority, and
is the fountain of knowledge and wisdom.
We are to worship Him.
He is on the throne of life, and
gives grace and glory.
Let us give thanks to Him.
He is the sun and the shield, and
gives peace to reign in our hearts.
Let us praise Him.
He is the Lord of heaven and earth.
Power and joy are in His sanctuary.
To Him be all honor and majesty!

English-Chinese Glossary 英中词汇表

English	Chinese	Pinyin	Part of Speech	Lesson
advice	忠告	zhōng gào	N	2.3
age	年龄	nián ling	N	2.1
Almighty	全能者	quánnéng zhě	N	1.1
angel	天使	tiān shǐ	N	1.2
anticipatory hope	指望	zhǐ wàng	N	4.1
apostle	使徒	shǐ tú	N	Pre-Unit
arrangement	安排	ān pái	N	5.1
authority	权威	quán wēi	N	2.1
authority, power	权柄	quán bǐng	N	1.3
background	背景	bèi jǐng	N	2.1
benevolence and righteousness	仁义	rén yì	N	4.1
Bible story	圣经故事	shèng jīng gù shi	N	Pre-Unit
Bible/Holy Scripture	圣经	shèng jīng	N	Pre-Unit
bloodshed	流血	liú xuè	N	5.2
book	书卷	shū juàn	N	Pre-Unit
brokenness	破碎	pò suì	N	4.3
calling	呼召	hū zhào	N	5.3
chapter	章	zhāng	N	Pre-Unit
Christ	基督	jī dū	N	1.2
Christianity	基督教	jī dū jiào	N	Pre-Unit
church	教会	jiào huì	N	Pre-Unit
coherent	连贯	lián guàn	Adj.	2.1
command	命令	mìng lìng	N	3.2
commandment	诫命	jiè mìng	N	2.3
completely, entirely	全然	quán rán	Adv.	5.2
constellation	星宿	xīng xiù	N	5.1
content	内容	nèi róng	N	2.3
core	核心	hé xīn	N	3.3
cost, price	代价	dài jià	N	4.2
covenant	盟约	méng yuē	N	Pre-Unit
Creator	创造主	chuàngzào zhǔ	N	1.1
creed	信条	xìn tiáo	N	Pre-Unit
darkness	黑暗	hēi'àn	N	5.2
deeds	行为	xíng wéi	N	4.1
demon, devil	魔鬼	mó guǐ	N	3.1
depravity	败坏	bài huài	N	3.1

English	Chinese	Pinyin	Part of Speech	Lesson
descendant	后裔	hòu yì	N	4.2
doctrine	教义	jiào yì	N	Pre-Unit
each other	彼此	bǐ cǐ	Pr.	4.2
earliest ancestor	始祖	shǐ zǔ	N	2.3
end, finality	终结	zhōng jié	N	5.1
ending, result	结局	jié jú	N	3.1
era	时代	shí dài	N	2.1
estate, property	产业	chǎn yè	N	5.2
eternal life	永生	yǒng shēng	N	3.2
everlasting	永恒的	yǒnghéng de	Adj.	1.3
evidence	凭据	píng jù	N	5.3
evil, malevolence	凶恶	xiōng è	N	5.2
faith	信仰	xìn yǎng	N	2.3
farmer	农夫	nóng fū	N	2.1
feast, banquet	筵席	yán xí	N	5.3
filthy	污秽	wū huì	Adj.	4.1
first of all	首先	shǒu xiān	Adj.	1.1
fisherman	渔夫	yú fū	N	2.1
flawless	无瑕	wú xiá	Adj.	2.3
forever, permanent	永	yǒng	Adj.	1.1
foundation	根基	gēn jī	N	4.3
General Epistles	普通书信	pǔ tōng shū xìn	N	Pre-Unit
genre	体裁	tǐ cái	N	2.3
God (also 神)	上帝	shàng dì	N	1.1
Gospel	福音	fúyīn	N	Pre-Unit, 3.3
grace	恩典	ēn diǎn	N	3.2
grass	草	cǎo	N	4.3
guidance	引导	yǐn dǎo	N	5.2
heart posture (attitude)	心志	xīn zhì	N	4.1
hell	地狱	dì yù	N	3.1
history	历史	lì shǐ	N	Pre-Unit
holiness; holy	圣洁	shèng jié	N/Adj.	4.1
hope	盼望	pàn wàng	N	1.2
humanity	人类	rén lèi	N	1.2
identity	身份	shēn fèn	N	2.1
idol	偶像	ǒu xiàng	N	3.2
image	形象	xíng xiàng	N	4.1
in vain	徒然	tú rán	Adj.	3.3

English	Chinese	Pinyin	Part of Speech	Lesson
infinite	无限的	wúxiàn de	Adj.	1.3
instruction	训悔	xùn huì	N	2.3
intention, will	意旨	yì zhǐ	N	5.3
Jesus	耶稣	yē sū	N	1.2
joy	喜乐	xǐ lè	N	4.3
judgement	审判	shěn pàn	N	3.1
king, lord	君王	jūn wáng	N	2.1
knowledge	知识	zhī shi	N	4.1
lamb	羔羊	gāo yáng	N	5.3
last of all	末后	mò hòu	Adj.	1.1
law	律法	lǜ fǎ	N	Pre-Unit
life	生命	shēng mìng	N	1.2
light	光	guāng	N	1.2
lost	失丧	shī sàng	Adj.	2.2
miracle	奇迹	qí jì	N	2.2
miraculous sign	神迹	shén jì	N	Pre-Unit
moral character	品格	pǐn gé	N	2.3
narrative; to narrate	叙述	xùshù	N/V	Pre-Unit
nation, kingdom	国度	guó dù	N	5.3
New Testament	新约	xīn yuē	N	Pre-Unit
news, message	消息	xiāo xi	N	4.3
Old Testament	旧约	jiù yuē	N	Pre-Unit
omnipotent	无所不能	wú suǒ bù néng	Adj.	1.3
omnipresent	无所不在	wú suǒ bù zài	Adj.	1.3
omniscient	无所不知	wú suǒ bù zhī	Adj.	1.3
only begotten son	独生子	dú shēng zǐ	N	1.2
only, sole	独一	dú yī	Adj.	1.1
outline	纲要	gāng yào	N	Pre-Unit
pain, suffering	痛苦	tòng kǔ	N	5.3
parable; to compare···to···	比喻	bǐ yù	N/V	Pre-Unit
Pauline Epistles	保罗书信	bǎo luó	N	Pre-Unit
peace	平安	píng'ān	N	4.3
Pentateuch	摩西五经	mó xī wǔ jīng	N	Pre-Unit
perfect	完美	wán měi	Adj.	4.1
person	位格	wèi gé	N	1.3
personally	亲自	qīn zì	Adv.	5.3
poetry	诗歌	shī gē	N	Pre-Unit
precious blood	宝血	bǎo xuè	N	3.3

English	Chinese	Pinyin	Part of Speech	Lesson
preservation, protection	保守	bǎo shǒu	N	5.2
priest	祭司	jì sī	N	2.1
prison	监狱	jiān yù	N	2.1
prophecy; to predict	预言	yù yán	N/V	Pre-Unit
prophet	先知	xiān zhī	N	Pre-Unit
proverb	箴言	zhēn yán	N	Pre-Unit
psalm	诗篇	shī piān	N	Pre-Unit
punishment	惩罚	chéng fá	N	3.1
pursuit	追求	zhuī qiú	N	5.2
rank and honor	尊荣	zūn róng	N	1.3
ransom price	赎价	shú jià	N	2.2
record	记载	jì zǎi	N	2.2
repentance	悔改	huǐ gǎi	N	3.2
revelation	启示	qǐshì	N	Pre-Unit
rich, abundant	丰盛	fēng shèng	Adj.	5.2
Savior	救主	jiù zhǔ	N	1.2
scripture verse	经文	jīng wén	N	Pre-Unit
seed	种子	zhǒng zi	N	4.3
sermon; to preach	讲道	jiǎng dào	N/V	Pre-Unit
shame, disgrace	耻	chǐ	N	4.3
shepherd	牧者	mù zhě	N	1.1
sin	罪恶	zuì'è	N	2.2
sin, iniquity	罪孽	zuì niè	N	4.1
soul	灵魂	líng hún	N	3.1
source, beginning	源头	yuán tóu	N	1.1
source, origin	根源	gēn yuán	N	1.3
spiritual	属灵	shǔ líng	Adj.	4.2
splendor	荣美	róng měi	N	4.3
splendor, radiance	光辉	guāng huī	N	5.1
style, pattern	样式	yàng shì	N	4.1
teaching/guidance	教导	jiào dǎo	N	2.3
temple	圣殿	shèng diàn	N	2.1
Ten Commandments	十诫	shí jiè	N	Pre-Unit
the cross	十字架	shí zì jià	N	3.3
the Lord	主	zhǔ	N	1.1
the people	子民	zǐ mín	N	2.2
theology	神学	shén xué	N	2.3
throne	宝座	bǎo zuò	N	5.3

English	Chinese	Pinyin	Part of Speech	Lesson
throughout time	亘古	gèn gǔ	N	1.3
title, salutation	称谓	chēng wèi	N	1.1
to admit (into), to adopt	接纳	jiē nà	V	5.1
to accept	接受	jiē shòu	V	4.2
to accomplish	成就	chéng jiù	V	4.2
to admit	承认	chéng rèn	V	3.2
to announce	宣告	xuān gào	V	1.2
to baptize	施洗	shī xǐ	V	4.2
to be attributed to	归与	guī yǔ	V	5.2
to be born	降生	jiàng shēng	V	1.2
to be fallen	堕落	duò luò	V	2.3
to be filled with	充满	chōng mǎn	V	4.3
to be fulfilled	应验	yìng yàn	V	2.3
to be justified	称义	chēng yì	V	3.3
to be obedient	顺服	shùn fú	V	3.2
to be sanctified	成圣	chéng shèng	V	5.2
to be sure of	确信	què xìn	V	4.3
to be worthy of	配得	pèi dé	V	5.2
to believe	相信	xiāng xìn	V	4.2
to betray	背叛	bèi pàn	V	3.1
to break away	脱离	tuō lí	V	5.2
to breathe	呼吸	hū xī	V	3.2
to bury	埋葬	mái zàng	V	3.3
to call, to address	称呼	chēng hu	V	1.1
to change	改变	gǎi biàn	V	1.3
to choose	拣选	jiǎn xuǎn	V	2.3
to come down	降临	jiàng lín	V	2.2
to comfort	安慰	ān wèi	V	1.3
to comply with	遵守	zūn shǒu	V	4.2
to conquer, to overcome	战胜	zhàn shèng	V	4.1
to control, to be in charge of	掌管	zhǎng guǎn	V	5.1
to decay	朽坏	xiǔ huài	V	5.1
to defy, to disobey	违抗	wéi kàng	V	3.2
to die out	灭绝	miè jué	V	3.1
to differentiate	分别	fēn bié	V	5.2
to dominate	主宰	zhǔ zǎi	V	3.2
to dry up	枯干	kū gān	V	4.3
to endure	忍耐	rěn nài	V	5.1

English	Chinese	Pinyin	Part of Speech	Lesson
to establish, to build	建立	jiàn lì	V	4.2
to experience	经历	jīng lì	V	3.3
to extol	歌颂	gē sòng	V	5.3
to fall short of; to be lacking	亏缺	kuī quē	V	4.2
to fear	惧怕	jù pà	V	4.1
to follow	跟随	gēn suí	V	3.2
to give, to bestow	赐给	cì gěi	V	3.2
to go, to attend	赴	fù	V	5.3
to govern, to rule	统管	tǒng guǎn	V	5.3
to have	拥有	yǒng yǒu	V	3.3
to help complete	成全	chéng quán	V	2.2
to honor; glory	荣耀	róng yào	V/N	4.1
to imitate	效法	xiào fǎ	V	5.3
to imply, to reveal	默示	mò shì	V	2.1
to instruct	吩咐	fēn fù	V	4.2
to lean on	倚靠	yǐ kào	V	5.2
to look after	看顾	kàn gù	V	5.1
to maintain, to protect	维护	wéi hù	V	5.1
to make a covenant	立约	lì yuē	V	2.2
to manifest	彰显	zhāng xiǎn	V	5.1
to mean	意味	yì wèi	V	2.1
to nail	钉	dìng	V	3.3
to obey, to comply	遵命	zūn mìng	V	3.1
to offer	献上	xiàn shàng	V	3.3
to offer in the name of	奉（…的名）	fèng	V	4.2
to ordain	命定	mìng dìng	V	5.2
to perish	灭亡	miè wáng	V	2.2
to pay tribute to (glorification)	称颂	chēng sòng	V	5.1
to praise	赞美	zàn měi	V	5.3
to promise	应许	yīng xǔ	V	1.3
to provide	提供	tí gōng	V	3.2
to rebel	悖逆	bèi nì	V	3.1
to receive	领受	lǐng shòu	V	3.3
to receive, to be covered by,	蒙	méng	V	4.2
to reconcile	和好	hé hǎo	V	4.1
to rely on	信靠	xìn kào	V	1.2
to remit(a punishment)	赦免	shè miǎn	V	3.1
to renew	更新	gēng xīn	V	4.1
to reveal	启示	qǐ shì	V	1.1

English	Chinese	Pinyin	Part of Speech	Lesson
to rot, to decay	腐烂	fǔ làn	V	4.3
to sacrifice oneself	舍命	shě mìng	V	2.2
to save	拯救	zhěng jiù	V	2.2
to search	寻找	xún zhǎo	V	2.2
to send, to dispatch	差派	chāi pài	V	5.1
to separate	隔绝	gé jué	V	3.1
to serve, to wait on	侍奉	shì fèng	V	3.2
to share the joy of	享	xiǎng	V	5.3
to show, to demonstrate	显明	xiǎn míng	V	2.2
to sin	犯罪	fàn zuì	V	2.3
to spread	传	chuán	V	3.3
to stand firm	立定	lì dìng	V	5.3
to support, to hold up	托住	tuō zhù	V	5.1
to sustain	支撑	zhī chēng	V	5.1
to take the place of	代替	dài tì	V	3.3
to tempt, to entice	引诱	yǐn yòu	V	3.1
to touch, to affect	感动	gǎn dòng	V	1.3
to violate	违反	wéi fǎn	V	3.1
to win a victory	得胜	dé shèng	V	4.3
to worship	敬拜	jìng bài	V	1.3
translation	译本	yì běn	N	Pre-Unit
truth	真理	zhēn lǐ	N	1.2
universe, cosmos	宇宙	yǔ zhòu	N	5.1
verse	节	jié	N	Pre-Unit
warning	警告	jǐng gào	N	3.1
way	道路	dào lù	N	1.2
wickedness, evil	邪恶	xié'è	N	3.2
wilderness	旷野	kuàng yě	N	2.1
wisdom literature	智慧文学	zhì huì wén xué	N	Pre-Unit
wither and fall	凋谢	diāo xiè	V	4.3
witness	见证	jiàn zhèng	N	4.2
worry, sorrow	忧患	yōu huàn	N	2.3
Yahweh	耶和华	yē hé huá	N	1.1

Chinese-English Glossary 中英词汇表

Pinyin	Chinese	Part of Speech	English	Lesson
ān pái	安排	N	arrangement	5.1
ān wèi	安慰	V	to comfort	1.3
bài huài	败坏	N	depravity	3.1
bǎo luó	保罗书信	N	Pauline Epistles	Pre-Unit
bǎo shǒu	保守	N	preservation, protection	5.2
bǎo xuè	宝血	N	precious blood	3.3
bǎo zuò	宝座	N	throne	5.3
bèi jǐng	背景	N	background	2.1
bèi nì	悖逆	V	to rebel	3.1
bèi pàn	背叛	V	to betray	3.1
bǐ cǐ	彼此	Pr.	each other	4.2
bǐ yù	比喻	N/V	parable; to compare...to...	Pre-Unit
cǎo	草	N	grass	4.3
chāi pài	差派	V	to send, to dispatch	5.1
chǎn yè	产业	N	estate, property	5.2
chéng fá	惩罚	N	punishment	3.1
chēng hu	称呼	V	to call, to address	1.1
chéng jiù	成就	V	to accomplish	4.2
chéng quán	成全	V	to help complete	2.2
chéng rèn	承认	V	to admit	3.2
chéng shèng	成圣	V	to be sanctified	5.2
chēng sòng	称颂	V	to pay tribute to (glorification)	5.1
chēng wèi	称谓	N	title, salutation	1.1
chēng yì	称义	V	to be justified	3.3
chǐ	耻	N	shame, disgrace	4.3
chōng mǎn	充满	V	to be filled with	4.3
chuán	传	V	to spread	3.3
chuàngzào zhǔ	创造主	N	creator	1.1
cì gěi	赐给	V	to give, to bestow	3.2
dài jià	代价	N	cost, price	4.2
dài tì	代替	V	to take the place of	3.3
dào lù	道路	N	way	1.2
dé shèng	得胜	V	to win a victory	4.3
dì yù	地狱	N	hell	3.1
diāo xiè	凋谢	V	wither and fall	4.3
dìng	钉	V	to nail	3.3
dú shēng zǐ	独生子	N	only begotten son	1.2

Pinyin	Chinese	Part of Speech	English	Lesson
dú yī	独一	Adj.	only, sole	1.1
duò luò	堕落	V	to be fallen	2.3
ēn diǎn	恩典	N	grace	3.2
fàn zuì	犯罪	V	to sin	2.3
fēn bié	分别	V	to differentiate	5.2
fēn fù	吩咐	V	to instruct	4.2
fèng	奉（…的名）	V	to offer in the name of	4.2
fēng shèng	丰盛	Adj.	rich, abundant	5.2
fù	赴	V	to go, to attend	5.3
fǔ làn	腐烂	V	to rot, to decay	4.3
fú yīn	福音	N	the Gospel	Pre-Unit, 3.3
gǎi biàn	改变	V	to change	1.3
gǎn dòng	感动	V	to touch, to affect	1.3
gāng yào	纲要	N	outline	Pre-Unit
gāo yáng	羔羊	N	lamb	5.3
gé jué	隔绝	V	to separate	3.1
gē sòng	歌颂	V	to extol	5.3
gèn gǔ	亘古	N	throughout time	1.3
gēn jī	根基	N	foundation	4.3
gēn suí	跟随	V	to follow	3.2
gēn yuán	根源	N	source, origin	1.3
gēng xīn	更新	V	to renew	4.1
guāng	光	N	light	1.2
guāng huī	光辉	N	splendor, radiance	5.1
guī yǔ	归与	V	to be attributed to	5.2
guó dù	国度	N	nation, kingdom	5.3
hé hǎo	和好	V	to reconcile	4.1
hé xīn	核心	N	core	3.3
hēi'àn	黑暗	N	darkness	5.2
hòu yì	后裔	N	descendant	4.2
hū xī	呼吸	V	to breathe	3.2
hū zhào	呼召	N	calling	5.3
huǐ gǎi	悔改	N	repentance	3.2
jī dū	基督	N	Christ	1.2
jī dū jiào	基督教	N	Christianity	Pre-Unit
jì sī	祭司	N	priest	2.1
jì zǎi	记载	N	record	2.2
jiàn lì	建立	V	to establish, to build	4.2
jiǎn xuǎn	拣选	V	to choose	2.3

Pinyin	Chinese	Part of Speech	English	Lesson
jiān yù	监狱	N	prison	2.1
jiàn zhèng	见证	N	witness	4.2
jiǎng dào	讲道	N/V	sermon; to preach	Pre-Unit
jiàng lín	降临	V	to come down	2.2
jiàng shēng	降生	V	to be born	1.2
jiào dǎo	教导	N	teaching/guidance	2.3
jiào huì	教会	N	church	Pre-Unit
jiào yì	教义	N	doctrine	Pre-Unit
jié	节	N	verse	Pre-Unit
jié jú	结局	N	ending，result	3.1
jiè mìng	诫命	N	commandment	2.3
jiē nà	接纳	V	to admit (into), to adopt	5.1
jiē shòu	接受	V	to accept	4.2
jìng bài	敬拜	V	to worship	1.3
jǐng gào	警告	N	warning	3.1
jīng lì	经历	V	to experience	3.3
jīng wén	经文	N	scripture verse	Pre-Unit
jiù yuē	旧约	N	Old Testament	Pre-Unit
jiù zhǔ	救主	N	savior	1.2
jù pà	惧怕	V	to fear	4.1
jūn wáng	君王	N	king, lord	2.1
kàn gù	看顾	V	to look after	5.1
kū gān	枯干	V	to dry up	4.3
kuàng yě	旷野	N	wilderness	2.1
kuī quē	亏缺	V	to fall short of; to be lacking	4.2
lì dìng	立定	V	to stand firm	5.3
lì shǐ	历史	N	history	Pre-Unit
lì yuē	立约	V	to make a covenant	2.2
lián guàn	连贯	Adj.	coherent	2.1
líng hún	灵魂	N	soul	3.1
lǐng shòu	领受	V	to receive	3.3
liú xuè	流血	N	bloodshed	5.2
lǜ fǎ	律法	N	law	Pre-Unit
mái zàng	埋葬	V	to bury	3.3
méng	蒙	V	to be covered by; to receive	4.2
méng yuē	盟约	N	covenant	Pre-Unit
miè jué	灭绝	V	to die out	3.1
miè wáng	灭亡	V	to perish	2.2
mìng dìng	命定	V	to ordain	5.2

Pinyin	Chinese	Part of Speech	English	Lesson
mìng lìng	命令	N	command	3.2
mó guǐ	魔鬼	N	demon, devil	3.1
mò hòu	末后	Adj.	last of all	1.1
mò shì	默示	V	to imply, to reveal	2.1
mó xī wǔ jīng	摩西五经	N	Pentateuch	Pre-Unit
mù zhě	牧者	N	shepherd	1.1
nèi róng	内容	N	content	2.3
nián líng	年龄	N	age	2.1
nóng fū	农夫	N	farmer	2.1
ǒu xiàng	偶像	N	idol	3.2
pàn wàng	盼望	N	hope	1.2
pèi dé	配得	V	to be worthy of	5.2
pǐn gé	品格	N	moral character	2.3
píng jù	凭据	N	evidence	5.3
píng'ān	平安	N	peace	4.3
pò suì	破碎	N	brokenness	4.3
pǔ tōng shū xìn	普通书信	N	General Epistles	Pre-Unit
qí jì	奇迹	N	miracle	2.2
qǐ shì	启示	N/V	revelation; to reveal	Pre-Unit,1.1
qīn zì	亲自	Adv.	personally	5.3
quán bǐng	权柄	N	authority, power	1.3
quán rán	全然	Adv.	completely, entirely	5.2
quán wēi	权威	N	authority	2.1
quánnéng zhě	全能者	N	Almighty	1.1
què xìn	确信	V	to be sure of	4.3
rén lèi	人类	N	humanity	1.2
rěn nài	忍耐	V	to endure	5.1
rén yì	仁义	N	benevolence and righteousness	4.1
róng měi	荣美	N	splendor	4.3
róng yào	荣耀	V/N	to honor; glory	4.1
shàng dì	上帝	N	God (also 神)	1.1
shè miǎn	赦免	V	to remit (a punishment)	3.1
shě mìng	舍命	V	to sacrifice oneself	2.2
shēn fèn	身份	N	identity	2.1
shén jì	神迹	N	miraculous sign	Pre-Unit
shěn pàn	审判	N	judgement	3.1
shén xué	神学	N	theology	2.3
shèng diàn	圣殿	N	temple	2.1

Pinyin	Chinese	Part of Speech	English	Lesson
shèng jié	圣洁	N/Adj.	holiness; holy	4.1
shèng jīng	圣经	N	Bible/Holy Scripture	Pre-Unit
shèng jīng gù shi	圣经故事	N	Bible story	Pre-Unit
shēng mìng	生命	N	life	1.2
shí dài	时代	N	era	2.1
shì fèng	侍奉	V	to serve, to wait on	3.2
shī gē	诗歌	N	poetry	Pre-Unit
shí jiè	十诫	N	Ten Commandments	Pre-Unit
shī piān	诗篇	N	psalm	Pre-Unit
shī sàng	失丧	Adj.	lost	2.2
shǐ tú	使徒	N	apostle	Pre-Unit
shī xǐ	施洗	V	to baptize	4.2
shí zì jià	十字架	N	the cross	3.3
shǐ zǔ	始祖	N	earliest ancestor	2.3
shǒu xiān	首先	Adj.	first of all	1.1
shú jià	赎价	N	ransom price	2.2
shū juàn	书卷	N	book	Pre-Unit
shǔ líng	属灵	Adj.	spiritual	4.2
shùn fú	顺服	V	to be obedient	3.2
tǐ cái	体裁	N	genre	2.3
tí gōng	提供	V	to provide	3.2
tiān shǐ	天使	N	angel	1.2
tǒng guǎn	统管	V	to govern, to rule	5.3
tòng kǔ	痛苦	N	pain, suffering	5.3
tú rán	徒然	Adj.	in vain	3.3
tuō lí	脱离	V	to break away	5.2
tuō zhù	托住	V	to support, to hold up	5.1
wán měi	完美	Adj.	perfect	4.1
wéi fǎn	违反	V	to violate	3.1
wèi gé	位格	N	person	1.3
wéi hù	维护	V	to maintain, to protect	5.1
wéi kàng	违抗	V	to defy, to disobey	3.2
wū huì	污秽	Adj.	filthy	4.1
wú suǒ bù néng	无所不能	Adj.	omnipotent	1.3
wú suǒ bù zài	无所不在	Adj.	omnipresent	1.3
wú suǒ bù zhī	无所不知	Adj.	omniscient	1.3
wú xiá	无瑕	Adj.	flawless	2.3
wúxiàn de	无限的	Adj.	infinite	1.3

Pinyin	Chinese	Part of Speech	English	Lesson
xǐ lè	喜乐	N	joy	4.3
xiǎn míng	显明	V	to show, to demonstrate	2.2
xiàn shàng	献上	V	to offer	3.3
xiān zhī	先知	N	prophet	Pre-Unit
xiǎng	享	V	to share the joy of	5.3
xiāng xìn	相信	V	to believe	4.2
xiào fǎ	效法	V	to imitate	5.3
xiāo xi	消息	N	news, message	4.3
xié'è	邪恶	N	wickedness, evil	3.2
xìn kào	信靠	V	to rely on	1.2
xìn tiáo	信条	N	creed	Pre-Unit
xìn yǎng	信仰	N	faith	2.3
xīn yuē	新约	N	New Testament	Pre-Unit
xīn zhì	心志	N	heart posture (attitude)	4.1
xíng wéi	行为	N	deeds	4.1
xíng xiàng	形象	N	image	4.1
xīng xiù	星宿	N	constellation	5.1
xiōng è	凶恶	N	evil, malevolence	5.2
xiǔ huài	朽坏	V	to decay	5.1
xuān gào	宣告	V	to announce	1.2
xùn huì	训悔	N	instruction	2.3
xún zhǎo	寻找	V	to search	2.2
xùshù	叙述	N/V	narrative; to narrate	Pre-Unit
yán xí	筵席	N	feast, banquet	5.3
yàng shì	样式	N	style, pattern	4.1
yē hé huá	耶和华	N	Yahweh	1.1
yē sū	耶稣	N	Jesus	1.2
yì běn	译本	N	translation	Pre-Unit
yǐ kào	倚靠	V	to lean on	5.2
yì wèi	意味	V	to mean	2.1
yì zhǐ	意旨	N	intention, will	5.3
yǐn dǎo	引导	N	guidance	5.2
yǐn yòu	引诱	V	to tempt, to entice	3.1
yīng xǔ	应许	V	to promise	1.3
yìng yàn	应验	V	to be fulfilled	2.3
yǒng	永	Adj.	forever, permanent	1.1
yǒng shēng	永生	N	eternal life	3.2
yǒng yǒu	拥有	V	to have	3.3

Pinyin	Chinese	Part of Speech	English	Lesson
yǒnghéng de	永恒的	Adj.	everlasting	1.3
yōu huàn	忧患	N	worry, sorrow	2.3
yú fū	渔夫	N	fisherman	2.1
yù yán	预言	N/V	prophecy; to predict	Pre-Unit
yǔ zhòu	宇宙	N	universe, cosmos	5.1
yuán tóu	源头	N	source, beginning	1.1
zàn měi	赞美	V	to praise	5.3
zhàn shèng	战胜	V	to conquer, to overcome	4.1
zhāng	章	N	chapter	Pre-Unit
zhǎng guǎn	掌管	V	to control, to be in charge of	5.1
zhāng xiǎn	彰显	V	to manifest	5.1
zhēn lǐ	真理	N	truth	1.2
zhēn yán	箴言	N	proverb	Pre-Unit
zhěng jiù	拯救	V	to save	2.2
zhī chēng	支撑	V	to sustain	5.1
zhì huì wén xué	智慧文学	N	wisdom literature	Pre-Unit
zhī shi	知识	N	knowledge	4.1
zhǐ wàng	指望	N	anticipatory hope	4.1
zhōng gào	忠告	N	advice	2.3
zhōng jié	终结	N	end, finality	5.1
zhǒng zi	种子	N	seed	4.3
zhǔ	主	N	the Lord	1.1
zhǔ zǎi	主宰	V	to dominate	3.2
zhuī qiú	追求	N	pursuit	5.2
zǐ mín	子民	N	the people	2.2
zuì niè	罪孽	N	sin, iniquity	4.1
zuì'è	罪恶	N	sin	2.2
zūn mìng	遵命	V	to obey, to comply	3.1
zūn róng	尊荣	N	rank and honor	1.3
zūn shǒu	遵守	V	to comply with	4.2

"神爱世人，甚至将祂的独生子赐给他们，
叫一切信祂的，不致灭亡，反得永生。"

— 约翰福音 3:16

"For God so loved the world that he gave his one and only Son,
that whoever believes in him shall not perish but have eternal life."

— John 3:16

About Kharis Publishing:

Kharis Publishing, an imprint of Kharis Media LLC, is a leading Christian and inspirational book publisher based in Aurora, Chicago metropolitan area, Illinois. Kharis' dual mission is to give voice to under-represented writers (including women and first-time authors) and equip orphans in developing countries with literacy tools. That is why, for each book sold, the publisher channels some of the proceeds into providing books and computers for orphanages in developing countries so that these kids may learn to read, dream, and grow. For a limited time, Kharis Publishing is accepting unsolicited queries for nonfiction (Christian, self-help, memoirs, business, health and wellness) from qualified leaders, professionals, pastors, and ministers. Learn more at: https://kharispublishing.com/

CPSIA information can be obtained
at www.ICGtesting.com
Printed in the USA
JSHW050516201222
35187JS00002B/5

9 781637 461495